The Question of Skill in Cross-Border Labour Mobilities

Selecting migrants based on skill has become a widely practised migration policy in many countries around the world. Since the late 20th century, research on "skilled" and "highly skilled" migration has raised important questions about the value and ethics of skill-based labour mobility. More recent research has begun to question the concept of skill and skill categorisation in both government policy and academic research. Taking the view that 'skills' are socially constructed categories and highly malleable concepts in practice, this edited volume centres the discussion on the following questions: Who are the arbitrators of skill? What constitutes skill? And how is skill constructed in the migration process and in turn, how does skill affect the mobility? The empirical studies in this volume show that diverse actors are involved in the process of identifying, evaluating and shaping migrant skill. The interpretation of migrants' skill is frequently distorted by their ascriptive characteristics such as race, ethnicity, gender and nationality, reflecting the influence of colonial legacy, global inequality as well as social stratification. Finally, this edited volume emphasises the complex, and frequently reciprocal, relationship between skill and mobility. This book will be of interest to researchers and advanced students of Sociology, Human Geography, Politics, Social Anthropology, Economics, and Social Work. It was originally published as a special issue of the *Journal of Ethnic and Migration Studies.*

Gracia Liu-Farrer is Professor of Sociology at the Graduate School of Asia-Pacific Studies and Director of the Institute of Asian Migration at Waseda University, Tokyo, Japan. Her research examines immigrants' economic, social and political practices in Japan and the global mobility of students and professional migrants.

Brenda S.A. Yeoh is Raffles Professor of Social Sciences at the National University of Singapore (NUS) and Research Leader of the Asian Migration Cluster at the Asia Research Institute at NUS, Singapore. Her research interests include the politics of space in colonial and postcolonial cities and gender and transnational migration in Asia.

Michiel Baas is Senior Research Fellow at the Max Planck Institute for Social Anthropology, Halle, Germany. His research focuses on questions of (transnational) migration; the body, gender and masculinity; and artificial intelligence. His most recent book is titled *Muscular India: Masculinity, Mobility and the New Middle Class* (2020).

Research in Ethnic and Migration Studies

Series editor: ***Paul Statham****, Director, Sussex Centre for Migration Research (SCMR), University of Sussex, UK*

The *Research in Ethnic and Migration Studies* series publishes the results of high-quality, cutting-edge research that addresses key questions relating to ethnic relations, diversity and migration. The series is open to a range of disciplines and brings together research collaborations on specific defined topics on all aspects of migration and its consequences, including migration processes, migrants and their experiences, ethnic relations, discrimination, integration, racism, transnationalism, citizenship, identity and cultural diversity. Contributions are especially welcome when they are the result of comparative research, either across countries, cities or groups. All articles have previously been published in the *Journal of Ethnic and Migration Studies (JEMS)*, which has a rigorous peer review system. Collective volumes in this series are either the product of Special Issues published in the journal or published articles that the Editor has selected from individual submissions.

Migration and Marriage in Asian Contexts
Edited by Zheng Mu and Wei-Jun Jean Yeung

New Theoretical Dialogues on Migration in China
Edited by Hong Zhu and Junxi Qian

(Un)Settled Sojourners in Cities
Challenges of "Temporariness" among Migrants and Asylum Seekers
Edited by Elizabeth Chacko and Marie Price

Cross-Border Marriages
State Categories, Research Agendas and Family Practices
Edited by Apostolos Andrikopoulos, Joëlle Moret and Janine Dahinden

The Spiralling of the Securitization of Migration in the European Union
Edited by Valeria Bello and Sarah Léonard

The Question of Skill in Cross-Border Labour Mobilities
Edited by Gracia Liu-Farrer, Brenda S.A. Yeoh and Michiel Baas

For more information about this series, please visit:
www.routledge.com/Research-in-Ethnic-and-Migration-Studies/book-series/REMS

The Question of Skill in Cross-Border Labour Mobilities

Edited by
Gracia Liu-Farrer, Brenda S.A. Yeoh and Michiel Baas

Routledge
Taylor & Francis Group
LONDON AND NEW YORK

First published 2023
by Routledge
4 Park Square, Milton Park, Abingdon, Oxon, OX14 4RN

and by Routledge
605 Third Avenue, New York, NY 10158

Routledge is an imprint of the Taylor & Francis Group, an informa business

British Library Cataloguing in Publication Data
A catalogue record for this book is available from the British Library

ISBN13: 978-1-032-44869-5 (hbk)
ISBN13: 978-1-032-44890-9 (pbk)
ISBN13: 978-1-003-37436-7 (ebk)

DOI: 10.4324/9781003374367

Typeset in Minion Pro
by codeMantra

Publisher's Note
The publisher accepts responsibility for any inconsistencies that may have arisen during the conversion of this book from journal articles to book chapters, namely the inclusion of journal terminology.

Contents

Citation Information

The chapters in this book were originally published in the *Journal of Ethnic and Migration Studies*, volume 47, issue 10 (2021). When citing this material, please use the original page numbering for each article, as follows:

Chapter 1
Social construction of skill: an analytical approach toward the question of skill in cross-border labour mobilities
Gracia Liu-Farrer, Brenda S.A. Yeoh and Michiel Baas
Journal of Ethnic and Migration Studies, volume 47, issue 10 (2021) pp. 2237–2251

Chapter 2
Skilled or unskilled? The reconfiguration of migration policies in Japan
Nana Oishi
Journal of Ethnic and Migration Studies, volume 47, issue 10 (2021) pp. 2252–2269

Chapter 3
Shifting employabilities: skilling migrants in the nation of emigration
Yasmin Y. Ortiga
Journal of Ethnic and Migration Studies, volume 47, issue 10 (2021) pp. 2270–2287

Chapter 4
Becoming global talent? Taiwanese white-collar migrants in Japan
Yen-Fen Tseng
Journal of Ethnic and Migration Studies, volume 47, issue 10 (2021) pp. 2288–2304

Chapter 5
Who are the fittest? The question of skills in national employment systems in an age of global labour mobility
Gracia Liu-Farrer and Karen Shire
Journal of Ethnic and Migration Studies, volume 47, issue 10 (2021) pp. 2305–2322

Chapter 6
Intermediaries and transnational regimes of skill: nursing skills and competencies in the context of international migration
Margaret Walton-Roberts
Journal of Ethnic and Migration Studies, volume 47, issue 10 (2021) pp. 2323–2340

Chapter 7

The work that brokers do: the skills, competences and know-how of intermediaries in the H-2 visa programme
Rubén Hernández-León
Journal of Ethnic and Migration Studies, volume 47, issue 10 (2021) pp. 2341–2358

Chapter 8

From cooks to chefs: skilled migrants in a globalising culinary field
James Farrer
Journal of Ethnic and Migration Studies, volume 47, issue 10 (2021) pp. 2359–2375

Notes on Contributors

Michiel Baas, Max Planck Institute for Social Anthropology, Halle, Germany.

James Farrer, Faculty of Liberal Arts, Sophia University, Tokyo, Japan.

Rubén Hernández-León, Department of Sociology, University of California, Los Angeles, USA.

Gracia Liu-Farrer, Graduate School of Asia-Pacific Studies; Institute of Asian Migration, Waseda University, Tokyo, Japan.

Nana Oishi, Asia Institute, University of Melbourne, Parkville, Australia.

Yasmin Y. Ortiga, School of Social Science, Singapore Management University, Singapore.

Karen Shire, Institute of East Asian Studies/ Department of Sociology, University of Duisburg-Essen, Germany.

Yen-Fen Tseng, Department of Sociology, National Taiwan University, Taipei, Taiwan.

Margaret Walton-Roberts, Geography and Environmental Studies, Wilfrid Laurier University, Waterloo, Canada.

Brenda S.A. Yeoh, Department of Geography; Asia Research Institute, National University of Singapore, Singapore.

INTRODUCTION

Social construction of skill: an analytical approach toward the question of skill in cross-border labour mobilities

Gracia Liu-Farrer, Brenda S.A. Yeoh and Michiel Baas

ABSTRACT

Selecting labour migrants based on skill has become a widely practised migration policy in many countries around the world. Since the late twentieth century, research on 'skilled' and 'highly skilled' migration has raised important questions about the value and ethics of skill-based labour mobility. More recent research has begun to question the concept of skill and skill categorisation in both government policy and academic research. Taking the view that migrants' skill is socially constructed, we centre our discussion on three questions: Who are the arbitrators of skill? What constitutes skill? And how is skill constructed in the migration process and in turn, how does skill affect the mobility? We show that diverse actors are involved in the process of identifying, evaluating and shaping migrant skill. The interpretation of migrants' skill is frequently distorted by their ascriptive characteristics such as race, ethnicity, gender and nationality, reflecting the influence of colonial legacy, global inequality as well as social stratification. Finally, this special issue emphasises the complex, and frequently reciprocal, relationship between skill and mobility.

'Skilled' migration across borders

The question of skill and the notions of 'skilled' versus 'unskilled' did not emerge until the second half of the twentieth century when governments in leading industrialised countries started implementing selective migration programmes with skill level as an important criterion in determining one's chance of selection. An early strand of the scholarly literature mainly centred on the debate as to the extent such mobility drained the talent pool and created developmental problems in source countries in the developing world (e.g. Beine, Docquier, and Rapoport 2007; Skeldon 2009 among many). Widespread concerns about 'brain drain' or 'human capital flight' coalesced around fears that the depletion of skilled, educated, and talented individuals may adversely affect the development of local knowledge and science, retard economic growth, erode tax revenues, and cripple public institutions and service delivery (Appleyard 1998). These negative views were later challenged by those who argue that the emigration of talent is not so much a 'drain' but part of 'brain circulation' (Saxenian 2002), and that positive effects for source countries can include not only remittance flows and the mobilisation of foreign capital, but also skills transfer, exposure to new ideas and technologies, and the creation of new business opportunities as a result of diaspora networking (Trebilcock and Sudak 2006). In this early literature, what constituted 'skills' or 'skilled migration' is usually obfuscated by the rhetorical language of brain drain/gain/circulation, and the possession of skills simplistically conflated with 'having a university degree or extensive/equivalent experience in a given field' (Iredale 2001, 8).

A second impetus that gave visibility to the highly skilled migrant stemmed from the management literature when business review writers began to realise the value of 'talented' workers in securing competitive advantage for the firm through knowledge transfer (Yeoh and Lam 2016). According to Robert Reich (1991, 81–83), for example, companies striving to survive in the global knowledge economy of the twenty-first century must use knowledge creatively by relying on talented knowledge workers wielding three interrelated but different skills: problem-solving skills (e.g. technicians, engineers), problem-identifying skills (e.g. market and product analysts and evaluators) and skills in strategic brokering (e.g. executives and entrepreneurs). This approach to valorising the talent worker at the firm level was taken up by scholars interested in world city networks. In this iteration, highly skilled international migrants are crucial to the (re)making of the world city, where they function as transnational elites serving as 'conduit[s] through which capital is accumulated, networks built, [and] connections made' (Beaverstock 2012, 240). Moreover, it is argued that the presence of a large 'creative class' – from scientists and engineers to poets and architects and other 'people in design, education, arts, music and entertainment' (Florida 2002, 8) – helps revitalise post-industrial cities and contributes to the countries' economic growth (Florida 2002). In this literature, the notion of the highly skilled transnational worker – usually constructed relationally to and given meaning by the so-called global knowledge economy – is 'by definition (and in fact *produced* by being) internationally mobile' (Yeoh and Lam 2016).

While both sets of literature above are largely concerned with the intrinsic value of highly skilled international migrants – also referred to in multiple ways as 'expatriates', 'global talent', 'human capital', 'knowledge workers', 'professional, managerial and technical specialists (PMTs)', 'transnational elites' and the 'creative class' (Beaverstock 2005; Khadria 2004; Kuznetsov and Sabel 2006; Mahroum 1999) – a third strand of the emerging literature on migration and skills at the dawn of the new millennium focused on the outcomes of skilled migrants in destination countries with the establishment of skill-based migration programmes (e.g. Birrell, Hawthorne, and Richardson 2006; Al Ariss et al. 2012). Given shortages in skilled professionals as a result of ageing populations, the added complexity of low fertility rates, and the fear of lagging behind other advanced economies in the competition for talent, countries such as Australia, Canada, Japan and Singapore have introduced new measures to (selectively) attract those migrants that they hope to offer a long-term or even permanent home. Nonetheless, research shows that while different countries have different experiences and degrees of success with attracting variously 'skilled' migrants, they also face similar issues relating to utilising and integrating the so-called skilled migrants. Empirical case studies revealed the prevalence of skill wastage and mismatch, especially among women and ethnic minorities

(Kofman and Raghuram 2005, 2006; Williams 2007). Employing Bourdieusian theories of different forms of capital and the differentiated fields, studies highlight not only the difficulty of capital conversion across cultural boundaries, but also the institutional barriers and structural inequality that obstruct such conversion (Bauder 2003; Riaño and Baghdadi 2007; Erel 2010; Nohl, Schittenhelm, and Schmidtke 2014). Professional associations can deny immigrants' access to the occupations they are qualified for by controlling licensing (Bauder 2003). The same immigrant medical professionals can be included or excluded on the labour market in the same country over the decades depending on the labour pool (Peppler 2018).

In sum, since the late twentieth century, research on 'skilled' and 'highly skilled' migration has raised important questions about the intrinsic value of such form of labour mobility. The extant literature is primarily concerned with its developmental impacts on the sending regions and the lack of intended economic outcomes of such migration in the host labour market. The last observation in particular directs the attention to the problematic notion of skill, indicating that the idea of 'skilled labour migration' cannot be regarded as a self-evident pattern of migration. Scholars note that although the concept of skill is used to sort and determine individuals' chances of crossing borders and entering overseas labour markets, the criteria used to measure it is both technical and inherently simplistic, focusing on objectively quantifiable proxies from the years of education to credentials and occupational categories (Adams 2003; Carrington and Detragiache 1998; Docquier and Marfouk 2004, 2006; Dumont and Lamaitre 2005). Such objective measures are rarely correlated with actual practices because migrants' ability to utilise skill depends on complex social and political negotiations (Ribeiro 2018; Walton-Roberts 2019).

Studies have also questioned the arbitrary nature of skill categories, pointing out that the definitions, criteria, utilities and applications of skills in the migratory process are rife with ambiguities and malleability. What becomes defined and categorised as high, low or mid-level skills are left to the vagaries of situational economic demand and political calculation, and relies 'on complex power relations between social actors with competing objectives' (Hercog and Sandoz 2018, 454). For example, in the case of Singapore, legal criteria utilised to determine visa applications conflate skill and education with income, causing migrants who are well educated but do not have the bargaining power for high incomes to fall into middle categories (Baas 2017). In addition, as the import of 'global talent' exudes and confers legitimacy, in countries where immigration is a politically contentious subject, selective migration policy based on education and differential skills has become a seemingly neutral front to facilitate the de-facto import of various kinds of gendered and racialised labour. In Japan, international higher education becomes a de facto channel for low-wage labour (Liu-Farrer and Tran 2019). Moreover, research points out that some groups of migrants who are labelled unskilled do not always remain so. They succeed in acquiring skills in the process of migration and gain socioeconomic mobilities through geographic and sometimes multinational mobility (Hagan, Lowe, and Quingla 2011; Liu-Farrer 2012; Hagan, Hernández-León, and Demonsant 2015). Others – particularly migrant domestic workers who are unable to embark on stepwise migration for one reason or another – remain 'stuck' at the bottom of the skills ladder in retrogressive occupations as a result of legally imposed 'categorical control' (Paul 2015; Yeoh and Chee 2015).

Building on previous scholarship that has begun the work of problematising the concept of skill, this special issue pushes the inquiry further by taking a step back to examine the fundamental meaning of skill and how it operates in the process of cross-border mobilities. It should be noted that skill is defined and construed variedly by organisations and national governments. While the International Labour Organization (ILO) uses one's ability to fulfil a task to define skill and job complexity to measure skill level, OECD operationalises skill with education levels and occupational categories (Oishi 2021). The measure of skill in countries' skill-based selective migration policy also ranges from clearly quantifiable credentials typical in point-based systems to market-need as implied in employer-sponsored visa programmes. Such variations and apparent elasticity of the concept confirm that skill is at best a context-dependent operational concept. This issue, therefore, proposes a social constructive approach to the investigation of skill in cross-border labour mobilities. We take as a point of departure the notion that 'skill' in cross-border labour mobility, and consequently the idea of the high- or low-skilled migrant, is a concept socially constructed by a constellation of actors in specific local, national, transnational and global contexts (Walton-Roberts 2021; Farrer 2021). It is not intrinsically correlated with educational level or occupational category. In order to highlight the constructed nature of skill, we centre our discussion on three questions that are integral to this analytical framework: *Who* are the arbitrators of skill?; *What* constitutes skill?; And *how* is skill constructed in the migration process and in turn, how does skill affect the mobility? The seven empirical studies included in this special issue examine different strands of labour mobility, and critically engage one or all of these questions in their analysis. In the sections that follow, we elaborate on an analytical framework based on the concept of the social construction of skill-in-migration by drawing the papers in this special issue into dialogue.

Social construction of skill in migration: towards an analytical framework

The central argument collectively made by the papers in this special issue is the notion that migrants' skills are socially constructed. The social construction of skill is an idea emerged in sociology as early as the 1970s when researchers observed that class, gender and race affected how workers' skills were acknowledged and valued and, consequently, the jobs they performed were rewarded (e.g. Braverman [1974], 1998; Moss and Tilly 2001; Steinberg 1990; Kilbourne et al. 1994). This literature argues that skills, the technical requirements in the labour process, are established through a non-objective process. First, 'the way "skill" is conceptualised and named is itself a process of "social construction", which precedes recognition in qualifications or job descriptions' (Hampson and Junor 2015). In other words, skill is not an intrinsic quality a person possesses. Whether an ability is considered skill and can be called as such depends on the contexts of its use. When it is identified as skill, it then can be quantified or credentialed and used to define the content of a job. Second, the evaluation, identification and developing of skills, again, depend on by whom and in what contexts these processes take place (Rigby and Sanchis 2006).

As a central concept in sociology of labour and work, extant research has mostly examined the social construction of skill in the labour process within national labour market. Given this socially constructed nature of skill, the changing institutional and socio-cultural environment accompanying cross-border mobility means that individual migrants' skills will be interpreted, recognised and evaluated in more complex contexts and according to more varied standards. Consequently, this perspective has recently begun to be adopted in international migration among scholars investigating 'highly skilled' labour mobilities. For example, based on her observations of Polish skilled migrants in U.K., Nowicka (2014, 171) notes that skills are not 'fixed attribute[s]' that migrants simply 'bring with them'; and instead, 'notions of skill are geographically and historically specific [and dependent on] migration regimes, professional regulations and national policies'. In her empirical case, individual migrants understood the different ways skills are defined, acquired and valorised in source versus destination countries, and mobilised them according to their perceptions of the chances for negotiating strong positions in the labour market of the host country. In a recent special issue in *Migration Letters*, several case studies show that the legal and administrative practices, especially the national qualification recognition process, contribute to the selection of 'wanted' migrants in different countries (Hercog and Sandoz 2018; Kulu-Glasgow, Schans and Smit 2018; Andriescu 2018). Whether migrants can be recognised as skilled professionals are subject to the negotiation of multiple actors in a network of power (Ribeiro 2018).

While gaining some traction in migration research, the notion of the social construction of skill has largely remained an implicit notion that is mostly referred to in discussions of highly skilled labour migration. We argue that the utility of this framework is productive for the analysis of different forms of labour mobility, not just limited to 'skilled' migration. In fact, the understanding that skill is socially constructed and context-dependent serves to negate the arbitrary categorisation used in the skill-based selective migration policies. This special issue hence attempts to make it a more explicit analytical framework toward understanding the dynamic labour process in international migration. We propose that the following three questions can be useful in deconstructing the constructive process of skill in the cross-border labour migration: *who* arbitrates migrants' skill in the migration process and how it is interpreted and evaluated; *what* constitutes skill in different social contexts; and *how* individual migrants respond to the varied treatment of their skill.

The arbitrators of migrant skill

An expanding roster of actors – national and local governments (Andriescu 2018), employers, migration entrepreneurs and brokers (Ortiga 2018), professional associations (Bauder 2003), media and non-governmental organisations (Ribeiro 2018) – play crucial roles in not only shaping the skills of migrants but also deciding what constitutes skill and who are skilled migrants. This special issue examines the traditional arbitrators – the government, the employer and the migration entrepreneurs – as well as emerging actors in the globalising labour market.

As the key institution controlling population flows in and out of the country while gaining political legitimacy from a functioning economy, the government has vested interest in shaping and augmenting the country's talent pool. Labour receiving states design and alter skill categories to determine what constitutes desirable labour and what does not. Migrant sending countries sometimes become labour brokerage states, and, tying their developmental strategies to labour export, are actively involved in shaping and regulating the skill profile of its citizenry in line with global demand (Rodriguez 2010). In the

Philippines, such a developmental ethos pressures universities and colleges to produce more students with exportable skills, impairing the quality of its higher education and disrupting the domestic labour market (Ortiga 2017).

Oishi's (2021) and Ortiga's (2021) studies specifically describe the ways the governments of both migrant-receiving and sending countries manipulate conceptions and categories of skill to fulfil their respective political and economic agendas. In Japan, against the global trend of more stringent control over labour migration, the government has in recent years liberalised its labour migration policy by providing incentives to 'highly skilled professionals' to stay, while also cautiously opening its door to blue-collar workers. Oishi argues that this immigration policy change is influenced by the global competition for talent and the concerns about sustaining the nation-state as well as regions amidst a demographic crisis (Oishi 2021). While accepting and retaining 'highly skilled' workers is a relatively uncontroversial policy in Japan, this ethno-nationalist country has historically resisted the import of 'unskilled' or 'simple' labour. To respond to population decline and acute labour shortage in different sectors of economy while not jeopardising political legitimacy, this expansion of labour import is achieved through changing the definition of skill from a credential-based to an ability-based concept. Through programmes such as 'Specified Skilled Workers', the government stretches the bottom tiers of the 'skilled' category to incorporate occupational groups that had been formally labelled as 'unskilled' or 'semi-skilled', including agricultural workers, housekeepers and construction workers. Ortiga's paper, on the other hand, describes how the government in the Philippines manipulates the political discourses surrounding skill cultivation and skill utility in order to both reap the benefit of labour export and shun accountability for a volatile global market. Aiming to increase export nursing staff, the government encourages individual citizens to invest in education and training for nursing professions. When the global demand for nursing declines, the government changes the discourses to channel underemployed nurses to other professions in order to increase their employability.

Employers, as the actors that directly utilise labour, contribute to the skill construction process by determining the worth of migrants' skill as well as shaping its contours. This is particularly evident in selective migration programmes where the visa is sponsored by employers. Often, there is a gap between how employers and employees perceive skill (Rigby and Sanchis 2006). While employees have a broad definition of their own skill, including in it 'elements they use in their present jobs, in previous jobs and even elements they have never used but could if required', employers 'tend to define skill more narrowly, from the point of view of the requirements of the job after due analysis' (Rigby and Sanchis 2006, 23). Tseng's (2021) study of Taiwanese youth seeking job opportunities in Japan points to the different training regimes and differentiated evaluation of skills by employers in the sending and receiving contexts. Such discrepancies create opportunities for Taiwanese youth in corporate Japan, despite rejection by Taiwanese employers as not possessing the relevant skills. Similarly, in Germany and Japan, the national employment systems and firm-specific training regimes shaped in the post-war context of growing national economy have conditioned employers to look for particular skill profiles – often homophilous in logic and ethnocentric in content – among job applicants, creating obstacles for foreign graduates who do not necessarily fit the profiles to successfully make the transition in the host labour market (Liu-Farrer and Shire 2021). Employers, however, adjust their expectations of skill depending on their market positions. Liu-Farrer and Shire's comparative study of Germany and Japan shows that in both countries, small firms that tend to experience more dire labour shortage or belong to more flexible or emerging sectors of the economy are more willing to, and at times forced to, consider migrants who might not 'fit' the culturally and industrially specific expectations.

Migration entrepreneurs comprise another important actor in the shaping of skill profiles, especially with respect to low-skilled migrant labourers whose mobility they control for profit. Research has shown that migration entrepreneurs such as labour recruiters perform important roles in the facilitation of transnational mobility by connecting people and places and establishing networks (Hernandez-Leon 2005; Lindquist 2010; Lindquist, Xiang, and Yeoh 2012; Kern and Müller-Böker 2015; Baas 2020). Studies in this issue show that they are also responsible for training migrants to adapt to different skill regimes. For example, while migrant nurses have become the most globally mobile labour force, Walton-Roberts (2021) demonstrates that the main destination countries such as Canada have specific expectations and criteria for nursing. Her study of Indian nurses' mobility into Canada reveals that 'a complex chain of actors that includes households, state and non-state educational cum migration intermediaries and professional regulators … play variable roles in the formation and enforcement of the regime of skill' (Walton-Roberts 2021). Among them, she highlights the crucial roles played by migration intermediaries who seek to profit by facilitating Indian nurses' successful entry into Canadian labour market. While the state controls the policy pathways for migration purposes and the professional regulators in the host country control the credential evaluation and testing processes, educators and intermediaries in both India and Canada are actively engaged in the process of enforcing the regime of skill by tailoring the training of Indian nurses to meet the specific criteria dictated by the regime of skill.

Capitalising on the discrepancy between the skill supplied by international migrant employees and that expected by local employers, some former domestic human resource agencies transform themselves into de facto migration entrepreneurs. Liu-Farrer and Shire's study shows that when traditional German firms fail to absorb foreign students graduating from German universities into their firm-based employment systems, personal service agencies step in as an intermediary and bridge the skill gaps by employing them and moulding these foreign graduates into the skilled workers German companies desire.

The migration industry itself is a complex and high-risk enterprise. To recruit, select and mould random individuals into desirable migrant workers with appropriate skill profile and to handle the legal procedures for bringing them across borders require a high degree of social skill and expert knowledge. Hernandez-Leon's (2021) study examines the skill-building process taking place in the migration industry itself. His analysis focuses on two types of migration entrepreneurs who are involved in U.S. government-sponsored guest-worker schemes: recruiters, typically from rural backgrounds, whose job is to find and select guest workers; and document processors, often having urban middle-class backgrounds, who are responsible for completing visa application forms. His study reveals that both types of entrepreneurs are constantly honing their craft by interacting with and navigating through complex social relationships with colleagues, migrants, labour contracting firms, employers, migrant advocates, and government officials. The know-how gained through daily practices allows them to 'perform their jobs, to assume a more expansive role in the brokerage apparatus and to gauge risks and opportunities offered by labour intermediation' (Hernandez-Leon 2021).

With the globalisation of professions and labour markets, an expanding array of actors are taking on the roles of arbitrator of skill. James Farrer's (2021) case study on mobile chefs in fine dining restaurants in Shanghai is a case in point here. It shows how a constellation of actors shape a transnational field within which chefs ascend the occupational ladder. To be a chef instead of a cook involves not only former credentials recognised by the state and industry, more importantly, validation needs to be obtained from legitimating authorities in the transnational field (reviewers, bloggers, etc.). In a decentralised culinary field, global rating agencies such as Michelin's and World's Best Restaurants have increasingly assumed centralised authority in recognising culinary skills.

Skill, capital and status

Given a constellation of actors arbitrating skill, what then becomes recognised as skill? How is skill constituted, and what affects the way skill is categorised as high or low? Steiger (1993) has already argued that skill is often an ideological discourse used to justify pay, power and privilege. Proxies such as credentials, experiences, licenses, union or professional memberships, and in the case of construction workers, toolboxes, are used to identify groups who are believed to possess desired skills (Steiger 1993). However, to what degree different individuals at stake are able to claim skill ownership and how different skill proxies are evaluated is determined by power relationships existing in the pertinent field in which they play and take positions. Existing social hierarchy certainly affects the capacity that individuals in different social strata possess in claiming 'ownership' of particular skills. Studies of the social construction of skill in the national labour market have pointed out that the individuals' demographic characteristics such as gender and ethnicity directly influence how their skills are valued and the jobs they perform compensated. For example, while the value of skill is often measured by the substantive complexity and autonomy required for a job, Steinberg points out that the skills required for so-called women's jobs are systematically undervalued. Occupations such as nursery school teacher and child-care worker that are female-dominated are often assessed as less complex jobs compared to others such as the dog pound attendant and zoo keeper (Steinberg 1990, 456).

When labour crosses borders, global inequality, as well as the social formation and power relations in both sending and receiving societies, result in skills becoming partially determined by racialised assumptions, instead of what they are able to do. In traditional South-to-North labour migration, immigrants from less-developed countries are automatically considered to be unskilled workers (Samers 1998, 53), as reflected by Piore's (1979) theorisation that immigrant labour is structurally demanded to fill vacated jobs in host society's secondary labour market. Racism, nationalism and gender hierarchies continue to affect immigrants' skill recognition and consequently their labour market outcomes even when they enter specifically as highly skilled professionals (Bauder 2003; Man 2004; Riaño and Baghdadi 2007; Erel 2010; Nohl, Schittenhelm, and Schmidtke 2014; van Riemsdijk 2013).

Research also shows that the post-colonial legacy of racial hierarchy manifests itself again in the new context of cross-border migration. Demographic characteristics such as being white and having European citizenship are status symbols that continue to matter. People with such ascriptive statuses are perceived to possess specific or sought-after 'skills' which results in social and economic advantage to varying degrees. In the transnational culinary field that James Farrer describes in an earlier study, race and ethnicity become 'embodied capital', signifying one's qualification and projecting the authenticity of cuisine (Farrer 2015, see also 2021).

Hof (2019)'s study of young Europeans in Japan paints a more complex picture of the ways race affects how skill is perceived and consequently one's positioning in the social landscape. In Japan, a historical fascination with whiteness conferred a particular status to European youth. While some received preferential treatments, others were either pigeonholed into particular occupational categories or remained racialised tokens (Hof 2019).

Mobility and skill

The third question threaded into the social construction of skill relates to how skill is impacted by the process of cross-labour mobility. While there are many ways migrants acquire skills, this issue underscores the important role migration itself plays in building skills – a fact largely disregarded in selective immigration policy. As Williams (2007) argued, every migrant is a knowledge learner, carrier and potential transferrer. Increasingly, studies have not only shown that migrants actively engage in the process of skill acquisition, mobility itself is often an integral part of this skill building process and can be treated as a form of capital (Hagan, Lowe, and Quingla 2011; Hagan, Hernández-León, and Demonsant 2015; Leung 2013; Paul 2015). Moreover, the hard work of migration is also a source for attaining a range of social skills and competences. Through migration and overcoming constraints, migrants cultivate self-confidence, build networks, learn, adapt, become self-reliant (Williams and Baláž 2005), gain cosmopolitan sensibilities (Yeoh and Soco 2014) and upon return, some gain an edge in the home country labour market (Hagan, Hernández-León, and Demonsant 2015). This skill-building potential in the migratory process is evident not only among professional workers, but also migrants engaged in manual labour or other service industries.

In this issue, James Farrer's study shows that transnational mobility is now essential to the careers of culinary workers at all levels, from line cooks, to head chefs, to celebrity chefs building global brands. Such migrants use skills gained from mobility among different global cities to enhance their position in the field to access better jobs or to create conditions for further geographic mobility. On their mobility path are 'creative hotspots, famous restaurants, classic culinary regions, or upcoming culinary destinations' (Farrer 2021).

While migrants are able to acquire or valorise their skill through mobility, the relationship between skill and mobility is much more complex. Empirical studies in this issue also point out that 'higher' skill does not necessarily mean smoother mobility. Despite the fact that highly skilled migrants are considered desirable 'talent' which provides favourable conditions for migration in most countries, earlier studies on talent migration have debunked the myth that individuals with 'higher' skill – the so-called 'knowledge nomads' – 'inhabit a frictionless global space by virtue of their privileged positionings within processes of globalisation and in contradistinction to their lower-skilled counterparts' (Yeoh and Huang 2011, 682). This is because mobility is not simply motivated by economic logic, but 'negotiated within multiple life domains' (Yeoh and Huang 2011, 684).

Studies in this special issue show that because skills are socially constructed, migrant workers' social and physical mobility largely depend on how their skill is recognised, evaluated and utilised in different cultural, social and political contexts. Ortiga's study (2021), for example, highlights the precarity of skilled professionals in a volatile global labour market and the costs exacted by changing political and economic situations. Aspiring migrants who have invested in skill training in order to be transnationally mobile find themselves immobilised by the declining market demand for nursing staff. Liu-Farrer and Shire (2021), on the other hand, point out the disjuncture between the logic embedded in national employment systems and those of the globally mobile workforce despite the national policy to attract and retain highly skilled workers. Possessing the conventional proxies of skill such as educational credentials, even the ones from educational institutions in the host countries, do not necessarily guarantee that these foreign graduates are 'fit' for employment in the host labour market. Moreover, firm-specific skill training regimes that are oriented toward domestic labour markets essentially thwart migrant workers' potential career mobility outside the narrow confine of the firm and industry. Such skill training consequently generates frustration among individual migrants who hope to acquire transferrable skills that will allow them to deal with the vicissitudes of global labour market and at the same time build socially and geographically mobile careers (Tseng, 2021; Liu-Farrer and Shire 2021).

Conclusion

Amidst nativism and populism, anti-immigration sentiments are on the rise in many receiving nations. Increasingly, migration has become a controversial political issue, despite escalating demand for foreign 'skills' resulting from ageing native populations, declining fertility rates and technological innovations. National policy responses to these incompatible economic and political logics have resulted in selective migration programmes granting individuals varied entry conditions based on their levels of skill, measured by proxies such as education credentials or occupational experience. Empirical evidence indicates that the skill categories in operation neither reflect migrants' actual ability nor their post-migration labour market outcomes. The phenomena of skill mismatch and skill wastage among 'skilled' professionals, in particular, put the ethics as well as the meaning of skill-based selective migration policy into question.

Scholars studying 'highly skilled' labour migration have employed Bourdieu's theory of cultural capital (and fields) in the analysis of the utility (or the lack of it) and the (non)-transferability of immigrants' skill across borders (e.g. Bauder 2003; Nohl, Schittenhelm, and Schmidtke 2014). Research has also begun to pay attention to the social and institutional contexts within which skill is acquired and validated as well as the power relations involved in its definition and categorisation (Nowicka 2014; Hercog and Sandoz 2018). This special issue builds on this fruitful research, and provides a more encompassing analytical framework to understand the skill question in the labour mobilities across borders – not only those of so-called 'high skilled', but also those legally or administratively categorised as 'low skilled'. We argue that an explicit invocation of the concept of social construction of skill already puts pre-migration skill categorisation into question. By focusing on the three constitutive components – the different actors who participate in arbitrating skills; the various attributes and abilities that are variably identified and valued as skill; and the process of skill construction and in particular how migration itself contributes to skill-building – this framework helps clarify the contingent process of skill acquisition, transfer, and utility in transnational labour migration.

Dissecting the social construction process of skill emphasises contingency as well as the developmental potential of migrant skill regardless of skill categories. This perspective provides some basis for designing migration policy that is more conducive to talent development. Selective migration policy, by sorting immigrants according to their quantifiable skill levels, might be seen as progressive compared to racialised migration regimes that treat migrant workers of particular ethnicities as uniformly unskilled labour fit only to fill the bottom ranks of the labour market. However, by treating skill as fixed attributes that can be sorted into different categories of desirability and subjected to different degrees of control, selective migration policies still run the risk of taxonomising human beings and thereby reinforcing racial and gender prejudice and perpetuating global hierarchy. At the practical level, the rigid skill hierarchy, inflexibility of conversion even between different so-called skilled categories, and the locking mechanisms demonstrated in some migration regimes are not only susceptible to misuse and potential abuse, but also defeat the purpose of augmenting the national talent pool. It leads one to wonder if skill itself has not come to replace the category of race as employed in earlier forms of migration management. While the notion of skill is imbued with the notion that it is the objective product of merit, the papers included in this issue instead underline the arbitrariness as well as inflexibility of what determines its hierarchical scaling and interpretation. As such, 'skill' can be as meaningless as 'race' (or ethnicity, cultural background, etc.) in terms of a migrant's actual abilities and contribution to the host nation.

For researchers studying labour migration, the emphasis on the socially constructed nature of migrant skill urges intellectual awareness and reflexivity. Skill and its categorisation are too often taken for granted as commonsense concepts ready for use in practical and academic communications. When we lament how highly skilled professionals 'waste their skill' upon migration, while a legitimate concern, we unintentionally reproduce the political categories which embody an arbitrary and static notion of skill. Such unreflexive use has even more damaging consequences on the 'unskilled' and 'low-skilled' workers because it unintentionally justifies low pay and sometimes a form of non-personhood which is implicit in the tight surveillance and control placed on such workers in many countries (Hagan, Hernández-León, and Demonsant 2015). It is worthwhile to bear in mind that the categories of 'highly skilled professionals', 'skilled labour' and 'guest workers' are but visa categories, not actual people. A human-centred approach to migration might reveal that not only do we need to rethink the way nation-states categorise migrants, but also how we employ these concepts in our own studies.

Disclosure statement

No potential conflict of interest was reported by the author(s).

ORCID

Gracia Liu-Farrer http://orcid.org/0000-0003-3241-8703
Brenda S. Yeoh http://orcid.org/0000-0002-0240-3175

References

Adams, Richard. 2003. "International Migration, Remittances, and the Brain Drain: A Study of 24 Labor-exporting Countries", Policy Research Working Paper 3069, Washington, D.C.: World Bank.

Al Ariss, Akram, Iris Koall, Mustafa Özbilgin, and Vesa Suutari. 2012. "Careers of Skilled Migrants: Towards a Theoretical and Methodological Expansion." *Journal of Management Development* 31 (2): 92–101. doi:10.1108/02621711211199511.

Andriescu, Monica. 2018. "How Policies Select Immigrants: The Role of the Recognition of Foreign Qualifications." *Migration Letters* 15 (4): 461–475. doi:10.33182/ml.v15i4.3.

Appleyard, R. T. 1998. *Emigration Dynamics in Developing Countries (4 Vols).* Aldershot: Ashgate.

Baas, Michiel. 2017. "The Mobile Middle: Indian Skilled Migrants in Singapore and the 'Middling' Space Between Migration Categories." *Transitions: Journal of Transient Migration* 1 (1): 47–63. doi:10.1386/tjtm.1.1.47_1.

Baas, Michiel. 2020. "*Understanding the Cost of Migration: Facilitating Migration From India to Singapore and the Middle East.*" In *The Migration Industry in Asia: Brokerage, Gender and Precarity*, edited by M. Baas, 59–75. Singapore: Palgrave Pivot.

Bauder, Harald. 2003. ""Brain Abuse", or the Devaluation of Immigrant Labour in Canada." *Antipode* 35 (4): 699–717.

Beaverstock, Jonathan V. 2005. "Transnational Elites in the City: British Highly-Skilled Inter-Company Transferees in New York City's Financial District." *Journal of Ethnic And Migration Studies* 31 (2): 245–268. doi:10.1080/1369183042000339918.

Beaverstock, Jonathan V. 2012. "*Highly Skilled International Labour Migration and World Cities: Expatriates, Executives and Entrepreneurs.*" In *International Handbook of Globalization and World Cities*, edited by Ben Derudder, 240–250. Cheltenham: Edward Elgar.

Beine, Michel, Frédéric Docquier, and Hillel Rapoport. 2007. "Measuring International Skilled Migration: A New Database Controlling for Age of Entry." *The World Bank Economic Review* 21 (2): 249–254. doi:10.1093/wber/lhm007.

Birrell, Robert, Lesleyanne Hawthorne, and Sue Richardson. 2006. *"Evaluation of the General Skilled Migration Categories"*. Canberra: Department of Immigration and Multicultural Affairs.

Braverman, Harry. 1998. *Labor and Monopoly Capital: The Degradation of Work in the Twentieth Century.* Charlesbourg, QC: Braille Jymico Inc.

Carrington, William J., and Enrica Detragiache. 1998. "How Big is the Brain Drain?" Working Paper 98–102, Washington, D.C.: International Monetary Fund.

Docquier, Frédéric, and Abdeslam Marfouk. 2004. "Measuring the International Mobility of Skilled Workers (1990–2000)", Policy Research Working Paper 3381, Washington, D.C.: World Bank.

Docquier, Frédéric, and Abdeslam Marfouk. 2006. "*International Migration by Education Attainment in 1990–2000.*" In *International Migration, Remittances, and the Brain Drai*, edited by Çaglar Özden and Maurice Schiff, 151–199. New York, NY: Palgrave Macmillan.

Dumont, Jean-Christophe, and Georges Lamaitre. 2005. "Counting Immigrants and Expatriates in OECD Countries: A New Perspective, Directorate for Employment Labour and Social Affairs." *OECD Economic Studies* 2005 (1): 49–83. doi:10.1787/eco_studies-v2005-art3-en.

Erel, U. 2010. "Migrating Cultural Capital: Bourdieu in Migration Studies." *Sociology* 44 (4): 642–660.

Farrer, James. 2015. "Introduction: Travelling Cuisines in and out of Asia: Towards a Framework for Studying Culinary Globalization." In *Globalization and Asian Cuisines: Transnational Networks and Contact Zones*, edited by J. Farrer, 1–20. New York: Palgrave Macmillan.

Farrer, James. 2021. "From Cooks to Chefs: Skilled Migrants in a Globalising Culinary Field." *Journal of Ethnic and Migration Studies* 47 (10): 2359–2375. doi:10.1080/1369183X.2020.1731990.

Florida, Richard L. 2002. *The Rise of the Creative Class: And How It's Transforming Work, Leisure, Community and Everyday Life*. New York, NY: Basic Books.

Hagan, Jacqueline Maria, Rubén Hernández-León, and Jean-Luc Demonsant. 2015. *Skills of the Unskilled: Work and Mobility among Mexican Migrants*. Berkeley: University of California Press.

Hagan, J., N. Lowe, and C. Quingla. 2011. "Skills on the Move: Rethinking the Relationship Between Human Capital and Immigrant Economic Mobility." *Work and Occupations* 38 (2): 149–178. doi:10.1177/0730888410397918.

Hampson, Ian, and Anne Junor. 2015. "Stages of the Social Construction of Skill: Revisiting Debates Over Service Skill Recognition." *Sociology Compass* 9 (6): 450–463. doi:10.1111/soc4.12266.

Hercog, Metka, and Laure Sandoz. 2018. "Selecting the Highly Skilled: Norms and Practices of the Swiss Admission System for Non-EU Immigrants." *Migration Letters* 15 (4): 503–515. doi:10.33182/ml.v15i4.2.

Hernandez-Leon, Ruben. 2005. "The Migration Industry in the Mexico-US Migratory System." UCLA CCPR Population Working Papers.

Hernández-León, Ruben. 2021. "The Work that Brokers Do: The Skills, Competences and Know-How of Intermediaries in the H-2 Visa Programme." *Journal of Ethnic and Migration Studies* 47 (10): 2341–2358. doi:10.1080/1369183X.2020.1731989.

Hof, Helena. 2019. "Mobility as a Way of Life: European Millennials' Labour Migration to Asian Global Cities." Dissertation submitted to Graduate School of Asia-Pacific Studies, Waseda University.

Iredale, R. 2001. "The Migration of Professionals: Theories and Typologies." *International Migration* 39 (5): 7–26.

Kern, A., and U. Müller-Böker. 2015. "The Middle Space of Migration: A Case Study on Brokerage and Recruitment Agencies in Nepal." *Geoforum* 65: 158–169.

Khadria, Binod. 2004. "Human Resources in Science and Technology in India and the International Mobility of Highly Skilled Indians". OECD Science, Technology and Industry Working Papers 2004/7. OECD Publishing.

Kilbourne, Barbara Stanek, Paula England, George Farkas, Kurt Beron, and Dorothea Weir. 1994. "Returns to Skill, Compensating Differentials, and Gender Bias: Effects of Occupational Characteristics on the Wages of White Women and Men." *American Journal of Sociology* 100 (3): 689–719. doi:10.1086/230578.

Kofman, Eleonore, and Parvati Raghuram. 2005. "Gender and Skilled Migrants: Into and Beyond the Work Place." *Geoforum; Journal of Physical, Human, and Regional Geosciences* 36 (2): 149–154. doi:10.1016/j.geoforum.2004.06.001.

Kofman, Eleonore, and Parvati Raghuram. 2006. "Gender and Global Labour Migrations: Incorporating Skilled Workers." *Antipode* 38 (2): 282–303. doi:10.1111/j.1467-8330.2006.00580.x.

Kulu-Glasgow, Isik, Djamila Schans, and Monika Smit. 2018. "The Dutch Battle for Highly Skilled Migrants: Policy, Implementation and the Role of Social Networks." *Migration Letters* 15 (4): 517–532.

Kuznetsov, Y., and C. Sabel. 2006. "International Migration of Talent, Diaspora Networks, and Development: Overview of Main Issues." In *Diaspora Networks and the International Migration of Skills: How Countries Can Draw on Their Talent Abroad*, edited by Y. Kuznetsov, 3–20. Washington, D.C: World Bank.

Leung, Maggi W. H. 2013. "'Read Ten Thousand Books, Walk Ten Thousand Miles': Geographical Mobility and Capital Accumulation among Chinese Scholars." *Transactions of the Institute of British Geographers* 38 (2): 311–324. doi:10.1111/j.1475-5661.2012.00526.x.

Lindquist, Johan. 2010. "Labour Recruitment, Circuits of Capital and Gendered Mobility: Reconceptualizing the Indonesian Migration Industry." *Pacific Affairs* 83 (1): 115–132. doi:10.5509/2010831115.

Lindquist, Johan, Biao Xiang, and Brenda S.A. Yeoh. 2012. "Opening the Black Box of Migration: Brokers, The Organization of Transnational Mobility and the Changing Political Economy in Asia." *Pacific Affairs* 85 (1): 7–19. doi:10.5509/20128517.

Liu-Farrer, Gracia. 2012. "Ambiguous Concepts and Unintended Consequences: Rethinking Skilled Migration in View of Chinese Migrants' Economic Outcomes in Japan." *Asien* 124: 159–179.

Liu-Farrer, Gracia, and Karen Shire. 2021. "Who are the Fittest? The Question of Skills in National Employment Systems in an Age of Global Labour Mobility." *Journal of Ethnic and Migration Studies* 47 (10): 2305–2322. doi:10.1080/1369183X.2020.1731987.

Liu-Farrer, G., and A. H. Tran. 2019. "Bridging the Institutional Gaps: International Education as a Migration Industry." *International Migration* 57 (3): 235–249.

Mahroum, S. 1999. "Highly skilled globetrotters." In *Mobilising Human Resources for Innovation: Proceedings of the OECD Workshop on Science and Technology Labour Markets.* Paris: OECD.

Man, G. 2004. "Gender, Work and Migration: Deskilling Chinese Immigrant Women in Canada." *Women's Studies International Forum* 27 (2): 135–148.

Moss, Philip, and Chris Tilly. 2001. "Stories Employers Tell: Race, Skill, and Hiring in America." A Volume in the Multi-City Study of Urban Inequality. Russell Sage Foundation Publications Office.

Nohl, Arnd-Michael, Karin Schittenhelm, and Oliver Schmidtke. 2014. *Work in Transition: Cultural Capital and Highly Skilled Migrants' Passages Into the Labour Market.* Toronto: University of Toronto Press.

Nowicka, Magdalena. 2014. "Migrating Skills, Skilled Migrants and Migration Skills: The Influence of Contexts on the Validation of Migrants' Skills." *Migration Letters* 11 (2): 171–186. doi:10.33182/ml.v11i2.237.

Oishi, Nana. 2021. "Skilled or Unskilled? The Reconfiguration of Migration Policies in Japan." *Journal of Ethnic and Migration Studies* 47 (10): 2252–2269. doi:10.1080/1369183X.2020.1731984.

Ortiga, Yasmin. 2017. *Emigration, Employability and Higher Education in the Philippines.* London: Routledge.

Ortiga, Yasmin. 2018. "Education as Early Stage Brokerage: Cooling out Aspiring Migrants for the Global Hotel Industry." *Pacific Affairs* 91 (4): 727–748.

Ortiga, Yasmin Y. 2021. "Shifting Employabilities: Skilling Migrants in the Nation of Emigration." *Journal of Ethnic and Migration Studies* 47 (10): 2270–2287. doi:10.1080/1369183X.2020.1731985.

Paul, Anju Mary. 2015. "Capital and Mobility in the Stepwise International Migrations of Filipino Migrant Domestic Workers." *Migration Studies* 3 (3): 438–459. doi:10.1093/migration/mnv014.

Peppler, Lisa. 2018. "Changes in Highly Skilled Migration Policies: Turkish-German Medical Migration Since the 1960s." *Migration Letters* 15 (4): 491–502. doi:10.33182/ml.v15i4.1.

Piore, Michael J. 1979. *Birds of Passage: Migrant Labor and Industrial Societies.* Cambridge: Cambridge University Press.

Reich, R. 1991. *The Work of Nations: A Blueprint for the Future.* New York: Vintage Books.

Riaño, Y., and N. Baghdadi. 2007. "Understanding the Labour Market Participation of Skilled Immigrant Women in Switzerland: The Interplay of Class, Ethnicity, and Gender." *Journal of International Migration and Integration/Revue de l'integration et de la migration internationale* 8 (2): 163.

Ribeiro, Joana Sousa. 2018. "Being Called "Skilled": A Multi-Scalar Approach of Migrant Doctors' Recognition." *Migration Letters* 15 (4): 477–490. doi:10.33182/ml.v15i4.6.

Rigby, Mike, and Enric Sanchis. 2006. "The Concept of Skill and Its Social Construction." *European Journal of Vocational Training* 37: 22.

Samers, Michael. 1998. "'Structured Coherence': Immigration, Racism and Production in the Paris Car Industry." *European Planning Studies* 6: 49–72.

Saxenian, A. 2002. "BRAIN CIRCULATION. How High-Skill Immigration Makes Everyone Better Off." *Brookings Review* 20 (1): 28–31.

Skeldon, Ronald. 2009. "Of Skilled Migration, Brain Drains and Policy Responses." *International Migration* 47 (4): 3–29.

Steiger, Thomas L. 1993. "Construction Skill and Skill Construction." *Work, Employment and Society* 7 (4): 535–560. doi:10.1177/095001709300700403.

Steinberg, Ronnie J. 1990. "Social Construction of Skill: Gender, Power, and Comparable Worth." *Work and Occupations* 17 (4): 449–482. doi:10.1177/0730888490017004004.

Trebilcock, M. J., and M. Sudak. 2006. "The Political Economy of Emigration and Immigration." *New York University Law Review* 81: 234.

Tseng, Yen-Fen. 2021. "Becoming Global Talent? Taiwanese White-collar Migrants in Japan." *Journal of Ethnic and Migration Studies* 47 (10): 2288–2304. doi:10.1080/1369183X.2020.1731986.

van Riemsdijk, M. 2013. "Everyday Geopolitics, the Valuation of Labour and the Socio-political Hierarchies of Skill: Polish Nurses in Norway." *Journal of Ethnic and Migration Studies* 39 (3): 373–390.

Walton-Roberts, M. 2019. "Occupational (Im)Mobility in the Global Care Economy." *Journal of Ethnic and Migration Studies*, doi:10.1080/1369183X.2019.1592397.

Walton-Roberts, Margaret. 2021. "Intermediaries and Transnational Regimes of Skill: Nursing Skills and Competencies in the Context of International Migration." *Journal of Ethnic and Migration Studies* 47 (10): 2323–2340. doi:10.1080/1369183X.2020.1731988.

Williams, Allan M. 2007. "International Labour Migration and Tacit Knowledge Transactions: A Multi-Level Perspective." *Global Networks* 7 (1): 29–50. doi:10.1111/j.1471-0374.2006.00155.x.

Williams, Allan M., and Vladimir Baláž. 2005. "What Human Capital, Which Migrants? Returned Skilled Migration to Slovakia From The UK." *International Migration Review* 39 (2): 439–468. doi:10.1111/j.1747-7379.2005.tb00273.x.

Yeoh, Brenda S.A., and H. L. Chee. 2015. "Migrant Wives, Migrant Workers, and the Negotiation of (Il)Legality in Singapore." In *Migrant Encounters: Intimate Labour, the State, and Mobility Across Asia*, edited by S. L. Friedman and P. Mahdavi, 184–205. Philadelphia: The University of Pennsylvania Press.

Yeoh, B. S., and S. Huang. 2011. "Introduction: Fluidity and Friction in Talent Migration." *Journal of Ethnic and Migration Studies* 37 (5): 681–690.

Yeoh, Brenda S. A., and Theodora Lam. 2016. "Immigration and Its (Dis)Contents: The Challenges of Highly Skilled Migration in Globalising Singapore." *American Behavioral Scientist* 60 (5-6): 637–658. doi:10.1177/0002764216632831.

Yeoh, Brenda S.A., and Maria Andrea Soco. 2014. "The Cosmopolis and the Migrant Domestic Worker." *Cultural Geographies* 21 (2): 171–187. doi:10.1177/1474474014520899.

Skilled or unskilled?: The reconfiguration of migration policies in Japan

Nana Oishi

ABSTRACT

While Japan has long been perceived as a country with restrictive immigration policies, it has been rapidly widening its immigration gates through various policy reforms in the past decade. The most prominent policy shift in Japan took place in 2018 when the government decided to officially open its labour market to migrants in 14 occupational sectors, including agriculture, elder care and construction, which used to be considered 'unskilled' and 'semi-skilled' in previous migration schemes. This study analyses how the major shifts in Japan's migration policies have been introduced through the redefinition of 'skills' and 'skilled migrants'. In doing so, it integrates the scholarly debates on immigration policymaking in Japan and the literature on the conceptualisation of skills. By reviewing the development of skilled migration policies and some impactful discourses driven by global, national and regional forces, this study argues that the ambiguous nature of 'skills' and the multi-level merits as outcomes have facilitated the major policy transformation in Japan.

Introduction

Skilled migration has long been a policy priority of many countries for the last few decades. Particularly in the 2000s, the global competition for talent began to accelerate as many countries recognised the significance of skilled migrants for increasing their competitive advantage and driving innovation in the knowledge economy (Brown and Tannock 2009; Shachar 2006). In addition to traditional immigration countries, Japan, Singapore, Korea, China and EU countries also developed various policies on skilled migration (Ackers and Gill 2008; Oishi 2014).

In recent years, however, growing nationalism has been slowing down the process of such 'policy convergence' (Hollifield, Martin, and Orrenius 2014): several countries have begun to tighten their gate for skilled migration. In the US, under the slogan of 'America First', President Trump issued an Executive Order in 2017, declaring that the government would 'propose new rules and issue new guidance … to protect the interests of United States workers' (White House 2017). Other states have followed the US: Australia significantly reduced the number of occupations available for skilled worker visas in 2017 (Dehm and Vogl 2018) and further reduced the issuing of skilled visas in 2019–2020 (DHA 2019). Singapore has also tightened its borders for skilled migrants, which led to a drop in the non-resident population in 2017 for the first time in 14 years (Toh 2017). While skilled migration continues, the eligibility requirements for skilled migrants have been narrowed in terms of occupations and income thresholds (Brown and Tannock 2009).

In contrast, Japan has been rapidly widening its immigration gates through various policy reforms. The total number of migrants in Japan hit the record high of 2.7 million in 2018 (MOJ 2019a). While they still comprise only two per cent of the population, their presence has been on the rise: the percentage of the migrant workforce tripled in 16 prefectures in 2009–2018. (*Nihon Keizai Shimbun* 2018).

The most prominent policy shift in Japan took place in 2018, when the government announced that it would drastically open its labour market to 'new categories of migrants', including those without tertiary education (Cabinet Office 2018a, 50). In the next five years, the country will admit up to 345,150 migrants under a new visa titled 'Specified Skilled Worker No.1 visa' (SSW-1 hereafter) in 14 occupational sectors, including agriculture, elder care and construction, which used to be considered 'unskilled' and 'semiskilled' in previous migration schemes. Moreover, after five years, these SSW-1 visa holders who can demonstrate their advance skill levels through their industry's skill tests can apply for a 'Specified Skilled Worker No.2 visa' (SSW-2 hereafter) which offers them family reunification and unlimited visa renewals (Cabinet Office 2018b). While this SSW-2 visa itself doesn't offer permanent residency, it enables its holders to stay in Japan as long as they have a job and also allows them to apply for to permanent residency in the future. This shift was quite noteworthy, considering the fact that the Japanese government had long held a firm principle that it would only accept 'skilled migrants' with a bachelor's degree on a temporary basis and restricted their permanent settlement (MOL 1988). What do these policy changes mean and what was behind them?

This study attempts to reveal how the major changes in Japan's migration policies have been introduced by the incremental revisions of various 'skilled migration schemes'. In doing so, it will integrate the scholarly debates on immigration policy making in Japan and the emerging literature on the conceptualisation of skills. While existing political and cultural explanations were useful in understanding Japan's closed-door policy for unskilled migration until the mid-2000s, they cannot offer clear reasons for the country's seismic transformation of its migration policies. By identifying some impactful discourses driven by global, national and regional forces, this research underscores the fluidity of 'skills' in Japan's migration policies in recent years. It argues that the ambiguous concept of 'skills' has enabled policymakers to manoeuvre the existing institutional constraints and admit semi-skilled and unskilled workers. Based on the academic literature, qualitative analyses of a broad range of policy documents including the Diet (Parliament) Records and the Ministerial announcements, reports, statements and statistics, this research will investigate the processes in which the overall skilled migration policies have been changed in Japan and the dominant discourses behind them.

Policy-making in skilled migration in Japan and fluidity of 'skills'

Japan has long been perceived as an anomaly among liberal democracies due to its restrictive policies for unskilled foreign labour. While the political structure of liberal democracies tends to support open immigration policies (Freeman 1995), Japan's immigration gates had been closed – at least officially – for unskilled workers. Scholars treated Japan as a 'negative case', and tried to explain its restrictive policy[1] (Bartram 2005; Lee 2019).

Bartram (2005) attributed Japan's closed-door policies to the 'mode of economic governance' – its institutional structure and policies as a developmental state: developmental states are less likely to admit foreign workers since their state-centric policy-making is controlled by bureaucrats who are insulated from client politics and private interest groups (Bartram 2005). Instead of resorting to foreign labour, they encouraged corporations to cope with labour shortages by raising wages, productivity and investment in technology instead of resorting to foreign labour (*ibid*).

National identity and culture were also identified in migration studies to explain the differences in migration policies across countries (Brubaker 1992; Weiner 1995). Weiner highlighted the importance of national identity – 'whether a nation is built on the notion of cultural homogeneity or cultural diversity and whether the notion of pluralism extends from the political to the cultural realm' (Weiner 1995, 73–74). In this regard, Japan's xenophobic or insular culture is said to account for its closure to migrant labour (Bartram 2000). Other scholars integrated cultural and political arguments by addressing the 'practices, habits, or cultural "repertories" of policy-makers' as determinants of developmental states' migration policies (Seol and Skrentny 2009). Reflecting their elite political culture, they argue, industrialised states in Asia share a common approach similar to the logic of export-oriented industrialisation, which was to protect local labour markets and maximise economic growth rather than admitting migrants and promoting their settlement. These arguments, however, assume that the country's political structure and culture are static, which leaves us to wonder how and why immigration policies change.

Japan's migration policy-making requires more novel analyses by differentiating skilled and unskilled migration. While Japan has been mostly described as a 'closed' country for immigration, recent studies demonstrate that Japan's skilled migration policies have been quite open for many decades: the government has never adopted any quotas, a labour market test or a shortage skills list that many industrialised countries have used to limit the numbers and the occupational types of migrants to protect local workers (Oishi 2012, 2014). Furthermore, the Japanese government has been opening new skilled migration schemes in recent years. And most importantly, the 2018 Immigration Policy Reform and the revision in the Immigration and Refugee Control Act fundamentally overhauled the long-existing dichotomy of skilled versus unskilled migration.

These transformations of Japan's migration policies reflect conceptual fluidity of 'skills', indicating its social constructive nature (Liu-Farrer, Yeoh, and Baas 2021). While there are two major international definitions of 'skills',[2] an increasing number of studies confirmed that the nature of 'skills' is ambiguous in reality: there is no universal consensus on its definition (Liu-Farrer 2013; Martin and Ruhs 2011). Some scholars emphasised the socially-constructed dimensions of 'skills' in the existing policy approaches, claiming that 'skills' often arise from negotiations among various economic actors (e.g. industries, unions, professional organisations and experts) in the process of developing skills shortage lists used for selecting migrants (Martin and Ruhs 2011). Others also contended that skill is not a neutral concept, as skill recognition processes are often affected by migrants' cultural capital, gender, race and ethnicity, contributing to the perpetuation of existing hierarchical social order (Nohl et al. 2014; Shan and Fejes 2015).

To fully explain the recent shifts in Japan's migration policies, it is indispensable to trace the policy development process of skilled migration, examine the ways in which skills have been defined and redefined in them, and analyse what kind of social, economic and political contexts and discourses have been shaping such processes.

Policy developments on skilled migration: redefining 'skills'

The process of reconfiguring migration policies in Japan evidently reflects this social construction of 'skills'. While maintaining the official principle that the country admits only 'skilled workers' (MOL 1988), its definition of 'skills' has been gradually broadened due to some distinct policy discourses driven by various social, economic and political forces.

Officially, most work visas had been issued only to 'skilled' migrants who hold a bachelor's degree, have received a job offer from a company in Japan related to their degree area, and are expected to receive a salary comparable to that of locals. Since employers often require fluency in the Japanese language, the majority of these skilled migrants have been former international students who graduated from Japanese universities. At the same time, the government never officially defined 'skilled migrants'. In 2003, the Minister of Justice stated that the Japanese government does not officially use the term 'skilled migrants' but offered a proxy by acknowledging that the country has accepted foreigners in the fields of professional and technical fields through 14 visa categories including 'medical doctors', 'researchers', 'engineers', 'humanities and international affairs' and 'intra-company transferees' (MOJ 2003). Most government officials used these categories as 'skills' in the 2000s. Since then, more categories have been added to this list, and there are now 340,000 skilled migrants,[3] largely from Asian countries such as China, Korea and India (MOJ 2019a).

Three policy discourses in skilled migration

While the Japanese government had long admitted skilled migrants under regular work visas, it began to develop more specific skilled migration policies in the 2000s, paying attention to different categories of migrants and skills. These policies are not linear or temporal but are driven by different imperatives. This section will examine the three major discourses that seem to have had impacts on skilled migration policies in Japan. They are not necessarily mutually exclusive and are partly overlapping.

Globalism: global competition for talent

The policy discourses were initially dominated by globalism, particularly in the context of globalising labour market and talent competition. The Japanese government acknowledged the growing demand for IT workforce across the world, and highlighted the challenges in securing highly skilled migrants in IT sectors in the country due to the competition with other industrialised countries as well as emerging economies (Cabinet Office 2003a, 2003b; D'Costa 2008; Oishi 2014). To tap into a greater pool of engineers in the Asia-Pacific region, the government proposed the Asian Common IT Skill Standards Initiative at the meeting of the ASEAN plus Three (Japan, China, and Korea) to develop a mutual skill recognition system for engineers in 2000. In the same year, Japan also joined the APEC Engineers Mutual Recognition Project and became one of the participants of the APEC Engineer Register, which certified the qualified engineers in the region (IPEJ 2011). Subsequently, the government launched 'e-Japan Strategy' in

2003, aiming to enhance the country's IT environment and competitiveness by bringing 30,000 talented IT workers from overseas by 2005 (Cabinet Office 2003a). The government specifically stated that it would promote 'a system to help facilitate the acceptance of foreign IT specialists to work in Japan' by 'relaxing and improving immigration policies' (Cabinet Office 2003b, 38). Indeed, the immigration law was revised in 2006 to facilitate the immigration of IT workers.

This initiative to attract more IT workers was further expanded as the government and business leaders became more keenly aware that Japan was behind the global competition of talent. The government-led policy council expressed its concern as follows:

> The global competition to secure highly skilled talent such as researchers, engineers and managers has become fierce, and other countries have been adopting various policy measures to attract them. … For us not to be behind the global talent competition, … it is necessary to adopt strategic policies for institutional planning and promotion of their admission. (The Council for Promoting Highly Skilled Talent 2009, in Japanese)

In this context, 'the Points-Based Preferential Immigration Treatment for Highly Skilled Foreign Professionals' (the points system hereafter), was launched in 2012. This system aimed to attract more highly skilled migrants from overseas by offering them more incentives[4] to live and work in Japan. At the same time, through this system, Japan's skilled migrants were dichotomised into upper and lower strata, leading to differentiated access to benefits.

Nationalism: sustaining the nation-state in demographic crisis

Nationalism has become prominent in policy discourses since the mid-2000s, as Japan's total population began to drop in 2005 followed by the decline in its workforce in 2008. The labour force was projected to shrink by almost 40% in the period 2008–2060 and that the old-age dependency ratio would fall to 1.3 by 2055, threatening the country's long-term economic growth and the sustainability of social security systems (JBF 2008).

While the nationalism discourse is often associated with anti-immigrant sentiments in the West, the situation has been slightly different in Japan. Similar sentiments do also exist, but maintaining sufficient levels of population and workforce has become a primary focus, reflecting its demographic crisis. The discourse has been gradually shifted to Japan's long-term sustainability as a nation by fostering foreigners' long-term settlement and naturalisation, instead of relying on temporary guest worker programmes. The Alliance of Liberal Democratic Party Parliamentarians (2008) advocated for admitting 10 million migrants by 2050, arguing for a new 'Japanese-style immigration policy' which would turn foreigners into 'Japanese':

> [This new policy aims to] have them [foreigners] <u>settle down in local communities as Japanese citizens</u> as soon as possible. The core of the Japanese style-immigration policy is to produce 'new citizens' who can establish positive relationships with existing Japanese residents by providing generous education. (ALP 2008; Underlined by the author, in Japanese)

This proposal never materialised due to objections from the conservatives within the LDP, and thus it did not represent the party's official view. Nevertheless, the fact that a group of some LDP politicians felt urged to submit this proposal to the party leaders revealed the seriousness of population ageing in Japan and the pressing need for policy actions.

The East Japan Great Earthquake and the Fukushima disaster in March 2011 added an additional layer of incentives for developing new policies to promote the long-term settlement of skilled migrants and to minimise their exodus. In March and April 2011, over a half million migrants left the country (MOJ 2011). While many returned eventually, the number remained below the pre-disaster level for a while, which triggered a widespread sense of urgency among policymakers to attract more skilled migrants from overseas to contribute to the Japanese economy, resulting in the launch of the points-based system in 2012.

While the points-based system was partly meant to address the concern for global talent competition, it also entailed the component of Japan's socio-economic sustainability as a nation. The Council for Promoting Highly Skilled Talent (2009, 17), which advocated the points-based system, stated the following:

> It is necessary to implement the promotion of skilled migration as a national strategy to maintain our country's vitality and achieve sustainable growth in the midst of population decrease and population ageing.

Partly due to the fact that the number of eligible applicants was extremely small in the first year (MOJ 2013), the stringent requirements were significantly relaxed. The lowest income threshold was halved from six million yen to three million yen, and the minimum work experience requirement was also reduced from five to three years. The merits for highly skilled migrants also increased, and now they can apply for permanent residency in Japan after only one year.

While these changes boosted the cumulative stock of HSFPs to 6,669 in 2016, 17% of them have also left Japan (Cabinet Office 2017). Various studies demonstrated that limits in career prospects, inequality, institutional barriers (e.g. tax and social security) and social integration issues hamper the permanent settlement of skilled migrants in Japan (e.g. D'Costa 2008; Oishi 2012). Skilled migrant women, who comprise only a minority (30%) of skilled migrants in Japan, are also disincentivised to stay in Japan, since they do not feel they have been treated equally in their workplace (Hof 2018; Oishi 2018).

Regionalism[5]: 'disappearing municipalities' and the quest for migration

The nationalistic discourse driven by demographic crises further developed a distinct strand of discourses on regionalism, since regional areas (prefectures and smaller municipalities) have been more seriously affected by population ageing and labour shortages. The National Governors' Association (NGA) has been calling for further policy actions by the central government (NGA 2000), and even addressed the specific labour shortage in agriculture and care sectors in its policy recommendations (NGA 2014). While existing studies have attributed Japan's closed-door migration policy to the opposition from farmers and rural residents, the situation has changed since they started welcoming migrants through the Technical Intern Training Program (TITP) to cope with labour shortages in agriculture, fishery and manufacturing. Regional areas are now heavily dependent on these migrants: the total number of technical interns and trainees now exceeds 300,000, and the vast majority of the recipients are regional prefectures (MOJ 2019a). Moreover, reflecting the shortage of care workers in rural areas, the NGA also advocated admitting migrant care workers, not only as temporary guest workers but also long-term settlers (NGA 2014).

The central government was further pressed when Mr Hiroya Masuda, the former governor of Iwate (a regional prefecture) and the former Minister of Internal Affairs and Communication, published a book titled *Disappearance of Regional Areas*, arguing that 896 villages and towns in Japan would soon 'disappear' due to a rapidly declining number of women of child-bearing age (Masuda 2014). His book, as well as his policy paper called 'Masuda Report,' emitted a major shockwave across the country. Additionally, regional governments also demanded more political and financial autonomy through major administrative system reforms to meet more socio-economic needs in their prefectures and/or municipalities.

In response to these regional outcries, the central government took two major actions. First, it announced its commitment to 'regional vitalisation' (*chihou sousei*) by creating a new cabinet minister position for 'the Promotion of Overcoming Population Decline and Vitalising Local Economy in Japan' in 2015. The second policy action was to establish a major policy scheme for regional migration. Particularly since the 2017 general election was approaching, enabling regional governments to bring migrants into agriculture to meet local labour needs served the LDP's political interest in securing regional votes. The Act on National Strategic Special Zones (NSSZs), which was originally passed as part of regulatory reforms and entailed the minimal migration component, was revised in 2015 to expand the scope of regional migration, enabling both prefectural and smaller municipal governments to take initiatives to meet specific demands in the local labour market. In particular, reflecting the acute labour shortage in agriculture in regional areas, for the first time in Japan's migration history, the government stretched the bottom tier of the 'skilled' category by admitting migrant farmers, by redefining them as 'skilled'. The admission of agricultural workers under the NSSZ scheme was a breakthrough in Japan's migration policies, given that they had long been categorised as 'unskilled workers' and were thus outside the country's official migration policy. In 2018, four prefectures (Kyoto, Niigata, Aichi, and Okinawa) started recruiting 'foreign talent in agricultural support' from overseas who (1) are aged 18+, (2) have at least one year of work experience in agriculture and relevant knowledge and techniques and (3) possess the basic Japanese language proficiency necessary to execute agricultural *support services*[6] (Cabinet Office 2014). This breakthrough reflected the severity of population ageing in regional areas, particularly in agriculture. The average age of Japanese farmers has reached 67, and it is widely believed that the sustainability of the sector and food security are endangered (MAFF 2017).

Regional-global and regional-national linkages

These policy discourses are not mutually exclusive but are rather intricately linked to each other. For instance, the NSSZ Act that created a regional migration scheme concurrently served neoliberal globalism and nationalism by 'stretching the bottom tier' of skilled migrants and opening a path to admit 'foreign housekeepers,' who had long been defined as 'unskilled'. While this was part of the government's 'womenomics' policy, which aimed to increase Japanese women's labour force participation, it also met the needs of global corporations as their expatriates needed English-speaking helpers for housework and childcare that they used to have in other countries (Sadamatsu 2018). Foreign housekeepers can now work in some specific areas where expatriates are concentrated, namely Tokyo, Kanagawa, Aichi, Osaka and Hyogo.

The regional and global linkages are also observed in the NSSZ Act in its emphasis on Japan's cultural heritage. Kyoto became the first prefecture to employ foreign chefs and the foreign graduates of Japanese culinary schools in Japanese restaurants.[7] This decision came partly as a response to the need to accredit more Japanese and foreign chefs, which had arisen after Japanese traditional cuisine (*washoku*) became designated as Intangible Cultural Heritage by UNESCO in 2013. Kyoto has taken its pride as the birthplace of *washoku* and the mecca where the cuisine had been developed for hundreds of years. Nevertheless, many Japanese restaurants in the region had also been suffering from chronic labour shortages. Therefore, while the quest to have its traditional cuisine recognised by the world was regional and national in nature, the actual outcome resulted in globalising its workforce.

The NSSZ Act also had another nationalistic component as it was partly meant to strengthen its cultural presence and 'soft power' (Nye 1990) by admitting 'Cool Japan foreign talent (CJFT)' – workers in media, fashion, animation and games. Initially, international students in Japan were only allowed to work in the sectors that were relevant to their field of study, and some sectors such as sales, tourism, and entry-level animation production were excluded. However, the further revision of the NSSZ Act in 2017 removed these barriers, significantly expanding the range of jobs that vocational school graduates could take (Cabinet Office 2018c). While this new policy can be perceived as nationalistic in the sense that it was meant to strengthen Japan's cultural industries and its soft power, it was also meant to meet chronic labour shortages in these industries as well as to further develop the country's tourism industry.

Overhauling the 'unskilled': immigration reform in 2018

These revisions of the NSSZ Act were obviously not in line with the government's conventional policy of only accepting 'skilled migrants' – being university graduates and/or having equivalent skills and experience. Prime Minister Abe repeatedly justified the NSSZ scheme as part of the deregulatory reforms resolving the institutional rigidities that had hindered regional development (Diet Record 2014, 2016). Nevertheless, as labour shortages continued to grow, the government decided to overhaul the existing definition of 'skills' to maintain its policy consistency.

The redefinition of 'skilled migrants' in 2018 was the most significant change in Japan's post-war migration history. The Council on Economic and Fiscal Policy, which is chaired by Prime Minister Abe, created a 'new type of visas' to admit 'work-ready foreign workers who possess certain expertise and techniques' (Cabinet Office 2018a, 26). Under this new policy, the government stated that it would accept 345,150 newly-defined skilled migrants – 'Specified Skilled Worker No.1' (SSW-1) and 'Specified Skilled Worker No.2' (SSW-2) – in the next five years in 14 sectors (Cabinet Office 2018e). They include agriculture, construction, elderly care, hotels, and shipbuilding, which had long been categorised as unskilled sectors. The government recognised that these sectors suffer from chronic and severe labour shortage 'even after having implemented measures to improve productivity and secure workers by promoting women's and the elderly's labour force participation and improving salaries and working conditions' (*ibid*).

The change was not only that migrants in these 'formally unskilled' sectors can officially enter Japan after passing the exams on basic Japanese language as well as knowledge and skills in a specific field.[8] While migrants with the SSW-1 visa can only work for five years with no possibility for family reunification and contract renewal, if they demonstrate their skills by passing a relevant skill proficiency test and Japanese language exam, they can obtain a 'SSW-2' visa, which enables them to work in Japan permanently and bring their family members (Cabinet Office 2018d). Currently, SSW-2 visas are limited to construction and shipbuilding, since other industry associations are still in the process of developing their skill proficiency tests. Once these processes are completed, more migrants will be allowed to work permanently in other sectors as well. Based on sectoral analyses of labour shortages, the Japanese government decided on the quota of migrants in each industry as summarised in Table 1. All these formerly 'unskilled' occupational sectors are now officially categorised as 'skilled', and migrants in these sectors are also recognised as 'specific skilled workers' – workers who have skills in specific fields.

This policy change was made at an extraordinarily fast pace: the government started accepting these new migrants in less than a year after it announced the new policy. There were some political reasons behind it. Nonaka (2019) argued that the Japan Chambers of Commerce and Industry aggressively lobbied the government to respond to acute labour shortages in regional areas. Accommodating such a demand also served PM Abe's goal to secure two-thirds of the House of Representatives' seats in the 2019 election to realise his long-term ambition for Constitutional Reform. According to Nonaka, votes from the JCCI, which has over a million corporate members, were critical to win the election.

Implications of skill redefinitions

While the Organisation for Economic Co-operation and Development (OECD)'s concept of human resources in science and technology (HRST) had long been used as a definition of 'skilled workers' in Japan and elsewhere, its validity in non-science and technology (S&T) sectors had not been debated in Japan until recently. It was partly because non-S&T sectors were assumed to require limited skills. Nevertheless, the severity of population ageing and the resultant labour shortage forced the Japanese government to reassess this

Table 1. Newly-defined skilled sectors and maximum number of migrants to be admitted in 2019–2024.

Industries	Maximum numbers (2019–2024)
Elderly care	60,000
Food service (restaurants)	53,000
Construction	40,000
Building cleaning	37,000
Food/drink manufacturing	34,000
Hospitality (accommodation)	22,000
Primary materials industry	21,500
Shipbuilding	13,000
Fisheries	9,000
Automobile maintenance	7,000
Electric/electronic-related industries	4,700
Industrial machinery manufacturing	5,250
Airlines	2,200
Total	345,150

Adopted from Cabinet Office (2018e) by the author.

long-standing practice of classifying migrants and their skills. Japan is now the most severely affected by a labour shortage in the world: 89% of companies are short of talent (Manpower 2018). The government was particularly concerned about the declining number of trained technicians who constituted the core of Japan's manufacturing and construction industries (METI 2015). The sustainability of the skilled workforce in manufacturing and craft industries has been particularly a concern in regional areas, since it has a bearing on the future of their economy, industries and even cultures that have been maintained for generations (Nakamura and Takano 2014). These situations sparked the debates on the re-evaluation of vocational skills in three consecutive Diet (Parliament) meetings in 2015–2017, referring to Germany's Meister System in which workers with advanced vocational skills hold a high status and income security. One of the Senators, Yasuko Komiyama, made a statement as follows:

> Artisans and technicians are disappearing. The shortage of these workers will lead to the situation where we cannot produce our traditional artworks and craft products in Japan. What can we do about this? I am convinced that Japanese manufacturing can be strengthened only when we follow Germany's Meister system and improve the status and wages of these artisans and technicians. (Diet Record 2016)

Through these policy debates and media discourses, policymakers began to realise that leaving the situation as it was could endanger the sustenance of Japanese traditional industries and cultural heritage. Furthermore, the severe shortage of workers in care sectors has also been recognised as a threat to the already shrinking welfare state: 550,000 more workers need to be secured to maintain the existing system (Cabinet Office 2018e). The values of vocational skills were thus gradually recognised, which contributed to the 'deservingness' (Bonizzoni 2018) of migrants with no tertiary education and as a result, the expansion of the 'skilled migrants' category.

These redefinitions of 'skilled migrants' in Japan are, in fact, fully in line with the ILO definitions. While craft workers, care workers and housekeepers are often labelled as 'unskilled' in many industrialised countries, the ILO designates them to the middle-level occupational category, which requires 'relatively advanced literacy and numeracy skills and good interpersonal communication skills' and 'a high level of manual dexterity'[9] (ILO 2012, 12). To fully justify the admission of 'foreign housekeepers' as 'skilled workers', the Japanese government also required prospective migrants to complete at least 200 hours of orientation in the following areas: (1) basic ability (communication, team work, occupational safety and hygiene); (2) common ability (ability to establish good relationship with clients, managing one's own performance), and (3) specialised ability (cleaning, washing, cooking, food serving, etc.) (Cabinet Office 2015).

Despite the recognition of these abilities and skills, the newly admitted migrants under the NSSZ scheme became further stratified. The ones in cultural industries were labelled as 'specialised talent' (*senmon jinzai*) – the same category as mainstream skilled workers – while those in agriculture and housekeeping were 'supporting talent' (*shien jinzai*), even though the latter may have specialised knowledge in farming technology, nutrition or child development. It should be noted that this differentiation is not necessarily based on educational qualifications and work experience, but only on occupational stereotypes. For instance, no educational qualification is required for migrants who apply for *washoku* chef positions; the only requirement is one year of work experience. No clear reason is given as to why *washoku* chefs are categorised as 'specialised talent' while farmers and housekeepers are not, but it is most likely associated with the social perceptions of occupational prestige. As discussed earlier, *washoku* was registered as the UNESCO's Intangible Cultural Heritage and represents Japan's haute culture. The occupational prestige that *washoku* chefs carry is thus placed above the regular skill classification system which is largely based on educational qualifications. Other occupations in 'Cool Japan' industries are also categorised as 'specialised talent,' although they require a technical school certificate only. This might be attributed to the fact that they are mostly white-collar workers.

The label of 'supporting talent' given to agricultural workers and housekeepers might also reflect their low occupational status. The occupational prestige score of agricultural workers is 45.6, and that of care workers and domestic workers is 38.1, the lowest among all occupations (SSDQ 1995). The low occupational prestige scores for care/domestic workers are likely to be attributed to the systematic undervaluation of female-dominated jobs (Steinberg 1990). While skills are often measured by the substantive complexity and autonomy required for a job, it also reflects the ways in which policymakers attach their subjective meanings (and sometimes prejudices) to certain occupations. This social construction of skills significantly affects the recognition process of migrants' skills and their labour market outcomes, perpetuating the existing hierarchy of social order along axes of gender, ethnicity and race (2021; Shan and Fejes 2015, 230).

The same problem remains in the new migration scheme of 'Specific Skilled Workers' (SSWs). It officially recognised the 'skills' of agricultural workers and care workers by defining 'skills' as entailing three components: (1) prior knowledge of the sector, (2) techniques to execute necessary tasks and (3) work experience (Cabinet Office 2018d). These components are operationalised in the form of 'skill tests' that industry/trade associations operate. This institutionalisation of skills by involving industry/trade associations brought some transparency into the process of determining skill levels. While these skills may be 'specific' and may not have the versatility and generalisability across diverse sectors that other skills may have (e.g. IT coding skills), they are now recognised as useful vocational skills that the Japanese economy needs. Given Japan's long history of migration policy admitting workers in agriculture and care only through its 'side doors', opening a 'front door' for them is an epoch-making development. Nevertheless, the skill stratification and unequal treatment still remain: unlike other skilled migrants, SSW-1 visa holders can stay only up to five years and are not entitled to family reunification. They constitute the bottom rung of skilled workers and thus have access to limited rights until they pass another skill test and obtain an SSW-2 visa.

The prospective challenges of the new migration policies

While Japan's new SSW scheme may alleviate acute labour shortages in Japan by admitting newly-defined 'skilled workers', it is likely to face a number of operational challenges. The most important one is their integration in the workplace and the local community. While the guideline stated that SSW-1 visa holders have an N4 (basic) level proficiency or equivalent (MOJ 2018a), it is the second lowest level in the Japanese Language Proficiency Test, which can be challenging for smooth transitions to work and daily activities in Japan. Furthermore, unlike the existing technical intern and trainee programmes, the NSSZ scheme and the new migration scheme do not entail any official mandatory language and socio-cultural training period. The government requires employers of SSW-1 visa holders to provide language training and life support during their contract period[10] (MOJ 2019b). However, it is unclear how this requirement will be implemented at this point: it does not specify any penalties for those who do not comply. The language proficiency requirement is a concern from the perspective of occupational safety as well. As there were already cases where technical interns had been engaged in the decommission work in Fukushima without being sufficiently informed of radiation (Yamawaki 2018), SSWs might face similar circumstances entailing health risks. In fact, the Tokyo Electric Power Company (TEPCO) had a plan to hire SSWs for decommissioning the Fukushima No.1 nuclear power plant (Ishizuka 2019), which the Ministry of Health, Labour and Welfare intervened to suspend. Such cases might emerge, since employers can easily manipulate workers with limited language proficiency.

The protection of these new skilled migrants' rights is another major challenge. While the government declared that it would remove the involvement of intermediary agencies to prevent exploitative practices (Cabinet Office 2018d), Japanese companies have had a record of mistreating technical interns and trainees for over two decades. Despite the government's measures to tackle the problems, mistreatment, rights violations, and exploitation remain rampant across the country. According to a government survey, 186 companies and 27 monitoring/management agencies violated the rules of the technical intern scheme (MOJ 2018b). While the government plans to allocate 9 million yen (US $80,000) to improve the monitoring of companies with migrant workers including SSWs (Cabinet Office 2018f), more rigorous systems should be instituted since their effective interventions will hold the key to the new programme's success.

Perhaps the most important future challenge for Japan is social integration of these new skilled migrants in local communities. Japan has already been struggling with 'multicultural coexistence' with migrants for the last three decades, particularly with *Nikkeijin* (migrants of Japanese descent), technical interns and trainees, international students and foreign spouses and children. While the national government adopted the 'Multicultural Coexistence Plan' in 2005, the actual measures and services to assist and support migrants with their settlement and social services were relegated to municipalities. However, partly because of limited resource availability, the majority of municipalities (54%) had not adopted any measures to support migrants in their communities (MIAC 2018) even 13 years after the plan was issued.

The national government's new country-wide policy to tackle the challenges in 'multicultural coexistence' is likely to change the situation. For FY2018–2019, it allocated 21.1 billion yen for comprehensive measures and programmes for accepting and integrating migrants (Cabinet Office 2018f). The policy guideline, titled 'Comprehensive Policies for the Acceptance of and Coexistence with Foreign Talent', had four major pillars: (1) public hearings from practitioners as well as awareness raising for multicultural coexistence, (2) life support for migrants as community members (*seikatsusha*), (3) programmes to promote the appropriate and smooth acceptance of foreign talent, and (4) creation of a new immigration control system.

The first pillar of public hearings is an entirely new development in the sphere of integration. It is expected to incorporate the voices of civil society organisations into state policies and entails the component of implementing activities for raising human rights awareness under the same banner. The second pillar, life support, includes a long list of services such as medical interpretation, Japanese language programmes, assistance for migrants' children. The most prominent development was to establish a 'one-stop centre' in 100 cities across Japan, offering a wide range of assistance for migrants in 11 languages (Cabinet Office 2018f).

The most significant institutional development was the promotion of the Immigration Bureau from one of the offices of the Justice Ministry to a higher-level arm, the Immigration Services Agency, in April 2019. It indicates the government's determination to accept more migrants and tackle their social integration in a more open and comprehensive manner. Nevertheless, the Ministry of Justice has long been handling immigration control and law enforcement and does not possess sufficient institutional expertise in social integration. To what extent it could effectively implement all the integration measures will depend on the degree of their collaboration with the Ministry of Internal Affairs and Communications which has closely worked with municipal governments as well as the Ministry of Health, Labour and Welfare in charge of workplace issues.

With these numerous integration measures adopted for the first time at the national level, Japan entered a new era of migration and integration in 2019. We need to wait for future research, however, to assess the extent to which the new programmes are successfully implemented. In 2015, Japan was ranked only 27th in the Migrant Integration Policy Index, lower than most industrialised countries (Migration Policy Group 2015), which suggests that it may still take time to bring in significant changes. The existing anti-migrant sentiments also need to be tackled more effectively. While the majority of Japanese support more migration, some anti-Korean and anti-Chinese sentiments have taken root to a certain extent. Though the anti-hate speech law was passed in 2016, its impact is limited since it lacks penal clauses. Developing clear anti-discrimination legislation that ensures migrants' rights protection would be indispensable for the success of the new programme.

Concluding remarks

This study attempted to unravel how Japan's overall migration policies have changed through the recurrent revisions of 'skilled migration' schemes. In doing so, it identified three migration discourses driven by global, national and regional forces, which seemed to have had major impacts on the recent changes in skilled migration policies in Japan. The discourse on global talent competition can fit in the existing developmental state theory, in that it would serve the state bureaucracy's long-term development goal and quest for further economic growth. The prominence of demographic crisis and the decline in regional economies in policy discourses, on the other hand, can be understood as part of 'client politics', as the new policy served the LDP's supporters in rural areas, such as farmers and the owners of small- and medium-sized enterprises, who began to feel the serious impacts of population ageing more acutely than residents in urban areas. In other words, 'clients' interests' are not static, and their changes pressure policymakers to respond to the same issues differently. It was intriguing that the arguments based on maintaining culture and nationhood, which typically go against more immigration, seemed to play a role in supporting more open migration policies in the case of Japan, since the country's demographic crisis has reached the level that could endanger its traditional cultural heritage and national social security programmes. In other words, the redefinition of 'skilled migrants' served the interests of all fronts: it met its overall development goals arising from global talent competition, regional socio-economic needs and nationalistic interests for maintaining cultural heritage and identity, all of which are intricately linked to each other. I argue that these multi-level merits as outcomes have facilitated the major breakthrough occurring in Japan's migration policies. Having said that, more detailed empirical research and analyses are needed to fully disentangle the linkages of these policy discourses and the actual policy-making processes.

The demographic crisis and intergenerational sustainability of the welfare state in Japan have cultivated a 'deservingness' (Bonizzoni 2018) of more diverse migrants among the public in recent years. Many polls have been consistently supporting more migration: the latest one indicated that 57% supported the new SSW scheme (*Yomiuri Shimbun* 2019). Such wider public support for migration derives from the recognition that the country would not be able to sustain its industries, social security system and cultural heritage without admitting migrants with a broader range of skill sets. Such public support should have given more assurance to the Abe administration that the new policy would not affect its election outcome in 2019.

While this paper only presented the case of Japan, Japan is not the only country that has a broad boundary of skilled migration. Australia and New Zealand already have admitted migrants without tertiary education in certain sectors (e.g. farmers, welders and masons) in their regional 'skilled migration' schemes (DHA 2019; MBIE 2019). Germany also passed a new immigration law in December 2019 to admit non-EU migrants in the 'mid-skilled segment' who do not have tertiary education. As long as they have vocational training and possess knowledge of the German language, they are allowed to work in any occupations and/or look for jobs (Reuters 2018). While it is not clear if they can obtain permanent residency at this point, this new scheme can be considered a major expansion of its 'skilled migration scheme'. Further comparative studies are needed to figure out how 'skilled migration' has been redefined in different countries, what factors operate behind the process of redefinition and, most importantly, whether these newly defined 'skilled migrants' have full access to the rights and entitlements.

Notes

1. While such analysis is certainly meaningful, in actuality Japan has admitted unskilled workers through 'side-doors' (student migration and the Technical Intern Trainee Program) to tackle labour shortages. Their number is now quite substantial, exceeding 600,000 in 2018 (MOJ 2019a, 2019b).
2. The International Labour Organization (ILO) defined the concept of skills as 'the ability to carry out the tasks and duties of a given job' and has the dimensions of 'skill level' and 'skill specialisation' (ILO 2012, 11). ILO also defines the 'skill level' as 'a function of the complexity and range of tasks and duties a worker can perform' and addresses the dimension of social construction, referring to the roles of employers, education/training institutions and national authorities that acknowledge individual's skill levels and qualifications. Indeed, these institutions play crucial roles in issuing degrees, diplomas and certificates as well as accrediting migrants when they move across borders. The most notable point of the ILO definition is that there is no category of 'unskilled' for any occupations or workers. OECD, on the other hand, defined 'skilled workers' based on occupations and qualifications (OECD 1995, 3). It presented two definitions of skilled workers, or using their term, 'human resources in science and technology (HRST).' The wider definition of HRST extended to

everyone who has completed post-secondary education or is working in an 'S&T occupation'. In this definition, 'S&T' encompassed not only natural sciences, engineering and medical sciences but the 'social sciences, humanities, and other fields' (OECD 1995, 21). Its narrower definition, on the other hand, covered only those with at least university-level qualifications in natural sciences or engineering or working in an 'S&T occupation' (ibid). In both definitions, tertiary education and certain occupational sectors were a proxy measurement for 'skilled workers.' Following suit of many other industrialised countries, Japan adopted the OECD's definition of HRST by admitting those with a bachelor's degree under its work visas.

3. The actual number of 'skilled migrants' in Japan is higher, since there are 1.5 million permanent residents, naturalised citizens, their foreign spouses and foreign spouses of Japanese citizens, many of whom used to hold 'skilled visas,' and yet are no longer counted as part of skilled migrants' statistics.
4. The incentives include expediting the visa process for applicants and their family members, offering a work permit to a spouse and a visa for a domestic worker and parents, and shortening the required residency period for permanent residency application.
5. While 'regionalism' often refers to a force for developing a common identity across multiple countries and/or supra-national institutions, it is also used as an ideology that promotes a shift of political autonomy in the context of domestic political administration, or secession. The term in this study refers to the latter.
6. After the SSW scheme started, it was decided that the admission of agricultural support workers through the NSSZ scheme would cease in March 2020 and these workers would be transitioned to the SSW scheme.
7. While foreign chefs have already been allowed to work in Japan, their skilled visa requires 10 years of work experience. In contrast, the NSSZ scheme enables migrants with only one year of experience to work as *washoku* chefs. The maximum length of stay was initially two years but was later extended to five years (Cabinet Office 2018c).
8. Technical interns/trainees who have completed their term in Japan will be exempted from these exams (Cabinet Office 2018d), and thus are expected to constitute a large segment of the first cohort of SSW-1 migrants. Indeed, among 96 workers who were certified as 'Specific Skilled Workers' between April and July 2019, the majority were former technical interns/trainees (Murakami 2019).
9. Agricultural workers are not a monolithic category and are thus placed at different levels: agricultural labourers in Skill Level 1 (elementary skill level), skilled agricultural workers in Level 2 and agricultural managers and technicians in Level 3 (ILO 2012). The NSSZ accepts both skilled agricultural workers (Level 2) and agricultural labourers (Level 1).
10. These support activities can be outsourced to registered third-party organisations.

Disclosure statement

No potential conflict of interest was reported by the author(s).

ORCID

Nana Oishi http://orcid.org/0000-0001-5905-719X

References

Ackers, Louise, and Bryony Gill. 2008. *Moving People and Knowledge: Scientific Mobility in an Enlarging European Union*. Cheltenham: Edward Elgar Publishing.

Alliance of Liberal Democratic Party Parliamentarians. 2008. *Japanese-Style Immigration Nation* (in Japanese). National Strategy Division. June 12.

Bartram, David. 2000. "Japan and Labor Migration: Theoretical and Methodological Implications of Negative Cases." *International Migration Review* 34 (1): 5–32.

Bartram, David. 2005. *International Labor Migration: Foreign Workers and Public Policy*. New York: Palgrave McMillan.

Bonizzoni, Paola. 2018. "Looking for the Best and Brightest? Deservingness Regimes in Italian Labour Migration Management." *International Migration* 56 (4): 47–62.

Brown, Philip, and Stuart Tannock. 2009. "Education, Meritocracy and the Global War for Talent." *Journal of Education Policy* 24 (4): 377–392.

Brubaker, Rogers. 1992. *Citizenship and Nationhood in France and Germany*. Cambridge: Harvard University Press.

Cabinet Office. 2003a. *E-Japan Strategy* [in Japanese]. January 2. Accessed August 30, 2018. https://www.kantei.go.jp/jp/it/network/dai1/1siryou05_2.html.

Cabinet Office. 2003b. *E-Japan Strategy. II*. July 2. Accessed August 30, 2018. https://japan.kantei.go.jp/policy/it/040318senryaku_e.pdf.

Cabinet Office. 2014. *The National Strategic Special Zone Act* (in Japanese). Accessed September 1, 2018. https://www.kantei.go.jp/jp/singi/tiiki/kokusentoc/pdf/nogyosien_seirei.pdf.

Cabinet Office. 2015. *The Interpretation of Accepting Foreign Housekeepers through the NSSZ Scheme* (in Japanese). November 12.

Cabinet Office. 2017. *The Admission of Highly Skilled Foreign Professionals and their Employment Situations* (in Japanese). Tokyo. December 13. Accessed August 15, 2018. https://www.kantei.go.jp/jp/singi/keizaisaisei/miraitoshikaigi/suishinkaigo2018/koyou/dai2/siryou4.pdf.

Cabinet Office. 2018a. *The Basic Policy on Economic and Fiscal Management and Reform 2018*.

Cabinet Office. 2018b. *The Guidelines for Operating the Specified Skilled Worker Visa Scheme* (in Japanese).

Cabinet Office. 2018c. *Cool Japan Talent Development Committee Final Report* (in Japanese). Accessed August 15, 2018. http://www.cao.go.jp/cool_japan/kaigi/jinzai/6/pdf/honbun.pdf.

Cabinet Office. 2018d. *The Basic Policies on the Operation of Specified Skilled Worker Visa Status* (in Japanese).

Cabinet Office. 2018e. *The Concerning the Policies on the Operation of Specified Skilled Worker Visa Status* (in Japanese).

Cabinet Office. 2018f. *The Comprehensive Response Measures for Acceptance of and Coexistence with Foreign Talent* (in Japanese). December 25. Accessed February 23, 2019. https://www.kantei.go.jp/jp/singi/gaikokujinzai/kaigi/dai3/siryou3-2.pdf.

The Council for Promoting Highly Skilled Talent. 2009. *Toward the Major Development of Immigration Policies for Foreign Skilled Talent* (in Japanese). Accessed August 31, 2018. https://www.kantei.go.jp/jp/singi/jinzai/dai2/houkoku.pdf.

D'Costa, Anthony P. 2008. "The Barbarians are Here: How Japanese Institutional Barriers and Immigration Policies Keep Asian Talent Away." *Asian Population Studies* 4 (3): 311–329. doi:10.1080/17441730802496524.

Dehm, Sara, and Anthea Vogl. 2018. "Migration Law and Women: Gendering Australia's Migration Program." *Precedent* 144: 22–27.

DHA (Department of Home Affairs, Australia). 2019. "Working in Australia." Accessed April 18, 2019. https://immi.homeaffairs.gov.au/visas/working-in-australia/skill-occupation-list.

Diet Record (Japan). 2014. *House of Councillors Proceedings*. Budget Committee No.3. February 6.

Diet Record (Japan). 2016. *House of Representatives Proceedings*. Budget Committee No.1. February 24.

Freeman, Gary P. 1995. "Modes of Immigration Politics in Liberal Democratic States." *International Migration Review* 29 (4): 881–902.

Hof, Helena. 2018. "'Worklife Pathways' to Singapore and Japan: Gender and Racial Dynamics in Europeans' Mobility to Asia." *Social Science Japan Journal* 21 (1): 45–65.

Hollifield, James Frank, Philip L. Martin, and Pia M. Orrenius. 2014. *Controlling Immigration: A Global Perspective*. 3rd ed. Stanford, CA: Stanford University Press.

ILO (International Labour Office). 2012. *International Standard Classification of Occupations: Structure, Group Definitions and Correspondence Tables*. Geneva: International Labour Office.

IPEJ (Institution of Professional Engineers, Japan). 2011. "APEC Engineers." (in Japanese). Accessed January 28, 2020. http://www.engineer.or.jp/sub06/.

Ishizuka, Hiroshi. 2019. "TEPCO Will Suspend the Acceptance of Specified Skilled Foreign Workers at Fukushima Nuclear Power Plants." (in Japanese). *Asahi Shimbun*. May 22.

JBF (Japan Business Federation). 2008. *The Economy and Society in Response to Population Decline* (in Japanese). Accessed August 15, 2019. https://www.keidanren.or.jp/japanese/policy/2008/073.pdf.

LDP-DMC (Liberal Democratic Party Diet Members' Caucus for Promoting Exchange of Foreign Talent). 2008. *The Proposal of Japanese-Style Immigration Policies* (in Japanese). Tokyo.

Lee, Jack Jin Gary. 2019. "Why Developmental States Accept Guest Workers: Bureaucratic Policy-Making and the Politics of Labour Migration in Singapore." *Journal of Ethnic and Migration Studies* 45 (13): 2508–2526.

Liu-Farrer, Gracia. 2013. "Ambiguous Concepts and Unintended Consequences: Rethinking Skilled Migration Policies from the Case of Chinese Student Migrants in Japan." *Journal of Asia-Pacific Studies* 19: 221–239.

Liu-Farrer, Gracia, Brenda S. Yeoh, and Michiel Baas. 2021. "Social Construction of Skill: An Analytical Approach Toward the Question of Skill in Cross-Border Labour Mobilities." *Journal of Ethnic and Migration Studies* 47 (10): 2237–2251. doi:10.1080/1369183X.2020.1731983.

MAFF (Ministry of Agriculture, Forestry and Fisheries, Japan). 2017. *Trends in Agriculture and Forestry* (in Japanese). Tokyo.

Manpower Group. 2018. *Solving the Talent Shortage: Build, Buy Borrow and Bridge*. Accessed January 30, 2019. https://go.manpowergroup.com/hubfs/TalentShortage%202018%20(Global)%20Assets/PDFs/MG_TalentShortage2018_lo%206_25_18_FINAL.pdf.

Martin, Philip, and Martin Ruhs. 2011. "Labor Shortages and U.S. Immigration Reform: Promises and Perils of an Independent Commission." *International Migration Review* 45 (1): 174–187.

Masuda, Hiroya. 2014. *Disappearing Regional Areas* (in Japanese). Tokyo: Chuko Shinsho.

MBIE (Ministry of Business, Innovation and Employment, New Zealand). 2019. "Skilled Migrant Details Announced." Accessed February 17, 2019. https://skillshortages.immigration.govt.nz/?_ga=2.59930605.1579873265.1555979046-682629109.1555979046.

METI (Ministry of Economy, Trade and Industry, Japan). 2015. *Manufacturing White Paper* (in Japanese). Tokyo.

MIAC (Ministry of Internal Affairs and Communications, Japan). 2018. *The Situation of Implementing Policies and Guidelines related to Multicultural Coexistence* (in Japanese). Accessed September 15, 2018. http://www.soumu.go.jp/main_content/000555350.pdf.

Migration Policy Group. 2015. *Migrant Integration Policy Index 2015*. Accessed January 30, 2019. http://www.mipex.eu/.

MOJ (Ministry of Justice, Japan). 2003. *The Response to the Request from the Comprehensive Regulatory Reform Council to submit the Information* (in Japanese). Accessed December 15, 2017. https://www8.cao.go.jp/kisei/giji/03/wg/action/12/siryo2-2.pdf.

MOJ (Ministry of Justice, Japan). 2011. *Emigration Statistics* (in Japanese). Accessed July 30, 2019. http://www.moj.go.jp/housei/toukei/toukei_ichiran_nyukan.html.

MOJ (Ministry of Justice, Japan). 2013. *Re-Examining the Points-Based Preferential Immigration Treatment for Highly Skilled Foreign Professionals*. Unpublished meeting document.

MOJ (Ministry of Justice, Japan). 2018a. *The Guideline on the System Operation concerning the Residential Status of Specific Skilled Workers* (in Japanese). Tokyo.

MOJ (Ministry of Justice, Japan). 2018b. *Report on Misconducts* (in Japanese). Tokyo.

MOJ (Ministry of Justice, Japan). 2019a. *Immigration Statistics* (in Japanese). Accessed July 25, 2019. http://www.moj.go.jp/housei/toukei/toukei_ichiran_touroku.html.

MOJ (Ministry of Justice, Japan). 2019b. *Notification of Ministerial Ordinance on Specific Skilled Workers* (in Japanese).

MOL (Ministry of Labour, Japan). 1988. "The Sixth Employment Policy Basic Plan." (in Japanese). Tokyo.

Murakami, Takakazu. 2019. "96 Workers Became Certified as Specified Skilled Workers." *Mainichi Shimbun*. August 2.

Nakamura, Hajime, and Kenichi Takano. 2014. "A Study of the Policy for the Expert Skill Succession." (in Japanese). *Shakai Gijutsu Kenkyu Ronbunshu* 11: 82–95.
NGA (National Governors' Association). 2000. *Recommendations and Requests Concerning National Policies and Budgets for 2001* (in Japanese). Accessed August 31, 2019. http://www.nga.gr.jp/ikkrwebBrowse/material/files/group/2/kuni_h13_2000_8_x01.pdf.
NGA (National Governors' Association). 2014. *Recommendations and Requests Concerning National Policies and Budgets for 2015* (in Japanese). http://www.nga.gr.jp/ikkrwebBrowse/material/files/group/3/h27%20teianyoubo.pdf.
Nihon Keizai Shimbun. 2018. "Dependency on Foreigners: Sectoral and Prefectural Rankings." (in Japanese). August 2.
Nohl, Arnd-Michael, Karin Schittenhelm, Oliver Schmidtke, and Anja Weib. 2014. *Work in Transition: Cultural Capital and Highly Skilled Migrants' Passages Into the Labour Market*. Toronto: University of Toronto Press.
Nonaka, Daisuke. 2019. "The Hasty Revision of the Immigration Law: The True Aim is the Constitutional Reform and the House of Representatives Election." (in Japanese). *Shukan Toyo Keizai*. January 12.
Nye, Joseph S. 1990. "Soft Power." *Foreign Policy* 80: 153–171.
OECD (Organsation for Economic Cooperation and Development). 1995. *The Measurement of Science and Technological Activities: The Manual on the Measurement of Human Resources Devoted to S&T*. (Canberra Manual). Paris: OECD.
Oishi, Nana. 2012. "The Limits of Immigration Policies: The Challenges of Highly Skilled Migration in Japan." *American Behavioral Scientist* 56 (8): 1080–1100.
Oishi, Nana. 2014. "Redefining the "Highly Skilled": The Points-Based System for Highly Skilled Foreign Professionals in Japan." *Asian and Pacific Migration Journal* 23 (4): 421–450.
Oishi, Nana. 2018. "The Pitfalls of Skilled Migration Policies in Japan: Institutional Isomorphism and Reality." *Japanese Sociological Review* 68 (4): 549–566.
Reuters. 2018. "German Cabinet Approves Immigration Laws to Ease Worker Shortage." December 20. Accessed April 23. https://www.reuters.com/article/us-germany-immigration-law/german-cabinet-approves-immigration-laws-to-ease-worker-shortage-idUSKBN1OI1RO.
Sadamatsu, Aya. 2018. "National Strategic Special Zones and Foreigners Conducting Housekeeping Services." (in Japanese). *Economic Society and Gender* 3: 59–74.
Seol, Dong-Hoon, and John D. Skrentny. 2009. "Why is There So Little Migrant Settlement in East Asia?" *International Migration Review* 43 (3): 578–620.
Shachar, Ayelet. 2006. "The Race for Talent: Highly Skilled Migrants and Competitive Immigration Regimes." *New York University Law Review* 81 (April): 148–206.
Shan, Hongxia, and Andreas Fejes. 2015. "Skill Regime in the Context of Globalization and Migration." *Studies in Continuing Education* 37 (3): 227–235.
SSDQ (Social Research Database on Questionnaires). 1995. "Occupational Prestige Score." (Japanese). Accessed July 20, 2019. http://srdq.hus.osaka-u.ac.jp/PDF/SMM1995_r5_sukoa.pdf.
Steinberg, Ronnie J. 1990. "Social Construction of Skill: Gender, Power, and Comparable Worth." *Work and Occupations* 17 (4): 449–482.
Toh, Elgin. 2017. "Singapore's Non-Resident Population Falls by 1.6%, First Drop in 14 Years." *The Straits Times*. Accessed September 14, 2018. https://www.straitstimes.com/politics/spores-non-resident-population-falls-by-16-first-drop-in-14-years.
Weiner, Michael. 1995. *The Global Migration Crisis: Challenges to States and to Human Rights*. New York: Harper Collins College Publishers.
White House. 2017. *Presidential Executive Order on Buy American and Hire American*. Issued on April 18. https://www.whitehouse.gov/presidential-actions/presidential-executive-order-buy-american-hire-american/.
Yamawaki, Koji. 2018. "The Trap that Captured Foreign Trainees in the Nuclear Powerplant." (in Japanese). May 13. *Toyo Keizai Weekly*. Accessed April 25, 2019. https://toyokeizai.net/articles/-/220292?page=3.
Yomiuri Shimbun. 2019. "57 per cent Supported Admitting Migrants." (in Japanese). May 5.

Shifting employabilities: skilling migrants in the nation of emigration

Yasmin Y. Ortiga

ABSTRACT

This paper examines how Philippine state agencies sustain its labour-exporting strategies by encouraging aspiring migrants to invest in their own training and education, taking on the responsibility of turning themselves into desirable workers for employers overseas. Based on a document analysis of newspaper articles and Philippine government reports, this paper uses the case of Philippine nursing education to show how the Philippine state alters these discourses of skill when overseas opportunities decline, channelling aspiring migrants sideways to other sectors of the labour market. Discourses of employability justified these career detours to aspiring migrants by assuring them that such experiences will still contribute to their overseas employability and eventually lead to future emigration. This paper shows how the employability agenda allows the migrant-sending state to avoid accountability in a volatile global labour market, thus serving as an ideal tool in the neoliberal production of migrant labour.

Introduction

Studies on immigration provide us with a rich account of how 'skill' is socially constructed, simultaneously shaping the desirability of some immigrants, while limiting the incorporation and social mobility of many others (Bonizzoni 2018; Cerna 2016; Chatterjee 2015; Oishi 2021). Yet, in the context of *emigration*, there have been fewer scholarly responses to the question of skill. Most studies on migrant-sending countries portray skill as a resource that nations lose as people move across borders – a narrative that sustains a long-running debate on the issue of brain drain. Only recently have scholars begun to investigate how such skills are actually produced and how migrant-sending states can use such notions of skill to pursue their own interests.

Ironically, existing studies have largely focussed on the proliferation of training courses for construction and domestic work – jobs that are viewed as 'unskilled' by receiving countries. These studies criticise state-led skilling programmes as mere attempts to regulate aspiring migrants' behaviour by promoting the image of a docile and industrious employee (Chang 2018; Guevarra 2014; Killias 2018; Rodriguez 2010; Rodriguez and Schwenken 2013). In contrast, fewer scholars have investigated the deliberate skilling of professionals for overseas work within migrant-sending countries. Here, academic critique centres on educational institutions that exploit students' migration aspirations by selling expensive credentials with the promise of overseas jobs after graduation (see Kingma 2007; Masselink and Lee 2010; Xiang 2007).[1] Scholars portray these schools as commercial entities, competing in a migration industry driven towards maximising profits.

Yet, as noted by Hein De Haas (2005), state agencies are highly complicit in this process as well. Within large migrant-sending nations, governments have come to use skilling for export as a development strategy, encouraging the overproduction of particular professions in the hope that these individuals will migrate overseas and send remittances back to the country. Cabanda (2017) argues that export-oriented education can even define policy discussions on issues that have nothing to do with labour migration. His analysis of the Philippine Nursing Act of 2002 shows how lawmakers crafted *local* standards for nursing education in order to ensure Filipino nurses' ability to obtain jobs overseas.

Current research also tends to portray the skilling of aspiring migrants as a process that naturally leads to employment in a global market for migrant labour. Most research studies are based on short-term training programmes run by labour recruitment agencies or state institutions directly engaged in labour export. As such, it is easy to assume that all individuals skilled for export are deployed to overseas employers. For example, Rodriguez's (2010) study shows that the Philippine state's pre-employment process moves neatly from screening to pre-departure training to matching with employers. Yet, in the case of professional jobs such as nursing or engineering, skilling is a longer process that involves a 4-year university degree, multiple board examinations, language assessments, and certification of relevant work experience. In the course of skilling oneself for emigration, new immigration policies and changing economic conditions may affect one's access to overseas work. What happens when demands for particular professions wane, and there are too few opportunities for too many skilled would-be migrants? How can we think about the question of skill, not just in the context of people's mobility but their immobility as well?

In this paper, I argue that migration studies must look beyond employment, and investigate how notions of *employability* drive the production of migrant workers for the global economy. Loosely defined as an individual's capacity to obtain and retain work, employability has encouraged the belief that people must invest in enhancing their own capabilities, whether it is through work experience or education (Forrier, De Cuyper, and Akkermans 2018; Smith 2010). This paper demonstrates how migrant-sending states benefit from the pursuit of employability in two ways. First, the employability discourse makes aspiring migrants responsible for turning themselves into desirable job candidates for foreign employers, thereby allowing the state to outsource the cost of skilling future workers, while still benefitting from the remittances they will eventually send home. Second, this discourse also allows the state to avoid responsibility when overseas opportunities become unavailable, instead placing it upon aspiring migrants to reskill themselves for alternative careers.

I base my arguments on the case of nursing education in the Philippines, where schools have sought to produce nurse migrants for popular destination countries like the US, UK, and Canada. While most studies on nurse migration focus on periods of high demand for migrant nurses (see Guevarra 2010; Pyle 2006), this paper investigates how Philippine state agencies and private school owners use discourses of skill during a period of restricted emigration and poor job prospects for Filipino nurses in the West. I describe how, in promoting export-oriented education, the Philippine state found itself in a unique predicament: dealing with an excess of employable aspiring migrants who are unable to fulfil their aspirations of leaving the country. While low-wage positions (domestic work, housekeeping) remain widely available overseas, few aspiring nurse migrants were willing to take on jobs seen as 'below' the work of a professional registered nurse (Ortiga 2018). As such, I discuss how the Philippine government attempted to channel unemployed nursing graduates *sideways*, towards other sectors of the labour market deemed to fit the purpose and potential of professional nurse education. In particular, Philippine state officials tried to reconstruct and redefine the value of nursing skill, often contradicting its earlier agenda of tailoring local nursing education in line with foreign hospital needs. As these sideways shifts encountered resistance, state discourse resorted to appeasing concerned citizens with the promise that such career detours will still increase their chances of obtaining overseas jobs in the future, thereby reinforcing the belief that the nursing profession's true 'value' is found in its export to foreign employers. This paper concludes with a discussion of how the employability agenda allows the Philippine government to maintain its neoliberal production of migrant labour, despite an unpredictable and fast-changing migrant labour market.

Skilling and the employability agenda

While hardly a new concept, employability had recently become a prominent feature in neoliberal state policies, largely driven by the anxiety of how to prepare people for a competitive global market (Smith 2010; Tomlinson 2012; Waters 2009). In this paper, I discuss how notions of employability are crystallised into a state *agenda*, where government institutions dedicate resources and policy efforts towards producing workers who possess the qualities that potential employers supposedly need and desire. This agenda is rooted in an ideology of human capital development, where nations' economic growth purportedly depends on the skills and knowledge of its citizens (Becker 1964; 2002). An employable citizenry is one that has obtained enough 'human capital' through higher education, with the assumption that more education represents a higher level of skill. In places like the UK, scholars have shown how the employability agenda has altered the purpose of higher education, compelling universities to align academic programmes with the demands of the industry (Boden and Nedeva 2010; Tomlinson 2012).

Alongside state pressure on educational institutions, the employability agenda has also framed gainful employment as an *individual* responsibility, where citizens must take on the task of developing their own abilities to obtain work through further study and training. The state acts on the employability agenda by providing opportunities for individuals to skill themselves, rather than address the bigger problem of generating jobs for unemployed citizens. As a result, states have poured resources into offering and subsidising skills courses, prompting the rapid growth of a for-profit training and certification industry (Arora 2015; Lafer 2002). Proponents of employability have rationalised this process with the argument that higher investments in skilling will likely lead to positive outcomes, not only for individuals but the broader nation as well (Forrier, De Cuyper, and Akkermans 2018).

Yet, studies on education and work have shown how, beneath this rhetoric of personal development, the employability agenda largely serves the interests of the market. Individuals are increasingly expected to prepare themselves to perform jobs they have yet to obtain, often by seeking more and more education and training. Meanwhile, corporations have come to expect job applicants to be completely ready to do the required work, thereby outsourcing the cost of training new employees (Brown 2003; Handley 2018; Tomlinson 2008). Worsening this issue is that fact that there is little evidence that investment in skilling necessarily leads to better economic outcomes (Arora 2015; Shan and Fejes 2015). In fact, scholars have raised concerns regarding the rising number of college graduates who are struggling to find work commensurate with their qualifications and skills (Brown, Lauder, and Ashton 2011).

However, even within this burgeoning literature, critiques of state employability agendas have been mostly contained within the national boundaries. In these studies, state discourses of employability aim to produce desirable workers who will fill labour needs within a national labour market or attract multinational corporations into the country. Fewer studies have investigated how governments can also deliberately encourage local institutions to educate and train workers for *foreign* employers. In the case of the Philippines, the state's labour-exporting practices created an employability agenda that also worked to predict and define what skills overseas markets may demand in the future. State agencies urged Filipino students and their families to pursue particular skills in order to ensure overseas success, thereby encouraging a massive demand for particular professional degrees like nursing. In this paper, I focus on how the state transforms its employability agenda in response to changing demands and opportunities in the global labour market. In particular, I use the Philippine case to understand how an employability agenda frames not only individuals' mobility, but also their potential *immobility* as opportunities for immigration decline or disappear.

Methods

This paper is based on a larger project on how the Philippines' labour export strategies impact higher education institutions within the country. In particular, I draw from a document analysis of two sources of primary data. The first source comprises newspaper articles from 1999 to 2018, a time period that encompasses the beginning and end of the most recent cycle of 'demand' for nursing degrees (I outline the details and implications of this demand in later sections of this paper). These media reports revealed how state officials, government agencies, and private school owners sought to frame public discourse on nurse education and migration. I focussed specifically on sources from the Philippines' English language news publications such as the *Manila Bulletin*, the *Philippine Daily Inquirer*, and the *Philippine STAR*, among others. I used keyword indexing (i.e. nursing, skill, employability, migration) at Factiva and reviewed a total of 452 newspaper articles.

I complemented these sources with a review of annual reports, internal newsletters, and press releases from Philippine government agencies involved in the recruitment and deployment of migrant workers: the Department of Labour and Employment (DOLE) and the Philippine Overseas Employment Agency (POEA). I compared these sources to similar documents obtained from the Philippine Commission on Higher Education

(CHED), the agency tasked with regulating and monitoring higher education institutions within the country. I gathered documents beginning from the Philippines' labour export policies in the 1974 to the present period.

While these sources do not provide a complete picture of the public discourse and policy-making decisions that surround nurse education and emigration, they represent a significant part of how state officials and school owners rationalise and promote the skills needed among aspiring nurse migrants. More importantly, such discourse demonstrates how these same actors change or alter their views on skilling when overseas opportunities for Filipino nurses decline and more aspiring migrants are unable to leave the country.

Educating for export: from 'Excess' to employability

The Philippines' long history of emigration has made it a popular subject of study among migration scholars. Researchers have been particularly interested in the role of state agencies in recruiting, marketing, and deploying Filipino labour to foreign employers (Acacio 2008; Tyner 2009). Rodriguez (2010:, 8) defines these practices as the state's 'labour-brokering strategies,' where institutional and discursive practices work to generate profit from the remittances that migrants send to their families back home.

While labour-brokering is a strategy well established in the Philippines, the usefulness of the employability agenda in exporting migrant labour only emerged more recently. In the early years of the Philippines' labour export policies, DOLE described its overseas programme as 'a systematic export of excess skill' or, simply put, a means of channelling unemployed Filipinos to other countries. Training courses mainly catered to out-of-school youth and retrenched workers, offering lessons in welding, industrial sewing, and electronics (DOLE 1990; NMYC 1968). While one can question whether such skills were truly in excess, the notion of intentionally training students for export was relatively absent in both state and public discourse. Well into the 1980s, state agencies portrayed college graduates as individuals whose high-level skills would contribute to *national* needs (MEC 1984). Filipino graduates who sought overseas work were seen as those unable to find jobs locally, or whose skills could not be absorbed by domestic industries. While the outmigration of professionals continued to rise during this period, Philippine state discourse lamented the departure of highly educated individuals as brain drain, a loss of valuable human resources that could be detrimental to national development.

It was only in the 1990s when Philippine state documents revealed a distinct shift from channelling excess skill to deliberately educating employable workers for overseas jobs. This shift has to do with a combination of two factors. First, this period saw the prominence of what scholars have called the 'knowledge-based economy' or the belief that the world has moved beyond industrial manufacturing, towards a market driven by knowledge production and innovation. Nations seeking to get ahead in this economy were then expected to invest in creating a highly educated pool of citizens who could compete on a global stage (Powell and Snellman 2004). These beliefs reignited national interests in human capital development, where higher education and lifelong learning were seen to have direct links to economic prosperity and wellbeing (Guile 2006).

Second, the popularity of the knowledge-based economy coincided with a shift in the Philippine government's stance towards emigration. In the 1990s, Philippine state officials retreated from its earlier position that labour export was merely a temporary measure, and began to publicly refer to migration as a permanent institution that will shape national policy. Then president Fidel Ramos referred to overseas Filipino workers as 'internationally shared human resources' (DOLE 1995, 3), and broader government discourse celebrated migrants as *bagong bayani* (modern-day heroes) whose remittances kept the country's economy afloat.[2]

The intersection of this migrant-hero discourse with the global emphasis on education and skilling created a paradoxical version of human capital ideology within the Philippine context. In general, human capital logic dictates that a nation must produce a highly skilled workforce in order to attract investors *into* the country and develop local industries. Yet, in the Philippines, overseas Filipino workers are seen as key contributors to the country's economic progress and wellbeing. As such, Philippine state officials argued that education and training institutions must also ensure that Filipinos have the skills that would make them desirable for jobs *outside* the country's borders. This shift towards employability defined the state's preparation of potential migrants across a wide range of workers. The 1990s saw the establishment of state-led programmes on technical-vocational skills (e.g. welding, electronic installation, and housekeeping) – most of which were driven towards training Filipinos for jobs in other Asian countries and the Middle East (Rodriguez 2010). The POEA also mandated household work training programmes for domestic workers before they left the country, combining basic cooking and cleaning techniques with lessons on 'empowerment' and strategies to minimize 'vulnerability' (Guevarra 2006; 2014). Often less researched in the migration literature is how this period also saw rising expectations for Philippine colleges and universities to produce graduates who could serve as human capital for *other nations* (Ortiga 2018). Moving away from the brain drain discourse of the 1970s, Philippine state officials highlighted the overseas success of Filipino teachers, accountants, nurses, and engineers. Former secretary of the Department of Education, Gonzalez (2000), even went as far as to emphasise the need for Philippine schools to develop a more 'systemic' way of educating professionals for these 'global opportunities.'

These changes coincided with the high migration aspirations of Filipino youth and their families (Asis and Batistella 2013), prompting scholars to note that the large proportion of Filipino migrant professionals was not due to a lack of employment within the country, but Filipinos' deliberate effort to 'become professionals to work abroad' (Di Gropello, Tan, and Tandon 2010, 25). Private higher education institutions also played an integral role in this process, actively seeking labour gaps overseas and restructuring school spaces and academic programmes to offer degrees that supposedly address these needs (Ortiga 2017). Reports have highlighted the problematic outcomes of such export-oriented education, from shoddy academic programmes to the rise of substandard schools that cheat parents of their hard-earned money (Masselink and Lee 2010; Overland 2005). Given that 80% of Philippine higher education is privately owned, most of these issues were attributed to the lack of government regulation and the political power of private school owners (Tan 2011).

Yet, in many ways, the Philippine state was very much present in the production of future migrant workers. While private schools dominated the skilling of aspiring migrants, state agencies provided an environment that allowed these schools to thrive. State officials also encouraged aspiring migrants to seek training and qualifications that would enhance their chances in obtaining work overseas. In the following sections, I use the case of nursing to discuss how this employability agenda allowed state agencies to reap the benefits of nurse migrants' remittances as well as avoid responsibility for those who fail to leave.

Philippine nursing education: skilling for the competition

Philippine nursing education can be traced as far back as the early 1900s, when American colonial officials established the first nursing schools in the country (Choy 2003). However, the move towards producing nurses for foreign employers is a more recent phenomenon, as growing healthcare needs within developed nations led to a worldwide demand for migrant nurse labour (Yeates and Pillinger 2019).[3] In the early 2000s, hospitals in the US were particularly aggressive in recruiting foreign nurses, with policymakers predicting a labour shortage of close to 1 million nurses by 2020 (Aiken 2007). While the Philippines and India retained their positions as the top sources of migrant nurse labour, the early 2000s also saw an increasing number of migrant nurses from other parts of the world. Brush and Sochalski (2007) note that in countries like Korea and China, state agencies actively sought to copy the 'Philippines model,' investing in education in order to deliberately produce nurses for export.

This growing competition, along with the high overseas demand for nurses, pressed Philippine state officials to ensure that Filipino nurses would continue to have a positional advantage over counterparts from other nations (Guevarra 2010). For example, in 2004, a POEA officer noted that while the deployment of nurses is likely to increase, the Philippines must 'prepare for very steep competition,' as countries like Bangladesh, India, Vietnam, and China begin training nurses for overseas employment (Capistrano 2004). Private labour recruitment agencies reinforced this discourse, openly pushing government agencies to keep Filipino nurses competitive in the migrant labour market. In a *Manila Standard* article in 2002, the Federated Association of Manpower Exporters (FAME) reported that Filipino nurses were 'losing their edge' to other foreign nurses in popular destination countries. They noted a case in the UK, where nursing homes reported 'an alarming breakdown in communications' between Filipino nurses and British staff, despite the Filipinos' ability to speak English. Such issues were contextualised against a growing concern that China was building more nursing schools in a bid to replace Filipino nurses in the UK market. The group then urged the Philippine government to 'counteract this disturbing trend' through better English courses and a curriculum more in line with the needs of overseas hospitals.

Rodriguez and Schwenken (2013) had previously noted how the Philippines' labour exporting agencies portray nurses as an ideal alternative to domestic workers, given that they were professionals, high wage-earners, and migrant women in less need of protections from the state. Yet, in the early years of the Philippine state's labour export policies, such statements rarely reached mainstream media, given negative public sentiment on nurse migration and brain drain. With the shift towards a strong employability agenda, the most recent outflow of nurses took on a polished sheen of positivity, where outmigration is not a result of desperation but an indicator of Filipino nurses' superior abilities and global popularity (Capistrano 2004). Nursing schools then took on the role of ensuring that Filipino nurses would continue to have an advantages over nurse migrants from other nations, not only in terms of their ability to provide care, but supposedly their unique skill and specialised training (Ortiga 2014).

This emphasis on producing employable migrant workers remained unquestioned, despite worrying signs of other issues within the country's higher education system. In 2008, the *Manila Bulletin* reported that only two Philippine universities were listed in a ranking of the top 500 universities in Asia. While Filipino academics raised concerns regarding falling research output and the lack of qualified faculty within local universities, state officials downplayed the gravity of such rankings. The same article featured an interview with William Medrano, then executive director at CHED who argued,

> The results may be discouraging, but it should not be a big deal. I think what is important here is the employability of graduates. If you produce quality graduates, quality nurses, maritime professionals, world-class accountants ... then ranking does not matter at all.

In many ways, this statement reveals how government agencies and private school owners incorporated higher education into the country's larger labour-export strategies, emphasising the value of producing Filipino nurses who are able to fill the labour gaps of destination countries all over the world.

The decline of nursing: an excess of employable workers

The demand for health professionals has remained an important issue among ageing nations in the Global North. Yet, beginning in 2008, a nursing career was no longer a viable step for Filipinos looking to work overseas. Several factors contributed to this decline. First, the global financial crisis slowed the hiring of foreign nurses in the US and Europe, regions that were popular among aspiring nurse migrants (Buchan, O'May, and Dussault 2013). Second, Filipino nurse migration to the US was ground to a halt when visa processing for Filipinos went into 'retrogression' – a term embassy officials use to describe situations where the number of visa applicants exceeds the number of visas available (Acacio 2011). Third and more importantly, the overexpansion of Philippine nursing schools generated an unprecedented number of nursing graduates that local health institutions could not absorb due to a lack of government funds for permanent nursing positions within public hospitals (Ortiga 2018). As a result, aspiring nurse migrants found themselves unable to complete the two years of work experience that most foreign employers required. As noted by Walton-Roberts (2021), intermediaries provided alternative pathways to destinations like Canada. Instead of waiting to obtain enough work experience, nurses could enter educational institutions as international students first then later obtain nursing jobs in Canadian hospitals. Yet, this two-step pathway was too costly for the majority of nurses in the Philippines.

By 2011, Philippine nursing groups began protesting the growing number of nurses who were paying hospitals to allow them to work for free, often under the guise of a professional 'training' programme. In an interview with the *Manila Bulletin* that same year, Teresita Barcelo, president of the Philippine Nurses Association (PNA) lamented, '... never in the past have nurses undergone additional training and paid just to get hired.'

These changes incited a sharp change in state discourse. Having first encouraged nursing as the path to social mobility and overseas employment, Philippine state officials backtracked on their original statements, warning parents to avoid enrolling their children in nursing programmes (Cimatu 2011). Hoping to stem the overproduction of nurses, CHEd imposed a 'moratorium' that stopped colleges and universities from opening new nursing programmes, with then CHEd commissioner Patricia Licuanan admitting that, '... basically, there's an oversupply of people,' (Ronda 2010). While other fields such as information technology were included in this moratorium, nursing had the biggest share, with almost half a million students pursuing nursing degrees (Quismundo 2010). In 2013, government agencies pushed schools with poor performance in the local board examinations to 'voluntarily phase out' their nursing programmes as well ('83 Nursing Schools Closed' 2013). However, such efforts were too little and too late. As of 2011, newspapers reported that there were close to 300,000 unemployed and underemployed nursing graduates in the country ('Monitor Nursing Schools' 2012).

Faced with rising discontent among nursing graduates and their families, state officials attempted to shift the blame to other parties. Aside from private schools, government officials accused Filipino nursing leaders for failing to provide accurate information on the demand for nursing overseas. Arnel Ty, a congressman, criticised Philippine nursing officials for not doing enough research on 'projecting future labour market conditions, both here and abroad,' thus misleading Filipino families to invest too late on nursing degrees (Romero 2012). State agencies also blamed students and parents themselves, for choosing majors based on their migration aspirations ('CHED Advices' 2011). Formerly praised as national heroes whose future remittances will uplift the Philippines' economy, nursing graduates were suddenly portrayed as Filipino youth who pursued their own migration dreams instead of working in jobs that the country needed (Pefianco 2012).

Yet, shifting the blame was a strategy that could only go so far. State agencies still needed to address the large pool of employable yet unemployed aspiring nurse migrants who were technically 'stuck' within the country's borders. In the past, the Philippines' solution to problems of high unemployment had mainly revolved around facilitating outmigration. In fact, state officials in the 1970s had justified the state's labour brokering strategies as a 'safety valve' for an overcrowded local economy with too few job opportunities (Ruiz 2014, 27). However, with the recent case of nursing graduates, this safety valve could no longer be easily applied. Few nursing graduates were willing to 'waste' their professional training by leaving for available low wage jobs overseas (Ortiga 2018). As such, the Philippine state needed to find new ways of reconstructing and utilising nurses' labours and skills.

Reconstructing skills for immobile nurses: new 'Employabilities'

Before opportunities for Filipino nurses declined in 2008, Philippine nursing schools were actively driven towards educating their students for 'export,' altering course curricula to cater specifically to hospital settings in wealthy nations, while prioritising specialities considered useful for nursing jobs overseas (e.g. geriatric care) (Ortiga 2014). These practices reinforced Filipino parents' belief that paying the price of a nursing degree would ensure their children a chance to leave the country *as a professional nurse*. Such expectations regarding the purpose and value of higher education are not unique to the Philippines. Education scholars have shown how human capital ideals have driven the increasing commodification of higher education, where the value of a university degree is measured in terms of the advantages it will bring to a student's future career (Molesworth, Nixon, and Scullion 2011; Naidoo and Williams 2015). Yet, in the case of the Philippines, this narrowing of educational purpose and the export-oriented bias of nursing schools eventually worked against the labour-brokering state, as nursing graduates could not be pushed 'downward' towards jobs that were not commensurate to the price they paid for their nursing degrees. As a result, state agencies shifted towards redirecting nurse graduates *sideways*, promoting jobs in other sectors in the Philippine labour market that fit the value of their professional training. This section outlines how, from a narrow construction of nursing skills geared towards 'first world' hospitals, Philippine state officials attempted to repackage and reconstruct the value of nursing as labour desired in contexts beyond the foreign hospital.

Redeployed skill: nurses as agents for rural development

The first strategy that the Philippine state enacted was finding ways to deploy unemployed nursing graduates to rural health centres. Under the presidency of Gloria Macapagal-Arroyo, the state first implemented the Nurses Assigned in Rural Service (NARS) Project in 2009, a quick fix to the outcry against the number of nurses working in hospitals for free (Poblete 2011). Marianito Roque, then secretary of DOLE framed the programme as a 'training-cum employment scheme' where nursing graduates were hired to provide 'basic health services to needy folks in rural areas' and perform 'clinical functions under the guidance of participating hospitals and other medical facilities.' Roque went on to add that with close supervision from the Department of Health, nurse participants will obtain 'the essential skills and knowledge for employment *locally and eventually overseas*' (emphasis added) (Philippine News Agency [PNA] 2009).

State officials were careful to frame NARS as an experience that would allow nursing graduates to continue to make use of their nursing education and training. In some ways, the programme was effective in that the state received an overwhelming number of applications, many from nurses who were just desperate for work (Burgonio and Nunez 2009). Yet, after a year of implementation, feedback from those who joined the NARS programme highlighted the shortcomings of such claims. For one, nurses found themselves stationed in remote village health centres, initiating public health campaigns, assisting with home births, and immunising children. Nursing graduates did not see such work as useful in applying for jobs overseas (Ortiga 2018). PNA national president Teresita I. Barcelo admitted to reporters that while NARS provided nurses with 'additional competence,' it was not providing the kind of skills needed for work in places like the US and UK (Tubeza 2009). Further exacerbating nurses' discontent was the fact that NARS only paid participants a small allowance of 8000 pesos,[4] an amount lower than what they would receive working in the hospital.

Nonetheless, state officials continued to justify rural deployment as an experience that improves nurses' clinical skills (Guinto 2009). One congresswoman, Emmylou Taliño-Mendoza sent media agencies a statement that argued for the NARS programme as a form of 'specialised training' that would help nursing graduates find 'lucrative jobs overseas.' In an interview with the Philippine Daily Inquirer in 2009, she addressed complaints that nurses were working more as midwives by arguing,

> In America, for instance, there is growing demand for certified nurse-midwives. They are considered advanced practitioners there, with specialised education, training, and experience in both nursing and midwifery.

New rural deployment programmes were enacted in 2011 and 2018, as different administrations inherited the problem of providing employment for nursing graduates. Throughout these different programmes, state officials worked to emphasise the development potential of deploying 'idle' nursing graduates to underserved communities in the country's rural communities (Boncocan 2011). The most recent iteration (renamed the Nurse Deployment Programme) listed among its objectives a need to provide better access to quality healthcare services in the country's rural provinces. Yet, underlying such discourse was also a clear emphasis on overseas employability – an explicit attempt to placate aspiring migrants who comprise politicians' main constituency. As argued by Arnel Ty, a congressman, 'The program will provide short-term work to our unemployed nurses and midwives, while they obtain extra training that will make their skills more marketable and enhance their future employability here or abroad' (Romero 2012).

Spillover skill: nurses as call centre agents

Faced with limitations for rural deployment, state officials also sought to have nursing graduates 'spillover' to the country's business process outsourcing (BPO) industry, colloquially known as the call centre agencies. At this time, large numbers of nursing graduates were already working in BPO centres (Thompson 2018), yet such work often suffered the stigma as a job that required few skills. Nursing graduates often felt ashamed to admit that they worked at a call centre because it felt like they had wasted the time spent on training to be a professional nurse (Ortiga 2018).

As such, state officials worked to emphasise how the BPO industry utilised nursing skills and needed nursing graduates to fill an important need. Doing so also meant highlighting the 'health' aspects of the business process outsourcing industry. In 2012, DOLE Secretary Rosalinda Baldoz appealed to nursing graduates to 'go out of the box' and pursue jobs in 'other emerging medical and health-related careers.' She argued that she was not encouraging nursing graduates to become the 'common "headset with microphone" type of worker in call centres' and instead, wanted nurses to take on jobs where they were expected to 'process and analyse knowledge, information, and technical data' (Crisostomo 2012). A year later, Baldoz continued to advertise opportunities in the call centre industry, arguing that the healthcare information outsourcing can 'offer over 100,000 medical-related jobs to nursing graduates' (Estuye 2013).

Ironically, part of framing this appeal was in emphasising that while such call centre jobs did not explicitly offer overseas mobility, a bulk of the clients in this industry were still foreign companies and institutions. State officials encouraged the notion that such work experience could enhance the profile of nursing graduates who still aspired to pursue overseas careers in the health industry in the future. For example, state media reports highlighted the rise of a 'healthcare information sector,' where nursing graduates could obtain work as medical transcriptionists for American hospitals (PNA 2015). Another private company advertised positions as 'medical butlers' and 'medical concierge management' where nursing graduates could 'help people arrange everything – from appointments to hospital options to rest and recreation activities in any part of the world.' The owner of the firm also believed that such experience could still work towards helping nursing graduates emigrate in the future, 'The additional training and skills they gain from the program will set these nurses apart from their peers, thus making them more appealing to employers' (Salazar 2009).

Skills for reskilling: nursing new careers

While rural deployment and the BPO industry provided an outlet for nursing graduates, the bulk of government discourse actually encouraged them to invest in additional skilling and certification. Such discourse was ironic given that the oversupply of nursing graduates was largely caused by the pursuit of credentials for overseas work. The push for reskilling took a variety of forms. In some instances, state officials encouraged nurses to enrol in short term technical vocational courses in order to qualify for jobs outside hospitals. They specifically promoted 'in demand skills' that had some relation to health, such as training in 'spa or massage therapy' for the wellness industry. In response to critique that conjured images of sleazy massage parlours, Secretary Baldoz argued that massage therapy has gained 'growing acceptance among medical practitioners.' She also underlined the fact that health and wellness jobs were available both locally and *overseas* and that these professions obtain an 'average earning of US$ 6,351 per month.' Nursing graduates who enrolled in tech-voc programmes for the wellness industry were 'likely to have very good job opportunities' given that they were licensed health professionals with formal training in massage therapy (PNA 2011).

Meanwhile, nursing graduates with more economic resources were simply advised to shift careers by taking on a second major. In a distinct change from earlier discourse on skilling oneself for emigration, state officials encouraged nursing students and unemployed graduates to move towards academic majors associated with *local* needs. For example, former CHEd commissioner Licuanan highlighted her commission's list of 'priority' fields such as Science and Technology, Agriculture, and Fisheries (PNA 2016a; 'The Real Score' 2011). Other state officials argued that nursing graduates would also qualify as skilful teachers for public elementary and high schools. One article in the *Manila Standard* noted that interested nursing graduates need not invest in a lengthy four-year degree, and can qualify for schools by only taking 18 units of education subjects and logging in a specific number of teaching practicum hours. The article went on to explain that nurses would actually serve as ideal public school teachers,

> By hiring nurses-cum-teachers, it will be getting the services of a health professional and an education professional all rolled into one. As it will be getting double board passers, it will be putting classes under dual discipline professionals who can both teach children and take care of their health, those who will be able to nurture body and mind at the same time.

It is interesting to note that despite the promotion of reskilling for other professions, media reports were careful to emphasise the ability of nursing graduates to return to nursing jobs when opportunities for overseas work return. As noted in the same article pushing nurses to reskill as teachers:

> For nurses, [the shift to teaching] affords the attainment of a second license, the practice of a second profession, one that will burnish one's CV and buttress one's chance of getting hired as a nurse, should one swerve back to it after detouring to teaching.

These statements show that while the Philippine state reconstructed nursing skill as abilities that provide benefits beyond the prospect of emigration, they couched such statements with the continued assurance of overseas employability. In this sense, state officials are well aware that despite the current lack of opportunities for migrant nurses, Filipino nurse graduates still aspired to fulfil what they believed was the true 'value' of their skills: practising clinical nursing in a first world hospital overseas (Ortiga 2018). As such, state reconstructions of 'skill' always came with the promise that reskilling, rural work experience, and spillovers to non-nursing (but still health-related) careers still contribute to enhancing one's capability to leave the country in the future.

Conclusion: the value of skilling and skills

While often represented through supposedly objective measures of credentials and certification, perceptions of human knowledge and ability have always been subjective, malleable, and context-dependent (Liu-Farrer, Yeoh, and Baas 2021). This special issue has highlighted the role of different actors and organisations in constructing current notions of skill in the context of global migration: receiving nations (Oishi 2021), corporations (Liu-Farrer and Shire 2021), and migrants themselves (Tseng 2021). In this paper, I place particular emphasis on the migrant-sending nation, revealing how labour-exporting states can also predict, define, and reconstruct skill in negotiating a volatile world of changing labour needs and fluctuating citizenship regimes. The Philippine case shows how skill is not just a resource that individual migrants seek to develop, utilise, and have recognised, nor is it simply a category used by destination countries in determining conditions for access and entry. Rather, in the context of the migrant-sending nation, the process of skilling has also become a state-driven effort to produce ideal global labour subjects – would-be migrant workers who are flexible and compliant to the needs of an unpredictable global economy.

In the case of aspiring nurse migrants, the Philippine state moved between two contradictory definitions of Filipino nursing skills. During periods of high outmigration, Filipino nurses were portrayed as specialised workers, specifically trained in line with the needs and priorities of foreign employers. Yet, when these overseas opportunities declined, so did the value of such particular skills, and the Philippine government could no longer capitalise on nursing graduates' supposed export value. State agencies then shifted towards promoting nursing skills as having a more general purpose – important in a wider range of settings and easily channelled sideways, towards rural health units, medical call centres, or the wellness industry.

This paper also shows how a discourse of overseas employability sustains this system, allowing the state to pacify unhappy nursing graduates and justify their career detours as experiences that will eventually lead to future emigration. There are many doubts as to whether this argument is true (see Ortiga 2018), yet in the end, the employability discourse serves its purpose of allowing the labour-exporting state to capitalise on aspiring migrants' labour, even when they are unable to leave the country.

One would think that after the problems brought by export-oriented nursing education, the Philippine state would reconsider its strategies of encouraging the skilling of professionals for overseas employment. Yet, the past few years has seen a gradual shift back to promoting nurse education as a steppingstone to overseas work, with state agencies marketing new venues for Filipino migrant nurses to bring their skills (Jaymalin 2015). In 2016, Secretary Baldoz sent out a press release reporting that

Germany would need 'at least 200,000 nurses until 2020' (PNA 2016b). Baldoz then called for the retooling of Philippine nursing curriculum in order to produce nurses with the skills needed by the German healthcare system, echoing the same discourse that led to the overexpansion of nursing programmes in the early 2000s. Such statements now raise concerns that the country is on its way towards creating another oversupply of nursing graduates.

A few Filipino politicians have questioned the sustainability of skilling young people for export (Hernandez 2015), yet most state officials have continued to search for more rigorous means of anticipating foreign labour market needs and training local citizens accordingly ('Aquino' 2013). It is important to note that the Philippines' employability agenda for migrant workers extends to other professions beyond nursing. In particular, media reports have highlighted the need to produce more competitive professionals in fields such as maritime engineering, accounting, civil engineering, and even hospitality services (see Ortiga 2018). The state advertises and promotes these skills to foreign employers, underlining the talent of Filipino workers in a global economy (PNA 2016c). While no longer the scope of this paper, these trends raise critical questions about how the value and purpose of particular skills are reconstructed when a profession is increasingly defined in terms of its export value to foreign employers. In many ways, this paper illustrates how the question of skill is very much part of this process and how more work is needed in terms of investigating how notions of human talent and capability shapes contemporary labour migration.

Notes

1. There is a rich literature on how educational institutions within popular destination countries like Australia also market particular academic degrees as a steppingstone towards permanent residency, despite much uncertainty as to what the local labour market will truly recognise and absorb (See Baas 2019; Robertson 2011).
2. This period also saw the creation of the Migrant Workers and Overseas Filipinos Act of 1995, where the Philippine government made official its mandate to facilitate the deployment of Filipino workers, while ensuring their rights and protection. Guevarra (2006) provides a rich outline of the events that led to this act and its outcomes for Filipina women seeking overseas work.
3. While the Philippine state deploys nurses to more than 50 countries across the world, the US remains the ideal destination for Filipino nurses – a belief strongly informed by the country's history as a former American colony, but also reinforced by the promise of higher wages and the best possibility of permanent settlement (Choy 2003). As such, the pursuit of nursing degrees in the Philippines has been linked to the opening and closing of opportunities for foreign nurses in the US (Acacio 2011).
4. Eight thousand Philippine pesos is roughly 153 USD (1 USD = 52 Pesos).

Disclosure statement

No potential conflict of interest was reported by the author(s).

ORCID

Yasmin Y. Ortiga http://orcid.org/0000-0003-1740-0521

References

"83 Nursing Schools Closed.". 2013. *Manila Bulletin*, March 23.

Acacio, Kristel Ann Santiago. 2008. "Managing Labor Migration: Philippine State Policy and International Migration Flows, 1969–2000." *Asian and Pacific Migration Journal* 17 (2): 103–132. doi:10.1177/011719680801700201.

Acacio, Kristel Ann Santiago. 2011. "Getting Nurses Here: Migration Industry and the Business of Connecting Philippine-Educated Nurses with United States Employers". Ph.D, University of California, Berkeley.

Aiken, Linda H. 2007. "U.S. Nurse Labour Market Dynamics are Key to Global Nurse Sufficiency." *Health Services Research* 42 (3): 1299–1320.

"Aquino: There are Jobs but No Applicants.". 2013. *Philippine Daily Inquirer*, February 6.

Arora, Bela. 2015. "A Gramscian Analysis of the Employability Agenda." *British Journal of Sociology of Education* 36 (4): 635–648.

Asis, Maruja M. B., and Graziano Batistella. 2013. *The Filipino Youth and the Employment Migration Nexus*. Makati City, Philippines: UNICEF Philippines.

Baas, Michiel. 2019. "The Education-Migration Industry: International Students, Migration Policy and the Question of Skills." *International Migration*, doi: 10.1111/imig.12540.

Becker, Gary S. 1964. *Human Capital: A Theoretical and Empirical Analysis, with Special Reference to Education*. New York: National Bureau of Economic Research.

Becker, Gary S. 2002. "*The Age of Human Capital.*" In *Education in the Twenty-First Century*, edited by Edward Paul Lazear, 3–8. Stanford, CA: Hoover Institution Press.

Boden, Rebecca, and Maria Nedeva. 2010. "Employing Discourse: Universities and Graduate 'Employability." *Journal of Education Policy* 25 (1): 37–54.

Boncocan, Karen. 2011. "10,000 Nurses to be Trained, Deployed in Rural Communities." *Philippine Daily Inquirer*, January 12.

Bonizzoni, Paola. 2018. "Looking for the Best and Brightest? Deservingness Regimes in Italian Labour Migration Management." *International Migration* 56 (4): 47–62.

Brown, Phillip. 2003. "The Opportunity Trap: Education and Employment in a Global Economy." *European Educational Research Journal* 2 (1): 142–180.

Brown, Phillip, Hugh Lauder, and David Ashton. 2011. *The Global Auction: The Broken Promises of Education, Jobs, and Incomes*. Oxford, UK: Oxford University Press.

Brush, Barbara L., and Julie Sochalski. 2007. ""International Nurse Migration: Lessons from the Philippines." *Policy, Politics & Nursing Practice* 8 (1): 37–46.

Buchan, James, Fiona O'May, and Gilles Dussault. 2013. "Nursing Workforce Policy and the Economic Crisis: A Global Overview." *Journal of Nursing Scholarship* 45 (3): 298–307.

Burgonio, T. J., and Eugene Nunez. 2009. "5000 Public Nurses Sought; 11000 Apply." *Philippine Daily Inquirer*, April 1.

Cabanda, Exequiel. 2017. "Higher Education, Migration and Policy Design of the Philippine Nursing Act of 2002." *Higher Education Policy* 30 (4): 555–575.

Capistrano, Francis Y. 2004. "OFW Diaspora." *Business World*, November 12.

Cerna, Lucie. 2016. *Immigration Policies and the Global Competition for Talent*. London: Palgrave Macmillan UK.

Chang, Andy Scott. 2018. "Producing the Self-Regulating Subject: Liberal Protection in Indonesia's Migration Infrastructure." *Pacific Affairs* 91 (4): 695–716. doi:10.5509/2018914695.

Chatterjee, Soma. 2015. "Skills to Build the Nation: The Ideology of 'Canadian Experience' and Nationalism in Global Knowledge Regime." *Ethnicities* 15 (4): 544–567. doi:10.1177/1468796815577702.

"CHED Advices Incoming College Freshmen.". 2011. *Manila Bulletin*, May 28.

Choy, Catherine Ceniza. 2003. *Empire of Care: Nursing and Migration in Filipino American History*. Durham, NC: Duke University Press.

Cimatu, Frank. 2011. "Health Secretary Tells Students: Avoid Nursing." *Philippine Daily Inquirer*, May 11.

Crisostomo, Sheila. 2012. "Aspiring Nurses Urged to Explore other Fields." *Philippine STAR*, March 4.
De Haas, Hein. 2005. "International Migration, Remittances and Development: Myths and Facts." *Third World Quarterly* 26 (8): 1269–1284.
Department of Labor and Employment, Philippines (DOLE). 1995. Annual Report. Manila, Philippines.
Department of Labour and Employment, Philippines (DOLE). 1990. Annual Report. Manila, Philippines.
Di Gropello, Emanuela, Hong Tan, and Prateek Tandon. 2010. *Skills for the Labour Market in the Philippines*. Washington DC: The World Bank.
Estuye, Josine. 2013. "DOLE Urges Filipino Nurses to Consider Working in BPO's Healthcare Information Management Outsourcing Sector." *Philippine News Agency*, August 30.
Forrier, Anneleen, Nele De Cuyper, and Jos Akkermans. 2018. "The Winner Takes it All, the Loser has to Fall: Provoking the Agency Perspective in Employability Research." *Human Resource Management Journal* 28 (4): 511–523.
Gonzalez, Andrew. 2000. "Some Educational Implications from Our Membership in the WTO." *Manila Bulletin*, Dec 7.
Guevarra, Anna Romina. 2006. "Managing 'Vulnerabilities' and 'Empowering' Migrant Filipina Workers: The Philippines' Overseas Employment Program." *Social Identities* 12 (5): 523–541.
Guevarra, Anna Romina. 2010. *Marketing Dreams, Manufacturing Heroes: The Transnational Labour Brokering of Filipino Workers*. Rutgers, NJ: Rutgers University Press.
Guevarra, Anna Romina. 2014. ""Supermaids: The Racial Branding of Global Filipino Care Labour."." In *Migration and Care Labour: Theory, Policy And Politics*, edited by Bridget Anderson, and Isabel Shutes, 130–150. London: Palgrave Macmillan.
Guile, David. 2006. "What is Distinctive About the Knowledge Economy? Implications for Education." In *Education, Globalization and Social Change*, edited by Hugh Lauder, Phillip Brown, Jo-Anne Dillabough, and A. H. Halsey, 355–366. New York: Oxford University Press.
Guinto, Joel. 2009. "Nurses Eyed to Be 'Warriors of Wellness.'" *Philippine Daily Inquirer*, February 9.
Handley, Karen. 2018. ""Anticipatory Socialization and the Construction of the Employable Graduate: A Critical Analysis of Employers' Graduate Careers Websites." *Work, Employment and Society* 32 (2): 239–256.
Hernandez, Butch. 2015. "K-to-12 and Beyond." *Philippine Daily Inquirer*, May 16.
Jaymalin, Mayen. 2015. "More Jobs await Pinoys in Canada." *Philippine STAR*, July 19.
Killias, Olivia. 2018. *Follow the Maid: Domestic Worker Migration From Indonesia*. Denmark: NIAS Press.
Kingma, Mireille. 2007. "Nurses on the Move: A Global Overview." *Health Services Research* 42 (3 II): 1281–1298.
Lafer, Gordon. 2002. *The Job Training Charade*. Ithaca, NY: Cornell University Press.
Liu-Farrer, Gracia, and Karen Shire. 2021. "Who Are the Fittest? The Question of Skills in National Employment Systems in an Age of Global Labour Mobility." *Journal of Ethnic and Migration Studies* 47 (10): 2305–2322. doi:10.1080/1369183X.2020.1731987.
Liu-Farrer, Gracia, Brenda S. Yeoh, and Michiel Baas. 2021. "Social Construction of Skill: An Analytical Approach Toward The Question of Skill in Cross-Border Labour Mobilities." *Journal of Ethnic and Migration Studies* 47 (10): 2237–2251. doi:10.1080/1369183X.2020.1731983.
Masselink, Leah E., and Shoou Yih Daniel Lee. 2010. "Nurses, Inc.: Expansion and Commercialization of Nursing Education in the Philippines." *Social Science and Medicine* 71 (1): 166–172.
Ministry of Education and Culture, Philippines (MEC). 1984. *Annual Report*. Manila, Philippines.
Molesworth, Mike, Elizabeth Nixon, and Richard Scullion. 2011. *The Marketisation of Higher Education and the Student as Consumer*. Abingdon, Oxon: Routledge.
"Monitor Nursing Schools, CHED Told.". 2012. *Manila Bulletin*, May 18.
Naidoo, Rajani, and Joanna Williams. 2015. "The Neoliberal Regime in English Higher Education: Charters, Consumers and the Erosion of the Public Good." *Critical Studies in Education* 56 (2): 208–223.

National Manpower and Youth Council (NMYC). 1968. *Survey on Youth.* Manila, Philippines.

Oishi, Nana. 2021. "Skilled or Unskilled?: The Re-Configuration of Migration Policies in Japan." *Journal of Ethnic and Migration Studies* 47 (10): 2252–2269. doi:10.1080/1369183X.2020.1731984.

Ortiga, Yasmin Y. 2014. "Professional Problems: The Burden of Producing the 'Global' Filipino Nurse." *Social Science & Medicine* 115: 64–71.

Ortiga, Yasmin Y. 2017. "The Flexible University: Neoliberal Education and the Global Production of Migrant Labor." *British Journal of Sociology of Education* 38 (4): 485–499.

Ortiga, Yasmin Y. 2018. "Learning to Fill the Labor Niche: Aspiring Nurse Migrants Caught in a Migration Trap." *Russell Sage Foundation Journal of the Social Sciences* 4 (1): 172–187.

Overland, Martha Ann. 2005. "A Nursing Crisis in the Philippines." *Chronicle of Higher Education* 51: A46.

Pefianco, Roming. 2012. "Rare Uprising." *Manila Bulletin*, February 25.

Philippine News Agency (PNA). 2009. *NARS to Train Inexperienced Nurses in Public Health and Clinical Functions.* Manila, Philippines: PNA.

Philippine News Agency (PNA). 2011. *Philippines: Jobs Aplenty beyond Nursing in Health and Wellness Industry - Baldoz.* Manila, Philippines: PNA.

Philippine News Agency (PNA). 2015. *PHL Improving Talents, Skills, Competencies to Fill IT-BPM Demands.* Manila, Philippines: PNA.

Philippine News Agency (PNA). 2016a. *Baldoz Encourages Jobseekers to Avail of Local Job Opportunities.* Manila, Philippines: PNA.

Philippine News Agency (PNA). 2016b. *Germany Needs 200,000 Nurses Till 2020 - Baldoz.* Manila, Philippines: PNA.

Philippine News Agency (PNA). 2016c. *PRC, CHED to Meet with Qatari Officials on Equivalency.* Manila, Philippines: PNA.

Poblete, Johanna Paola D. 2011. "Program to Deploy 10,000 Nurses to Poor Municipalities." *Business World*, January 13.

Powell, Walter W, and Kaisa Snellman. 2004. "The Knowledge Economy." *Annual Review of Sociology* 30: 199–220.

Pyle, Jean L. 2006. "Globalization, Transnational Migration, and Gendered Care Work: Introduction." *Globalizations* 3 (3): 283–295.

Quismundo, Tarra. 2010. "CHED Halts New Course Offerings in Nursing, 4 other Fields of Study." *Philippine Daily Inquirer*, November 12.

Robertson, Shanthi. 2011. "Student Switchers and the Regulation of Residency: The Interface of the Individual and Australia's Immigration Regime." *Population, Space and Place* 17 (1): 103–115.

Rodriguez, Robyn. 2010. *Migrants for Export: How the Philippine State Brokers Labour to the World.* Minnesota, MN: University of Minnesota Press.

Rodriguez, Robyn M., and Helen Schwenken. 2013. "Becoming a Migrant at Home: Subjectivation Processes in Migrant-Sending Countries Prior to Departure." *Population, Space and Place* 19 (4): 375–388.

Romero, Paolo. 2012. "'No More Shortage of Nurses in US.'" *Philippine STAR*, April 11.

Ronda, Rainier Allan. 2010. "CHED Imposes Moratorium on New Courses." *Philippine STAR*, November 13.

Ruiz, Neil. 2014. "Made for Export: Labor Migration, State Power, and Higher Education in a Developing Philippine Economy." PhD Diss. Massachusetts Institute of Technology.

Salazar, Tessa. 2009. "Health, Wellness Served on a Silver Platter, Anyone?" *Philippine Daily Inquirer*, December 4.

Shan, Hongxia, and Andreas Fejes. 2015. "Skill Regime in the Context of Globalization and Migration." *Studies in Continuing Education* 37 (3): 227–235.

Smith, Vicki. 2010. "Review Article: Enhancing Employability: Human, Cultural, and Social Capital in an Era of Turbulent Unpredictability." *Human Relations* 63 (2): 279–300.

Tan, Edita. 2011. "What's Wrong with the Philippine Higher Education?" *The Philippine Review of Economics* 48 (1): 147–184.

"The Real Score.". 2011. *Manila Bulletin*, July 16.

Thompson, Maddy. 2018. "Everything Changes to Stay the Same: Persistent Global Health Inequalities Amidst New Therapeutic Opportunities and Mobilities for Filipino Nurses." *Mobilities*, doi:10.1080/17450101.2018.1518841.

Tomlinson, Michael. 2008. "'The Degree is not Enough': Students' Perceptions of the Role of Higher Education Credentials for Graduate Work and Employability." *British Journal of Sociology of Education* 29 (1): 49–61.

Tomlinson, Michael. 2012. "Graduate Employability: A Review of Conceptual and Empirical Themes." *Higher Education Policy* 25 (4): 407–431.

Tseng, Yen-Fen. 2021. "Becoming Global Talent? Taiwanese Skilled Migrants in Japan." *Journal of Ethnic and Migration Studies* 47 (10): 2288–2304. doi:10.1080/1369183X.2020.1731986.

Tubeza, Philip. 2009. "4-Yr Wait before Nurses Land Job in US." *Philippine Daily Inquirer*, March 2.

Tyner, James A. 2009. *The Philippines: Mobilities, Identities and Globalization.* New York: Routledge.

Walton-Roberts, Margaret. 2021. "Intermediaries and Transnational Regimes of Skill: Nursing Skills and Competencies in the Context of International Migration." *Journal of Ethnic and Migration Studies* 47 (10): 2323–2340. doi:10.1080/1369183X.2020.1731988.

Waters, Johanna L. 2009. "In Pursuit of Scarcity: Transnational Students, 'Employability', and the MBA." *Environment and Planning A: Economy and Space* 41 (8): 1865–1883.

Xiang, Biao. 2007. *Global "Body Shopping": An Indian Labour System in the Information Technology Industry.* Princeton, NJ: Princeton University Press.

Yeates, Nicola, and Jane Pillinger. 2019. *International Health Worker Migration and Recruitment: Global Governance, Politics, and Policy.* London: Routledge.

Becoming global talent? Taiwanese white-collar migrants in Japan

Yen-Fen Tseng

ABSTRACT
As more governments implement skill-based migration policies, understanding how policymakers, employers and migrants evaluate and interpret skills is of great importance. Based on a study of Taiwanese white-collar migrant workers in Japan, this article treats skills as socially constructed and offers an opportunity to investigate how skill is experienced across borders. This article makes contribution to skilled migration research by investigating the social contexts in which skills are categorised, evaluated, and developed, and how such experiences feed into migration decisions and adaptation outcomes. To many Taiwanese college-educated migrants, coming to work in Japan is a first step in being recognized as 'global talent'. The initial successful migration outcome fails, however, to retain these new arrivals to corporate Japan. Taiwanese migrant professionals usually do not aspire to develop the firm-specific skills and in-house careers that Japanese-style training regimes offer.

Introduction

There is a marked shift from restrictive to selective immigration policies in many countries that have recently abandoned 'zero immigration policies' in favour of skill-based migration policies (de Haas, Natter, and Vezzoli 2016). In these drives to implement skilled migration policies, skill level is a core concern regarding who should be allowed to immigrate and what the resulting fit between migrants and a host labour market will look like (Boucher and Cerna 2014). A key question for researchers remains how host country policymakers and employers evaluate skills, and how migrants themselves experience the meaning of skill across borders. For example, a college education is often considered a good indicator of skill for many policymakers. A large number of college-educated migrants, however, continue to experience poor outcomes when searching for employment opportunities in host countries (Reitz, Curtis, and Elrick 2013). Even when the job match is initially positive, retention rates depend on how migrants experience skill development (Hof 2018). While a host country's immigration policy is crucial to the entry of skilled migrants, it does little to help them adapt and settle (Findlay and Cranston 2015). In the introduction to this special issue, Liu-Farrer, Yeoh, and Bass contend that research on skilled migration should problematise the notions of 'skilled' vs. 'unskilled' constructed by immigration policy-makers.

This article investigates the ability of Japan's skilled migration policy to attract college-educated foreigners and the country's distinctive employment practices to train and retain a newly gained global workforce. Although long known for its 'closed-door' immigration policy, Japan's new skilled migration scheme is one of the most open to receiving skilled migrants (Oishi 2012; Komine 2018). Facing challenges posed by recent changes in the global economy, the Japanese business sector has pressured the government to offer more lenient immigration policies to match their efforts to internationalise human resources (Oishi 2012). Beginning in the 2000s, large Japanese firms actively sought to increase the number of foreigners in headquarter managerial tracks, a process called 'internal internationalisation' [*uchinaru kokusai-ka*] (Yamao and Sekiguchi 2015). Since then, the phrase, 'global talent' [*Gurōbaru jinzai*], has become a buzz term in Japanese human resources management (Japanese Business Federation 2011; Sekiguchi 2014). Tapping the increased supply of foreign talent via new skilled migration policies, 33% of Japanese companies registered on the Tokyo stock exchange employed foreigners in 2013, a significant jump of 6% in a single year from 27% in 2012 (Sekiguchi, Froese, and Iguchi 2016). The outcome of this human resource strategy might not, however, be as rosy as these recruitment figures indicate. Holbrow and Nagayoshi (2018) found that detrimental employment practices often 'cancel out' the monetary returns of human capital among skilled migrants in Japan. Conrad and Meyer-Ohle (2017) propose that the employment system is an important variable in understanding the employment outcomes of foreign skilled workers.

This article, based on a study of young college-educated Taiwanese migrants in Japan, elaborates the theme of this special issue and places the question of who 'arbitrates' skills and what constitutes skill at the centre of cross-border labour mobility (Liu-Farrer, Yeoh, and Bass, 2021). It investigates the social contexts in which skills are categorised, evaluated, and developed across borders, and how such experiences feed into migration decisions and adaptation outcomes. By bringing in Thelen's (2004) training regime, the focus of my study goes beyond mere employment systems. The concept of the training regime is concerned with the skill formation system in which education, training, and work are connected via routes and mechanisms that differ across countries or capitalisms. Thelen (2004) proposes two ideal types: *liberal market economy* (LME) and *coordinated market economy* (CME). Prior to employment workers in LME training regimes are required to have vocational skills normally gained from formal education, while firms in CME training regime look for workers with the learning potential to acquire essential skills via on-the-job-training. In Thelen's (2004) evaluation, the U.S. and U.K. are typical LME training regimes, while Germany and Japan are two representatives of CME training regimes. Taiwan and Japan have different training regimes, with Taiwan being an LME regime and Japan a CME. Thus, it offers a valuable opportunity to investigate how migrants experience skill evaluation and training when they move between divergent training regimes. This article demonstrates that although Japan has 'made' it to bring in impressive numbers of foreign college-educated workers in a relatively short period of time, the later incorporation issues involve how migrants adapt to host country's training regime. To retain newly gained global workforce in headquarters, therefore, requires recognition on the part of Japanese employers that foreign workers may not share the aspiration for growing the firm-specific skills that Japanese-style training regimes offer.

This article proceeds as follows. After a discussion of data collection, I first review the context in which skills are socially constructed by comparing how skills are evaluated in the labour market in two divergent training regimes, Taiwan and Japan. In Taiwan, the dislocation of college-educated workers in the increasingly polarised labour market constitutes the main push factor behind the significant outmigration. Among those who choose to migrate to Japan, unique features of Japan's employment system and its migration policy provides special appeal, besides cultural affinity. I then analyse how Taiwanese experience what constitutes core skills valued and cultivated by Japanese corporations. The last part of the findings presents migrant evaluations of skill acquisition and adaptation outcomes in the area of skill development and the resulting job satisfaction.

Data

The research data consist of the following sources: 32 in-depth interviews with Taiwanese migrants, conducted during 2017–2018, mainly in Japan; government policies and mass media coverage from Taiwan and Japan; and important website information that facilitates Taiwanese migration to Japan. Key informants are intermediaries, including recruiters and Taiwanese active in the migrant community. I also made field observations by attending events organised by recruiters and gatherings held by migrant groups, in Tokyo and Taipei. The most important initial contacts were made through the founders of *Worklife in Japan*, a website established in 2016 by a group of recent Taiwanese migrants in Tokyo that provides a not-for-profit platform to share personal tales and know-how about migrating to work in Japan. More than a platform, *Worklife in Japan* offers advice to potential migrants from Taiwan. Since 2016, *Worklife in Japan* has held events in Tokyo, connecting audiences back in Taiwan via live stream. For example, during the 2018 annual sharing event connecting various university campuses, over 900 students in Taiwan registered for online viewing. In 2017, it conducted a survey of Taiwanese migrants in Japan to learn their basic profiles and experiences. The survey results, based on 841 respondents, are accessible online (Worklife in Japan 2017). When presenting my findings, I will cross-reference these survey results.

The interviewees were selected to match the demographic profiles of recent Taiwanese migrants in Japan. Sixty per cent of all interviewees were women and the great majority were between 25 and 35 years old (Ministry of Justice Japan 2018). The interviewees are recruited according to the following criteria. First, because the effect of Japan's recent active recruitment efforts to attract college-educated migration is the article's focus, most interviewees were new arrivals with a four-year college or more advanced degree. Second, to study career-track employees who were recruited as part of 'internal internationalisation' at headquarters of large firms, the interviewees were those working as regular employees in career-track positions in large and reputable firms.[1] Hence, their experiences cannot be readily generalised to those working in small and medium firms. Third, the sample was selected to reflect diverse migration channels including student and employment visas as modes of entry to Japan. The employment sectors included manufacturing, business services, retailing, and information technology. Since the study is interested in learning whether experiences diverge for those whose skills are more universally applied, interviewees included a disproportionate number of information technology engineers (10 out of 32). According to Iredale (2001), the skills of IT professional migrants are the most internationally applicable. Therefore, the cultural context in the host country should have relatively less impact on how they employ their skills. I conducted semi-structured interviews in Mandarin. A number of interviewees were interviewed more than once. In analysing interviewee transcripts, I developed codes in relation to migration decisions, recruitment processes, and senses of achievement/frustrations associated with working in Japan. Successive rounds of coding focused on identifying patterns by gender, industry type, and foreign/Japanese-owned companies.

Skill as a social construct in training regimes

To deepen our understanding about how migrants experience skills in different training regimes, we need to investigate how their skills are evaluated by migrants themselves and their employers. As Wood (1981) argues, the concept of skills should be understood as a product of social construction that involves processes of how skills are identified, recognised, and developed. Rigby and Sanchis (2006) argue that gaps always exist in the labour market between effective skills, that is, what workers think they can offer, and nominal skills, that is, the skills employers recognise and seek. According to Rigby and Sanchis, workers tend to view their own skills with a wider definition, whereas employers tend to apply narrower definitions. The bigger the gap between these two sets of evaluations, that is, between effective and nominal skills, the more likely it is that workers feel they are devalued. I argue that the size of the gap depends on the social context in which the training regimes operate. As Liu-Farrer and Shire (2021) show that despite the many common features Japan and Germany, both CME training regimes, share, foreign graduate job seekers are evaluated differently by the respective employers; Japanese look for 'potential fits' and Germans for 'exact fits'. The differences in what Taiwanese and Japanese employers seek in foreign workers will be even larger since they are embedded in different training regimes. Their contrast is succinctly put by an interviewee who had worked in Taiwan for more than five years before coming to work in Japan:

> Taiwanese employers treat employees as instruments, while Japanese employers consider employees their assets. Taiwanese companies invest very little in cultivating employees' abilities, as compared to Japanese companies' strong emphasis on training.

The following sections compare the training regimes in Taiwan and Japan to illustrate the different social contexts of skill evaluation in these two countries.

Taiwan

The training regime in Taiwan has long relied on state investments in the education system to provide qualified workers for employers in order to create rapid economic development (Ashton et al. 2002). Beyond the formal education system, collective action in training at both industry and firm level is scant, and the burden of skill formation is largely placed upon individual workers' shoulders once they finish their schooling (Ashton et al. 2002). According to survey data, Taiwanese employers leave filling the skill gap almost entirely to their employees (Liu and Huang 2011). Taiwan can be categorised as having an LME training regime in which workers are supposed to have skills directly applicable to the job before they enter the labour market. According to the *Oxford Report on Global Talent*, among surveyed countries, Taiwanese employers reported the most serious problem finding suitably skilled workers (Oxford Economics 2012). This is puzzling since Taiwan has a well-educated workforce, with a high proportion holding tertiary degrees or above, and is ranked number two for scholastic performance in international comparisons (IMD 2018). Taiwanese employers' tendency to select workers with specific skills learnt from their formal education, i.e. as part of their college majors (Chang 2016). Research shows that in Taiwan while holding a college degree does on average increase a worker's earnings, there is a major discrepancy between the benefit of degrees in the humanities and social sciences and those with degrees in more marketable majors like business and engineering (Tien 2008). Consequently, the gap between effective and nominal skill is large because only a few workers who possess degrees in the 'right' majors are considered by employers to be skilled workers. Such social valuations lead to a situation in which Taiwanese employers have the general sense that workers are under-qualified.

Japan

Japan is considered one of the few capitalist countries where employers routinely offer intensive and lengthy training to their employees (Nagano 2014). The Japanese training regime is typical of the CME model, which offers long-term employment as an incentive for workers to undergo intensive training once they enter companies to gain firm-specific skills. As Ashton, Sung, and Turbin (2000) contend, the Japanese model of skill formation is uniquely enterprise-based. The well-known company motto of Panasonic offers a glimpse of this emphasis on training – 'before producing products we need to produce people' (*Mono o tsukuru mae ni mazu hito o tsukuru*). Consequently, as compared with Taiwanese employers, who look for specific ready-to-work skills in their employees, Japanese employers do not look for specific skills that workers possess before entry but gauge the potential of workers to develop skills that serve the company's needs once they are employed (Conrad and Meyer-Ohle 2017). In such a situation, academic credentials indicate the potential to be trained but not specific vocational skills that workers demonstrate. A strong indicator of this orientation toward training is Japanese employers' preference for new graduates, whom employers assume are a 'white cloth' that can be 'dyed' with ease (Hassan and Hoshino 2009). Because Japanese employers look for general but not specific skills, the gap is narrower between the effective skill possessed by workers and the nominal skill recognised by employers.

Even after the bubble economy burst in the early 1990s, long-term employment, seniority-based promotion, and firm-specific training still constitute the solid pillars of Japanese employment in large firms (Nagano 2014). Although the overall proportion of employees included in such a system has declined, reputation and status recognition are among the main reasons why most large employers continue to maintain this traditional employment system for management track personnel, even when the firms are not as profitable as before (Hassan and Hoshino 2009). Distinctive Japanese employer preferences provide an interesting social context in which to investigate how foreigners' skills are evaluated, how Japanese employers select foreign employees, and how these employees are trained once they cross the border and enter the companies.

Taiwanese 'skilled' migration to Japan

Say goodbye to Taiwan's 'spoiled boss'

According to government data, in 2017 there were about 736,000 Taiwanese working abroad, with an overwhelming majority being tertiary-educated, and those between 25 and 34 were the largest and fastest growing group (National Statistics Bureau 2018). The main push factor is low wages, which have stagnated for nearly two decades, with young workers suffering the most, due to the declining added value of industrial products that Taiwan has experienced over the past decade, with its marginalisation in the international trading system (Lin and Yang 2018). Job satisfaction among young workers is generally low, indicated by a high turnover rate. According to the Ministry of Labour (2019), college-educated workers experience more difficulties in finding jobs than vocational training graduates. As college graduates in many countries are also undervalued (Allen and Ainley 2010), several conditions have paved a more troubling road for young Taiwanese college graduates as they have built their careers.

First, college diplomas have been devalued as higher education institutions expanded in the past decade and the supply of college graduates doubled (Yang, Lin, and Lin 2010). Second, the number of higher-paying jobs has shrunk and concentrated in only a few industries, such as finance and high-tech manufacturing (Chang 2016). Influenced by the abovementioned training regime, Taiwanese employers have the propensity to look for workers with skills gained in formal education. In general, however, higher education in Taiwan does not train students to connect their skills with job markets (Kuo 2019). Even when many would like to choose majors that offer sought-after skills, only a small proportion of high-achieving applicants are successful because universities cap the number of students admitted to 'hot' fields such as finance and IT engineering. As a result, those whose majors fall outside the skills required by higher paid jobs have become deeply frustrated about their career prospects in Taiwan.

Among interviewees, many shared similar observations about not being regarded in Taiwan as skilled workers. Some reported feeling insulted by their treatment in Taiwan's job market, simply because they did not possess the narrow set of skills employers considered valuable. They complained that in job postings in Taiwan, it was common to limit applicants to those with business/economics or IT majors. They feel excluded from many job sectors from the beginning. Interviewees frequently mentioned that young people use the term, '*guan lao ban*' (literally 'spoiled boss') to refer to employers/supervisors who act as though employees are expendable. They attribute such imbalance of power relations to the situation in which young college graduates do not have valuable skills as bargaining power. Even though many interviewees had not worked before their journey to Japan, they reported negative perceptions of Taiwanese supervisors/bosses through tales of 'spoiled bosses' that were widely shared by older classmates on social media. In general, interviewees appeared to think of their skills in much higher terms than Taiwanese employers do. They choose to migrate to find a place that appreciates their skills more. The main outmigration destinations for young workers have been major cities in China

(Tseng and Wu 2011). In 2018, half of the college-educated workers working abroad have gone to China, with the United States ranked second (National Statistics Bureau 2018).[2] Japan is a latecomer in the list of destination countries mainly because Japan's policy of liberalising immigration for college-educated foreigners has been known to Taiwanese only in recent years by active recruitment efforts of Japanese recruiters and companies. In 2018, 10,564 Taiwanese held working visas in Japan, a more than six-fold increase from 2012, with a great majority being engineer/specialist in humanities/international services visa holders (Ministry of Justice 2018).

Working as global talent in Japan

As Oishi (2021) points out, along with liberalising immigration policy, the Japanese government continues to define skills to allow more foreigners to work legally in Japan since the government insists that the country does not admit unskilled workers. As a result, Japan's skilled migration policy is now considered one of the most lenient. The current policy requires potential migrants to be college-educated and secure a job offer from a company operating in Japan prior to entry (Oishi, 2021). Most countries that adopt 'employer-driven' policies impose other criteria such as passing a labour market test (to ensure no domestic workers can fill the jobs) and filling an occupation on a nation's shortage list (Parsons et al. 2014). Japan, however, has none of these additional requirements. Japan's policy, with its exclusive dependence on employer preferences, reflects the characteristics of the training regime in Japan. Most notably, it does not take work experience into account. Japan's skilled-migration scheme is embedded in the norms of the country's corporate personnel practices, a typical institutional complementarity with the training regime that favours new graduates. As a consequence, Japan's skilled migrant policy grants recent foreign college graduates a greater opportunity to immigrate.

Another unique feature of Japan's policy is that the engineer/specialist in humanities/international services visa, with which most recent skilled migrants work for three or five years in Japan, recognises diverse and general skills (Debnar 2016). The engineer/specialist in humanities/international services visa category is meant to cast a wide net to include those who engage in jobs applying knowledge of natural sciences, social sciences (specifically economics, sociology, and law), humanities, or foreign cultures and languages. This also demonstrates the unique Japanese approach to skill in which employees' learning potential is valued over specific skills. As a result, unlike in other countries where foreign recruits are usually experienced workers with specific skills, migrants with diverse college majors have landed management-track jobs in Japan immediately upon graduation (Conrad and Meyer-Ohle 2017; Sekiguchi, Froese, and Iguchi 2016). This is unusual because college graduates with broad and non-specific qualifications (including degrees in the humanities, science, or commerce) often encounter difficulties finding skilled positions in managerial or professional jobs in host countries (Hawthorne 2006). Moreover, engineer/specialist in humanities/international services visa holders are allowed to apply to become permanent residents if they continue to reside and work for a required period of time.

Taiwanese consider Japanese skilled migration policy friendly because it welcomes college graduates with degrees from a wide range of majors and those with no prior work experiences. The opportunity is particularly attractive to those with some Japanese proficiency and who hold positive views about Japan. Interviewees confirmed that they had a degree of cultural affinity with Japan. They belong to the cohort influenced by the strong presence of Japanese popular culture, such as anime, comics, and games. Despite such cultural affinity, Japan's emergence as an attractive destination for Taiwanese young workers is surprising since in many job sectors, Japanese wages are not competitive, especially in light of the high cost of living (Hays Specialist 2018). Therefore, as Hof (2018) points out, without other incentives, monetary considerations alone do not attract foreign talent to Japan. For Taiwanese migrants, according to the *Worklife in Japan* survey, the opportunity to develop skills is as important a motivation to work in Japan as a better salary (Worklife in Japan 2017).

The aspiration to increase skills in Japan was an important conversation topic during my interviews. For example, when asked to describe in one sentence why he came to work in Japan, an interviewee who majored in business said: 'I want to be given proper training by companies to become a competent worker'. His response was surprising; he had received his formal education from a business school at a prestigious university in Taiwan. But young Taiwanese workers come to Japan specifically because of the unique training offered by Japanese companies. Although my interviewees acknowledge that Japan is well known for its hierarchical system operated by rigid norms and harsh working conditions, such as extensive overtime[3], they tend to emphasise that to work hard with a sense of purpose is better than being trapped in low-esteem jobs back home. While migrants share their personal tales on internet platforms, many are frank about the intensity of work and rigid rules in workplaces. However, reading the 73 personal tales published on *Worklife in Japan* between 2016 and end of March 2019,[4] I found that despite the hardship and frustration they face, the *Worklife* authors tend to highlight the ensuing joy and pride they experienced having overcome the obstacles of working in Japan. The main takeaway from these tales is that 'with extraordinary perseverance, you will make it in Japan'.

Most job posts for foreign applicants require applicants possess business-level Japanese-language ability. As a result, most of those who can land a job in Japan have put intensive efforts into acquiring the Japanese language and cultural familiarity prior to job-hunting. Except for some engineers, who were not required to have Japanese cultural literacy prior to their recruitment, most interviewees utilised various channels such as enrolling in postgraduate studies, exchange or language programmes at Japanese universities, short-term language schools, and working-holiday visits, to strengthen their ties with Japan prior to deciding to work in Japan. For example, the number of Taiwanese students studying in Japan doubled between 2012 and 2018 (Ministry of Education 2018).

Based on interviewees' commonly shared experiences in the recruitment process, training period, and work settings, the following two sections illustrate the distinctiveness of the Japanese employment system, in which migrants' skills are evaluated, sharpened through training, and encouraged to acquire. As consequence of their low satisfaction with Japanese employment system, none of the interviewees aspired to build an in-house career.

Becoming ideal Japanese workers

Starting from job-hunting, foreign job-searchers quickly realise that they will be subject to the same evaluative routines as native-born applicants. In the how-to guides offered by recruiters targeting foreigners, the information closely resembles what natives find in their own job-hunting books. In addition, the guides are usually supplemented by graphic comics and pictures, showing men and women adhering to a rigid dress code of black suits with white shirts. Eyeglasses are to be avoided and a tidy hair style and sitting on the front half of the chair while being interviewed are *de rigueur*. These requirements send a message to foreign job-hunters that Japanese employers expect foreign workers to behave exactly like native Japanese workers during recruitment. Going through recruitment is a rite of passage for cultural outsiders, a transit to becoming a Japanese worker in the fullest sense. At every step of the job-hunting process foreigners experience the distinctiveness of corporate Japan. For example, an interviewee commented, 'in Japan, a worker is hunting for a career with the company rather than just a job'. An IT engineer recalled the recruitment process and concluded: 'what they [employers] are looking for is, in the following order: your passion for the company, proper manners, and personality to fit their company culture'.

General intelligence instead of college major

Interviewees often emphasised that Japanese employers tend to value applicants' general intelligence more than their college majors. Except for technician positions post postings usually contain the following words: 'applicants welcomed with all majors'. An interviewee with master degree in Japanese literature expressed appreciation for being taken seriously during job-hunting in Japan:

> I went through over a dozen job interviews in Japan. None of the interviewers considers my major an issue. Instead they would try to relate my experiences of studying literature to learn about my potential to work in their companies.

A migrant with a degree in oceanography shared his thoughts about coming to Japan. Worried about limited career choices in Taiwan, he learnt, during the year when he was an exchange student in Japan, that 'except for technician jobs, Japanese employers do not care about your college major that much'. An IT engineer told me that her department recruited two new foreign workers with no prior education or training related to programming, so the company trained them from scratch.

Graduates from well-known universities are favoured, because their alma maters are taken as a proxy for intelligence. Quite a number of interviewees who did not graduate from high-ranking universities in Taiwan made efforts to enrol in language programmes or graduate programmes with prestigious universities in Japan. Beyond that, applicants are usually asked, especially if they are applying at large companies, to take a recruitment test known as *Sōgō Tekisei Kensa* (the Synthetic Personality Inventory, hereafter SPI), which includes verbal skills and mathematical knowledge as well as personality traits. The SPI test contains a series of questions that ask how an applicant will behave, the extent of his or her ambitions and emotional makeup, as indicators of personality. Japanese employers do not automatically select applicants with the highest scores; most interviewees told me their companies will use these tests to screen out applicants with below average scores and then use the results of the personality test to find the best candidates, that is, those who have the greatest ability to fit in the system. Ability to fit is the characteristic that best predicts the ability to acquire skills after employment.

Productive social skills

Among various aspects of personality, sociability is valued. Japanese HR people look for evidence that job candidates are socially active. Participation in extra-curricular activities and other indicators of social ability are skills job candidates usually highlight. The recruitment process often involves rounds of group discussions where an applicant's teamwork and social interactions are observed. An IT professional compared his experiences being interviewed in Taiwan and in Japan and concluded that Japanese companies consider individualism undesirable:

> When entering the phase of the interview for my current job in Japan, I was asked questions mostly about my behaviour and personality. As compared to the interview questions I had in Taiwan almost exclusively concerning programming skills, Japanese employers like to know how I will act when encountering problems. They seem to appreciate those responses indicating the readiness of seeking help from others, instead of solving problems all by yourself.

Japanese employers place emphasis on employees' social skills because work is accomplished in small groups. An interviewee pointed out:

> Working in Japanese firms does not require the input of personal uniqueness. The most important thing is that you work with the group. The group, not the individual, is the basic unit in work. The hard work you need to put in is communicating everything with your group members. But there is a positive side about it. When something goes wrong, no one in the same group points fingers at each other, since the responsibility does not lie on individual shoulders.

This fits Fligstein's (2001, 105) conception of social skill as 'the ability to induce cooperation in others'. This is especially important in Japanese companies, because the decision making is based on consensus among group members (Waldenberger 2016). As a result, Japanese workers need good social skills to moderate opinions to build consensus. Therefore, social skills are considered productive for the business rather than only fulfilling social functions.

In summary, after a tough recruitment process and landing their dream jobs, Taiwanese soon find that they are expected to increase their skills only in those aspects Japanese employers value. Their skill development in corporate Japan corresponds to what Japanese employers emphasise: 'good character' and valuing worker trainability over specific skills (Kariya 2010). As a result, an ideal Japanese worker should possess enthusiasm, perseverance, and commitment – proxies for being able to absorb firm-specific training. While many devote their efforts to learning to become ideal Japanese workers, it is questionable whether Taiwanese workers experience the skill growth they expect. The following section offers related findings.

Skill gain or skill loss?

The group of new migrants in this study could be considered the 'lucky' few who achieved careers most Japanese elites aspire to and many are excluded from, that is, to work as permanent employees in large firms. Such career opportunities are especially difficult for women to attain since most positions with the possibility of promotion are dominated by men, with 95% of female workers being employed in general staff positions (Ogawa 2017). Career achievement among Taiwanese female workers in Japan is unusual compared to the general population. Female participants in this study reported limited personal experiences of the gender inequality characteristic of Japanese firms, mainly because they had yet to reach the promotion stage. Liu-Farrer (2009) considers the demand for Japanese firms to expand transnationally to be a major factor that opens opportunities for highly educated female migrants.

Many, however, began to value skill development opportunities over the security and reputation of their jobs, after one or two years. As mentioned above, many came to Japan, not for monetary rewards but to learn the skills they consider important for them to become true professionals. When they invest time and energy learning Japanese ways, anxiety grows: will they become more or less skilled? If they sense a lack of challenge and opportunities to develop the kind of skills they wish to accumulate, they feel unfulfilled and may contemplate leaving the job or even the country. The following are several major sources of unfulfilling skill development.

Firm-specific skills

The first source of disillusionment about increasing skills in Japan is about the prospect of skill development by learning firm-specific training. Typically Japanese workers build in-house careers with one company by rotating between different departments in the training period, hence the skill development goal is to become a generalist instead of specialist (Waldenberger 2016). Consequently, firm-specific skills learnt are not necessarily useful in other corporations. An interviewee talked how learning the company culture constitutes the main part of training session including ways of business interactions such as how to write letters and emails to fit her company culture.

This situation sometimes leads to Taiwanese becoming reluctant to undergo lengthy training, because they are afraid they may lose the opportunity to learn something more important. An interviewee chose to reject a job offer from a big auto company that normally spends three years training a new worker. She did not wish to be trained for so long, so she accepted a job with a less well-known company because the training period was only one year. Another interviewee shared a similar worry:

> It is not difficult to learn the skills required by Japanese firms. It is just the fear that I might get stuck learning all these skills I will not be able to use elsewhere.

It is ironic that these migrants originally came to Japan to acquire skills through company training, but eventually came to fear that the longer and more seriously a company trains them the more likely they are locked in with the firm.

The rigid hierarchy of job assignments

The second aspect of disappointment has to do with a lack of challenges for junior workers, who labour under a rigid hierarchical system in which they perform only routine and boring tasks. In contrast to the situation that Taiwanese employers are eager to assign challenging tasks to new workers and then leave workers to struggle on their own with the work, junior employees in Japan work in non-significant functions for many years. An interviewee recruited to boost Asian sales in the overseas marketing department of a famous manufacturing firm said:

> Since I entered the company, eight months ago, in the department I work, I am the only one who is supposed to answer the phones and take down details simply because I am the most junior. But that occupies a big part of my time. I have a master's degree, and the way I work is not efficient!

Another interviewee expressed similar experiences. She was recruited to work in a marketing department but for months was trained to learn how to take meeting minutes, without having any 'real' opportunity to apply or learn important skills. It is worth noting that this is not particular to women's experiences, male interviewees shared similar experiences. A male IT engineer felt that it takes too long for Japanese firms to give their junior employees significant tasks. Another male interviewee who had three years of work experiences in a Taiwan's large firm before migrating to Japan offered the following:

> Every single business email written in my first two years had to be corrected by my mentor and he was always critical of small matters. In contrast, back in Taiwan when I began my first job, after a month of a transitional period, I was on my own to accomplish every task as a purchaser via learning-by-doing.

An IT engineer suggested that if Japanese employers wish to keep foreign skilled workers, they have to give junior employees opportunities to learn skills that they could claim 'ownership'.

Overemphasis of cultural skills

A third aspect of job dissatisfaction was a sense that they had achieved little skill growth because they spent too much energy learning cultural skills emphasised in workplace interactions. When acquiring cultural skills, Taiwanese consider having to follow overt and hidden rules in workplace interactions the major source of stress. As mentioned above, most foreigners recruited to work in the headquarters of large Japanese firms are equipped with business-level Japanese proficiency. They still encounter, however, communication problems in workplace interactions, because they are expected to understand hidden rules as much as natives do. The prevalent use of indirect expressions in the Japanese language creates difficulties for foreigners trying to interpret what their co-workers intend to communicate.

Many pointed out that the Japanese language encourages suppressing personal feelings and opinions. They worried that if they became too acculturated, they would lose the ability to express opinions directly. In work settings that encourage English as an alternative, many Taiwanese would choose to switch to English to make their points more directly and clearly. The longer they stayed in Japan, the more eager they were to cultivate their English ability and use it whenever allowed. An interviewee said:

> I am very aware that relying exclusively on Japanese to communicate for too long has gradually made me unable to tell people what I truly think. A lot of times, I would think in Chinese or in English before expressing my opinions in Japanese, in order to directly express opinions. This also helps send my co-workers a message that I am a foreigner.

In addition to verbal expressions, manners and etiquette are an important part of communication tools. An interviewee whose employer, a company regularly recruiting a sizable number of foreigners every year, even devote a whole day to teaching foreign newcomers crucial workplace manners, equipped with a thick manual containing details such as 'you should not let the phone ring more than twice before picking up'. In a Chinese version of work-in-Japan guide available in Taiwanese bookstores, before introducing 100 workplace manners, the authors take great pains to emphasise that in Japan, good etiquette is a crucial work skill to earn trust and maintain good working relations (EZ Japan 2016). Although interviewees confirm that it is essential to learn these cultural skills to survive, at the same time, the emphasis on etiquette strengthens their impression that most of the time, they are performing insignificant tasks and learning unimportant skills.

All of the above aspects constitute the main source of frustration about skill development for Taiwanese workers in Japan. They have been brought in to enhance the internationalisation of the workforce, but in daily routines they are expected, as soon as possible, to think and behave like their Japanese colleagues. Many migrants experienced a period in which they were eager to acculturate quickly but later learned that it is to migrants' benefit to subtly remind their Japanese colleagues that they are foreigners, who cannot be expected to be exactly like Japanese in all aspects. Even IT engineers, who are supposed to possess skills that can be universally applied across countries, found that their skills are deeply embedded in the Japanese cultural context. This realisation falls especially hard on these IT professionals since recruiters assured them that employers do not expect them to know the Japanese language and culture. An IT engineer said: 'we cannot afford to spend so much energy on the many tedious details of social interaction that the Japanese take for granted'. Many foreigners left the companies because they were not given opportunities to increase their skills. While many Europeans/Americans would leave within a year, Taiwanese, and other Asians, would stick around longer but at most for only two years. In their eyes, Japanese employers seem not to care about the high turnover rate among foreigners. In an IT engineer's words, 'in a way, we are a bit like *disposable chopsticks*'. This is far from the message conveyed during their recruitment that Japanese firms recruit them to enhance innovation capacity, not as cheap disposable workers.

As a result of these evaluations of limited skill growth, the longer skilled migrants stay in Japan, the greater the gap between their expectations of the workers they would like to become and the workers that Japanese firms expect them to be. An overwhelming majority of interviewees indicated that they were considering leaving Japan within five years. In the *Worklife in Japan* survey, 30% of 841 respondents said they would choose to migrate to work in Japan if they were given the chance to choose again, and only 10% expressed interest in obtaining permanent residency. It seems that after they experienced the reality of working in Japan, the idea of staying for a full 10 years to achieve residency, is rarely an attractive future.

Conclusion

This article makes two theoretical contributions to skilled migration research. First, the concept of training regime moves the question of skills beyond employment systems, by connecting education, work, and training to their national context. Second, this study incorporates migrants' experiences of skills in training regimes both at home and in the host country. Taiwanese skilled migrants in Japan have benefited from broad Japanese definitions of what constitutes desirable skills, evident from the openness of Japan's skilled migration policy and recruitment efforts targeting potential migrants with diverse college majors. Japanese employers take pride in recruiting, socialising, and training workers of diverse backgrounds. This article shows, however, the initial sense of achievement among Taiwanese workers does not last long for they aspire to cultivate more portable skills over which they can claim ownership. According to a survey done by the Ministry of Labour (2019), in Taiwan, workers younger than 29, on average, change jobs twice and the average job tenure is only 1.6 years. As a result, Taiwanese career aspirations diverge greatly from the firm-specific training and in-house careers most Japanese employers offer.

Unlike the mismatch that many skilled migrants encounter in host countries, mostly unemployment or underemployment (Reitz, Curtis, and Elrick 2013), migrants in this study are successfully matched but find little room to bolster core skills in Japanese corporate settings. Retaining newly minted global talent requires changes in current Japanese employer practices, since foreign workers come from training regime in their home country, and they have very different prospects for skill growth and career path than native-born workers. The limitations of Japanese training regime cause concerns not only for foreign workers, but also for native-born workers. As Kariya (2010) argues that in the ever-changing knowledge economy, Japanese ways of training employees suffer from the assumption that companies have a set of standard skills for employees to learn. This is especially problematic from the perspectives of foreign skilled workers. The difficulty for Japanese employers will be adjusting deeply seated social constructs in their training regime to fully utilise the skills of migrant workers that are now available to them.

Notes

1. Those who work in career-tracks have prospects to be promoted through career ladders, as opposed to general staff positions.
2. Most interviewees pointed out that their top choice is the United States. However, the usual requirement of obtaining the highest degree in the US before being eligible for employment requires family resources that most do not have. Many dislike China and exclude it from the list of destinations, even when it is much easier for Taiwanese to work in China legally and culturally as compared to moving to Japan. Those who reject China, note its worsening environmental quality, high living costs, and authoritarian regime.
3. For example, young people self-deprecatingly use the term *she chu* (i.e. 'wage slave'). They have little choice but to endure Taiwanese 'spoiled bosses'. The term *she chu* originates from the Japanese *shachiku* [literally, 'company cattle'], referring to the situation of being trapped in harsh working conditions.
4. The personal tales were submitted by authors or solicited, sometimes through interviews, by platform members. Typical content concerned motivations for working in Japan, recruitment processes, and work experiences. The platform published the stories more regularly, often twice a month, beginning in 2018. These personal narratives come from a variety of skilled migrants. Some authors updated their work situations in consecutive writings.

Disclosure statement

No potential conflict of interest was reported by the author(s).

Funding

This work is supported by the National Science Foundation, Taiwan [105-2410-H-002-129-MY2].

ORCID

Yen-Fen Tseng http://orcid.org/0000-0003-1334-8957

References

Allen, M., and P. Ainley. 2010. *Lost Generation: New Strategies for Youth and Education*. London: Continuum International Publishing Group.

Ashton, D., F. Green, J. Sung, and D. James. 2002. "The Evolution of Education and Training Strategies in Singapore, Taiwan and S. Korea: A Development Model of Skill Formation." *Journal of Education and Work* 15 (1): 5–30. doi:10.1080/13639080120106695.

Ashton, D., J. Sung, and J. Turbin. 2000. "Towards a Framework for the Comparative Analysis of National Systems of Skill Formation." *International Journal of Training and Development* 4 (1): 8–25. doi:10.1111/1468-2419.00093.

Boucher, A., and L. Cerna. 2014. "Current Policy Trends in Skilled Immigration Policy." *International Migration* 52 (3): 21–25. doi:10.1111/imig.12152.

Chang, Y. C. 2016. "The Trends in the Distribution of Job Opportunities and Industrial Transformation in Taiwan, 1978–2012." *Taiwanese Journal of Sociology* 60: 135–187.

Conrad, H., and H. Meyer-Ohle. 2017. "Overcoming the Ethnocentric Firm? Foreign Fresh University Graduate Employment in Japan as a New International Human Resource Development Method." *The International Journal of Human Resource Management* 30 (17): 2525–2543. doi:10.1080/09585192.2017.1330275.

Debnar, M. 2016. *Migration, Whiteness, and Cosmopolitanism*. New York: Palgrave Macmillan.

de Haas, H., K. Natter, and S. Vezzoli. 2018. "Growing Restrictiveness or Changing Selection? The Nature and Evolution of Migration Policies." *International Migration Review* 52 (2): 324–367. doi:10.1177/0197918318781584.

EZ Japan. 2016. *Nippon Suo Cang: Riben Zhichang Annei 100 Ze. Nippon*所藏：日本職場案內*100*則 [One Hundred Things You Need to Know About Japanese Workplaces]. Taipei: Heliopolis.

Findlay, A. M., and S. Cranston. 2015. "What's in a Research Agenda? An Evaluation of Research Developments in the Arena of Skilled International Migration." *International Development Planning Review* 37 (1): 17–31. doi:10.3828/idpr.2015.3.

Fligstein, N. 2001. "Social Skill and the Theory of Fields." *Sociological Theory* 19 (2): 105–125. doi:10.1111/0735-2751.00132.

Hassan, H., and Y. Hoshino. 2009. "Long-term Employment Contracts in Japanese Companies and the Corporate Profitability in Post Economic Bubble Era." *Journal of Financial Management and Analysis* 22 (2): 26–48.

Hawthorne, L. 2006. "Labour Market Outcomes for Migrant Professionals: Canada and Australia Compared." *SSRN Electronic Journal*. doi:10.2139/ssrn.2808943.

Hays Specialist. 2018. *The 2018 Hays Asia Salary Guide*. PDF. Hays. https://www.hays.co.jp/cs/groups/hays_common/@jp/@content/documents/digitalasset/hays_1808032.pdf.

Hof, H. B. 2018. "Mobility as a Way of Life: European Millennials' Labour Migration to Asian Global Cities." PhD Dissertation, Waseda University, Tokyo.

Holbrow, H. J., and K. Nagayoshi. 2018. "Economic Integration of Skilled Migrants in Japan." *International Migration Review* 52 (2): 458–486. doi:10.1177/0197918318781587.

IMD World Competitiveness Center. 2018. *IMD World Talent Report*. Lausanne: IMD.

Iredale, R. 2001. "The Migration of Professionals: Theories and Typologies." *International Migration* 39 (5): 7–26. doi:10.1111/1468-2435.00169.

Japan Business Federation. 2011. *Gurobaru-Jinzai No Ikusei Ni Muketa Teigen* [Proposal for Fostering Global Human Resources]. PDF. https://www.keidanren.or.jp/policy/2011/062honbun.pdf.

Kariya, T. 2010. "From Credential Society to 'Learning Capital'." In *Social Class in Contemporary Japan*, edited by H. Ishida and D. H. Slater, 87–113. New York: Routledge.

Komine, A. 2018. "A Closed Immigration Country: Revisiting Japan as a Negative Case." *International Migration* 56 (5): 106–122. doi:10.1111/imig.12383.

Kuo, C. F. 2019. "Factors Leading to Low and Stagnant Wages among Taiwanese Young Workers and Solutions." *Economic Research* 19: 83–105. https://www.ndc.gov.tw/Content_List.aspx?n=83EB0B3B2184E4BB.

Lin, Y. L., and T. T. Yang. 2018. ""Jingji Chengzhang, Xinzi Tingzhi? Chutan Taiwan Shizhixinzi Yu Laodong Shengchanli Tuogou De Chengyin." 經濟成長、薪資停滯？初探臺灣實質薪資與勞動生產力脫勾的成因. [Decoupling of Wage Growth and Productivity Growth in Taiwan: An Empirical Investigation]." *Academia Economic Papers* 46 (2): 263–322.

Liu-Farrer, G. 2009. "'I am the Only Woman in Suits': Chinese Immigrants and Gendered Careers in Corporate Japan." *Journal of Asia-Pacific Studies* 13: 37–48.

Liu-Farrer, G., and K. Shire. 2021. "Who are the Fittest? The Question of Skills in National Employment Systems in an Age of Global Labour Mobility." *Journal of Ethnic and Migration Studies* 47 (10): 2305–2322. doi:10.1080/1369183X.2020.1731987.

Liu-Farrer, G., B. S. Yeoh, and M. Baas. 2021. "Social Construction of Skill: An Analytical Approach Toward the Question of Skill in Cross-border Labour Mobilities." *Journal of Ethnic and Migration Studies* 47 (10): 2237–2251. doi:10.1080/1369183X.2020.1731983.

Liu, H. H., and C. K. Huang. 2011. ""Gaodengjiaoyu Kuozhang Hou Woguo DaxuebiyeshengRenliyunyong Zhi Yanjiu." 高等教育擴張後我國大學畢業生人力運用之研究. [Manpower Surveys on College-educated Employees Since Expansion of Higher Education in Taiwan]." *Journal of Education Research and Development* 7 (3): 153–180.

Ministry of Education. 2018. *Statistics of Taiwanese Studying Abroad*. https://depart.moe.edu.tw/ed2500/News_Content.aspx?n=2D25F01E87D6EE17&sms=4061A6357922F45A&s=F7EE493E853685E7.

Ministry of Justice (Japan). 2018. *Statistics of Foreign Residents*. http://www.moj.go.jp/nyuukokukanri/kouhou/nyuukokukanri04_00076.html.

Ministry of Labour (Taiwan). 2019. *Employment Survey on Young Workers Between 15–29*. https://statdb.mol.gov.tw/html/svy07/0711menu.htm.

Nagano, H. 2014. "Trends in Corporate Hiring of Recent Graduate: Focus on Developments Since the Global Financial Crisis." *Japan Labor Review* 11 (2): 23–36.

National Statistics Bureau. 2018. *Estimates of Taiwanese Working Overseas*. https://www.dgbas.gov.tw/public/Attachment/8121892937USMXRNUA.pdf.

Ogawa, R. 2017. "Japan: From Social Reproduction to Gender Inequality." In *Women, Work, and Care in Asia-Pacific*, edited by M. Baird, M. Ford, and E. Hill, 194–209. New York: Routledge.

Oishi, N. 2012. "The Limits of Immigration Policies: The Challenges of Highly Skilled Migration in Japan." *American Behavioral Scientist* 56 (8): 1080–1100. doi:10.1177/0002764212441787.

Oishi, N. 2021. "Skilled or Unskilled?: The Reconfiguration of Migration Policies in Japan." *Journal of Ethnic and Migration Studies* 47 (10): 2252–2269. doi:10.1080/1369183X.2020.1731984.

Oxford Economics. 2012. *Global Talent 2021: How the New Geography of Talent Will Transform Human Resource Strategies*. https://www.oxfordeconomics.com/Media/Default/Thought%20Leadership/global-talent-2021.pdf.

Parsons, C. R., S. Rojon, F. Samanani, and L. Wettach. 2014. *Conceptualising International High-skilled Migration*. International Migration Institute Working Paper No.104. University of Oxford.

Reitz, J. G., J. Curtis, and J. Elrick. 2013. "Immigrant Skill Utilization: Trends and Policy Issues." *Journal of International Migration and Integration* 15 (1): 1–26. doi:10.1007/s12134-012-0265-1.

Rigby, M., and E. Sanchis. 2006. "The Concept of Skill and It's Social Construction." *European Journal of Vocational Training* 37 (1): 22–33.

Sekiguchi, T. 2014. "Management Fashions and Human Resource Management." *Journal of Strategic Management Studies* 6: 2–16.

Sekiguchi, T., F. J. Froese, and C. Iguchi. 2016. "International Human Resource Management of Japanese Multinational Corporations: Challenges and Future Directions." *Asian Business & Management* 15 (2): 83–109. doi:10.1057/abm.2016.5.

Thelen, K. 2004. *How Institutions Evolve: The Political Economy of Skills in Germany, Britain, the United States, and Japan*. Cambridge: Cambridge University Press.

Tien, H. H. 2008. ""Gaodengjiaoyu Kuozhang Yu Daxuebiyesheng Xinzi De Yingxiangyinsu."高等教育擴張與大學畢業生薪資的影響因素. [Expansion of Higher Education and Wage Determination Factors among College-Educated Workers]." *Taiwan Higher Education Studies Newsletter* 24: 1–10.

Tseng, Y. F., and J. M. Wu. 2011. "Reconfiguring Citizenship and Nationality: Dual Citizenship of Taiwanese Migrants in China." *Citizenship Studies* 15 (2): 265–282. doi:10.1080/13621025.2011.549728.

Waldenberger, F. 2016. "In-house Careers: A Core Institution of the Japanese Firm in Need of Reform." *Journal of Strategic Management Studies* 8 (1): 23–32.

Wood, S. 1981. *The Degradation of Work: Skill, De-skilling and the Braverman Debate*. London: Harper and Collins.

Worklife in Japan. 2017. *Survey Results of Taiwanese Working in Japan*. https://crossing.cw.com.tw/index.php/blogTopic.action?id=678&nid=8769.

Yamao, S., and T. Sekiguchi. 2015. "Employee Commitment to Corporate Globalization: The Role of English Language Proficiency and Human Resource Practices." *Journal of World Business* 50 (1): 168–179. doi:10.1016/j.jwb.2014.03.001.

Yang, C. H., C. A. Lin, and C. R. Lin. 2010. "Dynamics of Rate of Returns for Postgraduate Education in Taiwan: The Impact of Higher Education Expansion." *Asia Pacific Education Review* 12 (3): 359–371. doi:10.1007/s12564-010-9132-y.

Who are the fittest? The question of skills in national employment systems in an age of global labour mobility

Gracia Liu-Farrer and Karen Shire

ABSTRACT

Faced with demographic as well as economic changes, Germany and Japan have liberalised immigration controls for skilled migrants, set targets for foreign student enrolments in university, and introduced visa categories to enable foreign graduates to enter their labour markets. Yet a relatively modest share of foreign graduates actually receives jobs appropriate to their skill-level and remain in these labour markets. In this article, we focus on organisational recruitment and employment practices, especially those related to skill formation and the structuring of careers, as factors affecting the remain rates of foreign graduates. Our analysis shows that while obtaining the same educational credentials as native students, foreign graduates are disadvantaged because the employment systems of the host countries operate according to the logic of national labour markets, entailing institutionally and culturally specific skill expectations as well as formation processes. Consequently, foreign graduates either fail to enter the market, or are placed in lower or niche categories in a differentiated labour market.

Introduction

'Brain abuse' (Bauder 2003) or 'brain waste' (Reitz 2001) refers to the phenomenon of highly skilled migrants' inability to utilise their skills in the host labour market. Aside from the influences of racism and nationalism under which immigrants are treated as "low-skilled' workers because they are immigrants' (Samers 1998, 53), this inability is considered to result from non-transferable cultural capital (Bauder 2003; Erel 2010; Nohl et al. 2014). In particular, the state and professional associations limit skilled immigrants' access to the professional occupations for which they are trained by devaluing their cultural capital developed in countries of origin (Bauder 2003). Studies also point out that in some cases higher education obtained in the home country does not equip migrants with the professional and linguistic skills needed in the host labour market (Nowicka 2014).

Responding to such difficult labour market entry for skilled immigrants with foreign credentials or inadequate host country language and cultural training, some countries have shifted skilled migration policies toward recruiting more international students, believing that graduates from domestic higher educational institutions have fewer hurdles in entering local labour markets (Hawthorne 2005, 2008). However, research shows that countries that actively recruit international students as potential skilled migrants are not necessarily successful in retaining them in their labour markets (Hawthorne 2010). According to a report on OECD countries, the average stay rate of international students – defined as the proportion of international students changing to a status other than 'student' – was about 21% (OECD 2011).

Studies attribute the low advancement of foreign students into employment to factors such as the ambiguous nature and purposes of international education (Robertson 2013), government programmes and their selection of international students (Basford and van Riemsdijk 2015), the existence of discrimination against non-Western migrants in local labour markets (Støren and Wiers-Jenssen 2010), or international students' inability to meet the requirements of employers despite obtaining local educational credentials (Blackmore, Gribble, and Rahimi 2017). Research also points out that international students themselves gauge job opportunities and make personal life choices when consider mobility options (Mosneaga and Winther 2013). This study investigates how the employment systems, with their specific *recruitment practices* and *skill formation* in host countries may be affecting these retention rates. Our focus is on the notion of skill itself and its socially constructed nature (see Liu-Farrer, Yeoh and Baas 2021). We show that, first, the lack of success in retaining foreign graduates essentially reflects how employment systems in these countries are still largely oriented toward a domestic labour market which entails specific cultural assumptions about employees' skill profiles. These institutionally and culturally delineated skill criteria in turn affect the ability of foreign graduates to enter the labour markets. Secondly, when international students successfully transition into employment, they tend to enter segments of the labour market where there are more acute labour shortages or more flexible forms of employment, or they enter occupational niches. Consequently, their employment status, work content or occupational roles within primary labour markets are 'distinguished by different labour market characteristics and behavioural rules (Reich, Gordon, and Edwards 1973, 359)'. Finally, both the rigidly programmed skill formation process and the reality of labour market segmentation restrict individuals' potential for career mobility and result in frustration or even an exit from their occupation or the host country.

This study uses Germany and Japan as empirical cases for such a comparative analysis. As large economies with declining working populations, Germany and Japan have tried to establish the 'education-migration nexus (Robertson 2013)' and have adopted liberal policies toward foreign students' labour market participation (Oishi 2021; Plöger and Becker 2015). They have done so by setting targets and introducing policies for attracting and retaining foreign students. Japan planned to accept 300,000 foreign students for 2020 and Germany aimed to have 350,000 non-EU foreign students enrolled by the same year (MEXT 2008; DAAD 2013). To facilitate entry into the labour market, both countries allow international students graduating from their higher educational institutions a period of time, one year in Japan, and 18 months in Germany, to look for jobs.[1] Germany achieved its target number of foreign students in 2018 (Statistisches Bundesamt 2018), and Japan had nearly done so by 2018 (JASSO 2019). Yet in both countries today, the percentage of international students who manage to stay and work has remained relatively low. In Germany, a publication of the Stifterverband (2016, 70) reports 25% of foreign graduates in 2014 staying to work in Germany after graduation. In Japan, 31.1% of the 48,598 students who graduated from post-secondary programmes in 2016 had entered the Japanese labour market (JASSO 2016).

This paper uses data from a larger comparative project of skilled migration in Germany and Japan conducted between 2015 and 2018. We interviewed 60 individual migrants (35 in Japan and 25 in Germany), career placement officers at 1 Japanese and 2 German universities, and human resource managers from 5 enterprises in Japan and 2 in Germany. In this paper we report our finding for a sub-sample of foreign graduates of Japanese (18) and German (12) universities, who found jobs in these host countries. The interviewees were obtained through personal networks, direct recruitment and snowball sampling, and interviewed in Chinese, English and German by the authors and five research assistants. All of the interviewees were between the ages of 24 and 35 at the time of interview. Table 1 presents the profiles of these individuals. In Japan, we oversampled Chinese nationals, since they comprise the majority of foreign graduates entering the labour market. Non-Chinese interviewees originated from Europe, North America and Africa. In Germany, we mainly interviewed non-EU graduates because the freedom of mobility for EU member state nationals removes the necessity for them to obtain study or work visas, and national policy has focussed on attracting more non-EU students and skilled labour. Non-EU citizens in this sample came from East and Southeast Asia, South Asia, the Middle East and Europe (Russia). Qualitative interviews were supplemented with documentary analysis of recent government and other reports about foreign skilled labour and international student labour market transitions.[2]

In the next sections we outline and compare employment institutions in Germany and Japan, with an emphasis on skill formation, the transition from higher education to employment, and skill and career development. We then present our evidence on how foreign graduates experience the job search process and standard employment practices, especially those related to skill development and career advancement. We conclude by reflecting on how employment institutions and cultural practices affect the retention of foreign graduates, and the ways in which employment institutions differentiate migrants from native employees.

Skill formation in the German and Japanese employment systems – how do skilled migrants fit in?

The German and Japanese employment systems have relatively well-structured transitions from schooling/higher education into the labour market and employment (Brinton 2005), with commitments on the part of employers to invest in workers' skills (Thelen and Kume 2003) and to extend rewards in the form of mobility and security (Streeck 2001). These employment systems are different from the more open and liberal labour markets in

Table 1. Demographic profiles of 30 interviewees in Japan and Germany.

	Japan		Germany		
Regional backgrounds	Chinese	Non-Chinese	East/South East Asia	South Asia	Others
	10	8	7	3	2
Gender	Female	Male	Female		Male
	9	9	7		5

countries such as the US and UK (Estévez-Abe, Iversen, and Soskice 2001). Yet Germany and Japan differ in how transitions to the labour market, skill development and mobility are organised, with the German employment system developing occupationally-structured labour markets versus organisationally-structured employment in Japan (Ernst 1998; Fligstein 2001). The question addressed in this section is how the similarities and differences in the German and Japanese employment systems shape transitions into the labour market, and how these institutionalised transitions affect whether and how skilled migrants enter employment.

Political economic research comparing skill formation systems begins with the classic distinction by Becker (1964) between general and specific skills. General skills are produced in schooling and institutions of higher education and influence the development of relatively open labour markets and job mobility driven by changes in employer demands for different sets of skills. The US labour market is the characteristic case (Estevez-Abe 2005). In Becker's second type, skills are specific when they are developed within an enterprise. For workers in firm-specific skill systems, enterprises (rather than general educational institutions) do the training, and commitment to an employer is a residual consequence of the fact that the skills one learns cannot easily be transferred to another employer, at least not without a loss in compensation. At the same time, firms develop a strong interest in retaining workers in order to reap returns on their investments in skill formation. Thus, both workers and firms favour mobility within internal labour markets (Streeck 2001).

The Japanese employment system, with an emphasis on long-term employment, age and skill-graded ranking (*shikaku seido*) within a highly differentiated internal labour market is the prototypical case of a firm-specific skill formation system. For core labour forces in blue-collar and white-collar work, entry into a firm upon graduation, on-the-job and firm-located training, and slow but steady mobility across pay grades and higher order tasks, or in the case of white-collar work, up through the ranks of managerial hierarchies, remains intact today. What has changed is that the proportion of workers in the core is shrinking, with more than 40% of all employment contracts now in non-standard and temporary contracts (Heinrich 2010; Waldenberger 2016). Within core labour forces, entry is at the bottom, usually right after graduation, and recruitment processes involve direct and close links between firm recruiters and specific educational institutions.

A specific characteristic of transitions from university to employment in Japan is the role played by the reputation of a university, and the relative lack of importance placed on the discipline of study. With highly competitive entrance examinations, elite institutions have a signalling function in the labour market (Ishida 2001; Kariya 2001), and the leading corporations in Japan have targeted these institutions almost exclusively for recruiting their core workforces, often through the alumni networks of student clubs. Graduates from elite Japanese universities who are well integrated into specific student networks thus exercise a clear advantage in accessing the best jobs. Job fairs are another contact point between students and potential employers.

Recruitment activities begin a year before graduation, and involve successive levels of assessment tests and screening interviews, culminating with a job offer (*naitei*) well before graduation. Through tests and interviews Japanese companies seek candidates with very general qualities, such as communication skills, evidence of drive and enthusiasm, and personality traits, such as malleability, perseverance and motivation (Conrad and Meyer-Ohle 2017). Currently, the system works to match nearly all college graduates to jobs in Japan. According to the annual government survey of graduating cohorts, by December 1, 2018, 87.9% of Japanese university students who were scheduled to graduate and enter employment in April 2019 had already received job offers (MEXT 2018). The actual employment rate of the 2019 graduating cohort reached 97.6% by April 1, 2019 (MHLW 2019).

Unlike in Japan, the subject of study at German universities has great importance in qualifying graduates for specific jobs, and employers pay close attention to evidence of special skills in university transcripts, and in internships completed during study (*Praktika*). Many students accumulate a portfolio of *Praktika* to compete for the best jobs on the labour market. Conversely, assessment tests are hardly utilised, and in the large firm sector of core employment, are often opposed by works councils representing company employees (Giardini, Kabst, and Müller-Camen 2005). Instead, formal job applications include transcripts, documentation of *Praktika* and carefully formulated CVs. The fundamental knowledge gained from higher education is then the basis for developing deeper operational knowledge on-the-job. In Germany, advancement into top management positions is tied to operational knowledge (Mayer and Whittington 1999), which depends on the specialisations of specific firms. Such operational knowledge, like rotations in Japanese firms, create firm-specific skills, and bind employees to in-house careers.

This brief characterisation of the Japanese organisation-centred and the German occupation-centred employment and skill formation systems shows that entry is strongly structured through recruitment practices assessing skills and competencies. Moreover, firm-specific components of skill formation (rotations in Japan, and operational experience in Germany) shape mobility chances within enterprises but are of less advantage in pursuing mobility through job changes. Important differences, however, lie in the content of university education in preparing students for the jobs they will do, which is relatively unimportant in Japan, but highly relevant for job searches in Germany. In both cases, however, job searches begin well before graduation.

In light of recruitment and employment practices, government policies to encourage potential foreign workers to complete their study domestically seem quite reasonable. It is also not surprising that studying in Germany and Japan has evolved into a strategy for individual migrants to gain employment in these countries. Surveys of international students in Japan and Germany repeatedly show that the majority aspire to enter employment in the host country after graduation (Doi and Enatsu 2010; Fukuoka 2015; Expert Council 2015). The question remains to what degree Japanese and German enterprises are actually willing or able to recruit foreign graduates, and once recruited, how they experience skill formation and career structures within their workplaces.

Different fits – how foreign graduates find a job in Germany and Japan

German and Japanese employers have different expectations with regard to the skills they seek in foreign graduates. In Germany, more emphasis is placed on university education, whereas Japanese employers tend to foreground other factors such as language competency and cultural adaptability. In this section, we analyse the mix of difficulties confronting foreign graduates in finding a job. Segmentation tendencies are evident in both national labour markets.

Germany – the search for Exact fits

In Germany, employers are keen to find workers who fit a very specific job profile, and careers develop as further specialisation is gained. International students, however, encounter obstacles while treading German specialised career paths, starting already in university education. Interviews with career placement officers revealed that even within the highly specialised German degree programmes, students were expected to develop an even more specific specialisation in anticipation of potential jobs. One university career placement officer explained,

> For example, if a student majors in mechanic engineering, she might learn general knowledge related to mechanic engineering in the university. But when an opening in a company occurs, it won't be general mechanic engineering, but a specific type of engineering process. Students with an academic transcript of Mechanic Engineering courses 1, 2, 3 are unlikely to be considered suitable.

In most cases, according to the officer, international students do not understand that specialisations are most effectively developed and documented through industry *Praktika,* a mandatory requirement in most degree programmes. Moreover, students are expected to find the *Praktika* themselves. Many international students reported problems in obtaining one. Liang, a Taiwanese student became emotional when asked about his *Praktika* experiences.

> Very hard! ... I must say, honestly, for foreigners ... Of course, I talked to other students about internships. Everyone told me, "it is very simple." But most of them are Germans. They told me that even a student with a 3.5 average[3] would still get an internship at Deutsche Bank in Frankfurt. [...] EVERYTHING was not true! For foreigners I would say, not only for me but also for all fellow students and friends who have studied in Germany to find a job here.

Liang went to various job fairs, searched online job platforms, and sent out about 100 applications for internships, but received no response. With his semester break now free, he decided to return to Taipei, where he found a casual job as a translator in an exhibition hall. There Liang met a German company representative visiting Taiwan on business, who after hearing that Liang was a student in Germany, gave him his business card, and eventually offered Liang an internship. Other students we interviewed were not as lucky. In another case, a student turned to applying for internships in the Netherlands in order to fulfil the mandatory requirement for a *Praktikum.*

After graduation, foreign job seekers soon confront another formidable obstacle – a recruitment and screening process that amplifies their cultural and skill disadvantages. The largest and most reputable German companies use online application portals and algorithms to sort and select suitable candidates. In the digital age, job searches have become an algorithmic game. According to career officers, graduates upload hundreds, some even thousands of job applications, meaning that each job vacancy garners thousands of applications nation-wide. International students, in the experience of career officers, are far less likely than German peers to be selected for interviews, because they either fail to include the right keywords, or make the mistake of applying in English. They are rejected before their applications reach human eyes. Even when a human being is involved in the screening, the failure to conform to employer expectations for application documents ends with the same result. Ms Schneider, a human resource manager at a financial services company, recounted receiving hundreds of applications for each vacancy she posted online, many of them from Indian engineers, 'but their resumes often just indicate some general backgrounds. It is hard to determine whether they really have the specific skills and experiences I ask for'.

What jobs do foreign graduates find in Germany? Their job profile reflects the profiles of companies that have the greatest demand for labour. An increasing number of them are with so-called personnel service agencies, another term for temporary agencies, in the small and medium-sized firm sector, or a combination of both (placed in small firms by personnel service agencies). While the online portals of large and reputable firms create high competition for the top jobs, small and medium size firms, which are less attractive for native graduates, often face a shortage of applicants. The German economy is projected to need 84,000–390,000 more engineers by 2029, depending on economic growth (VDI 2019). However, smaller enterprises, those that experience labour shortage the most, often lack knowledge of how to employ foreign graduates (for example, visa and earning requirements). This has provided a business opportunity for fee-charging personnel service agencies to offer the service for placing foreign graduates with potential employers. These agencies operate under temporary staffing regulations in Germany, which require that they act as employers, who then charge a fee for 'lending' out a worker for a specific period of time to a client. According to university career officers, German graduates do not consider agencies to be desirable employers, while the obstacles that foreign graduates face with large firms and online portals give agencies the chance to recruit very top international students. Moreover, agencies provide training to foreign graduates, to improve their fitness for working in a German company, including soft skills, language and German business culture. Wage thresholds for granting work visas mean that agencies have to pay foreign graduates more than native workers, but career officers claimed that agencies still favour foreign graduates over German candidates because foreigners are willing to work for small companies, and will move anywhere for a job. Finally, foreign graduates show high willingness to further their skill training, often at their own expense, for example, through online courses. The underlying significance of agency employment is how it becomes a mechanism for routing foreign graduates into temporary rather than permanent employment contracts, and into small and medium enterprises, where wages and status are generally lower than in the large firm sector. Agency employment also comes with much higher demands for flexibility, mobility and adaptability to market conditions.

Most international students in Germany study engineering or another STEM (Science, Technology, Engineering, Mathematics) field, but a significant number (26%) study economics or social sciences (Studying-in-Germany.org 2019). Non-EU foreign graduates in humanities and social sciences background had more difficulties finding jobs than engineers, especially in professional roles at the income levels needed to qualify for a work visa. Foreign graduates of these disciplines we interviewed searched more than a year, and rarely found work in large and reputable firms. Many spent their 18-month post-study period underemployed in various casual service jobs to support themselves while writing job applications. German universities do not charge tuition, and a strategy adopted by graduates who were coming to the end of the 18-month visa was to enrol themselves back into another German degree programme, thereby re-qualifying for a student visa. The jobs some of our interviewees eventually found were in small family firms, or in occupational niches (Liu-Farrer 2011), that is, in companies that engaged in business with their native countries, or whose owners were from their country of origin.

Occupational niching often places foreign graduates in work roles where they are expected to use their native language at least part of the time. One example in our study is Irena, a Russian woman who graduated with a Master's Degree in economics, and found a job with an insurance company that dealt with international clients. Aside from German and English, she also used Russian in her daily work. The Taiwanese student Liang, whose internship experience we recounted above, accepted a job as assistant to a manager at a Taiwanese company, where he became the liaison between the Taiwanese boss and his German employees. These foreign graduates often obtain a type of work visa on the basis of speciality skills – usually a non-European language – for which no German applicants can be found. In this way, foreign graduates in non-technical fields find their 'best fits' in niche jobs.

Japan – looking for the potential fits

Two factors make job searches for foreign students appear easier in Japan than in Germany. First, university courses are more general, and employers have lower expectations of graduates' specialised occupational skills. Instead, they expect to train graduates themselves in the skills required by the firm. Second, the standardisation of the job search process makes it easier for foreign graduates to understand how to compete for jobs. Nonetheless, foreign students are still at a disadvantage in entering the Japanese labour market. The biggest hurdle is the Japanese language and cultural expectations. While in Germany language proficiency is also expected, the degree of fluency demanded by Japanese enterprises is higher. One reason is that the level of English proficiency in the Japanese corporate world is low. In most multinational German companies, business meetings are conducted in English when necessary, but not in Japanese workplaces, where Japanese is the exclusive business language, even in many reputable multinational firms. A survey conducted by the recruitment firm MyNavi (2017) of employers in 2017 found that half of the 316 employers who responded wanted to employ foreign graduates for the purpose of 'securing good human resources regardless of nationality', yet 85% of those intending to recruit foreigners reported Japanese language competence as a key skill. Job applicants in Japan are typically required to take written tests that evaluate their language and other problem-solving skills (including mathematics and IQ tests) to qualify for interviews (see also Tseng 2021). All such tests, including the IQ test, are in Japanese, and most foreign graduates find passing these very difficult.

The MyNavi (2017) survey revealed four other skills demanded by firms of foreign applicants – communication skills, adaptability, understanding of Japanese culture, and the ability to take action (*kōdōryoku*). These skills are assessed through multiple rounds of interviews and assignments. For example, companies often organise foreign and Japanese applicants into groups to work on assigned projects, with the employers standing by and observing their dispositions and competencies. Foreign students reported feeling that they lacked the cultural instinct for acting appropriately in such situations. Given the strong emphasis of employers on language and 'cultural fit', foreign students felt less able to compete with Japanese students for the same jobs. The emphasis on language and cultural skills also operates to make a large segment of job openings inaccessible to foreign students, where employers assume that they lack 'cultural fit'. The MyNavi (2017) survey found that among those firms not hiring foreign students, 58.3% reported the reason as being 'not equipped with a system to accept foreigners in the firm'. According to a 2013 survey conducted by the Japanese Institute of Labour Policy and Training (JILPT 2013), three quarters (940) of the 1338 responding enterprises had never recruited 'highly skilled foreign talent' (*gaikokujin kōtō jinzai*), including foreign students.

Related to their handicaps in linguistic and cultural skills, foreign students' employment patterns in Japan are similar to those in Germany in two ways. First, we find evidence again of occupational niching. Foreign employees often report working in narrow occupational categories that utilise their home country as well as Japanese linguistic and cultural skills. As previous qualitative studies have shown, many foreign students opt for specific foreigner tracks in anticipation of obstacles elsewhere (Liu-Farrer 2011). Many foreign applicants even hope that occupational niches can transform their home country cultural and linguistic skills into a competitive advantage. Unlike in Germany, the majority of foreign students in Japan major in humanities and social sciences (JASSO 2019).[4] Several interviewees in our sample with such majors reported only applying for jobs specifically set aside for foreign applicants, for example, in global business sections.[5]

In other cases, even if students major in technical fields, given the loose association of Japanese university majors and later job roles, foreign students abandon their desired occupations in order to find work. Haruka, a Chinese woman, received her master's degree in civil engineering from a Japanese university. Upon graduation in 2013, she decided to work for an apparel company rather than in engineering, explaining:

> I was looking for a company that had overseas business. Civil engineering is all inside Japan, building ports, roads, etc. … Apparel companies, on the other hand, have most of their manufacturing done overseas, in China, or Vietnam. After all, the good thing about Japan is, you don't need to worry about your job not matching your major. Students from humanity backgrounds might not be able to apply for some jobs in science and technology, but science majors can participate in the interviews for any jobs that humanities students can do.

The company she chose was a large company with expanding overseas business. It specifically targeted foreign graduates through a separate 'foreigner only recruitment scheme'.

A second characteristic of international students' employment in Japan is the tendency to enter smaller firms – a phenomenon also observed in Germany. The Ministry of Justice's statistics show that, since 2010, over 60% of international students who obtained employment visas were working in firms with less than 300 employees. This reflects, first, the disadvantages for foreign graduates in competing for jobs in large and reputable firms. Aside from the cultural hurdles as mentioned before, there is also the obstacle of institutional hierarchy. Higher education institutions are more vertically differentiated in Japan. Large firms usually recruit students from the most prestigious universities. The majority of foreign students in Japan, on the other hand, are not enrolled in elite universities, and therefore have little access to large corporations (Liu-Farrer 2011).

Secondly, small firms in Japan are also plagued by labour shortages. Similar to German graduates, young Japanese graduates also favour employment in large and reputable companies, which pay higher wages and benefits, and extend job security and upward internal advancement. A survey conducted by Recruit Works Institute (2016) of 4504 Japanese companies showed that the ratio of job openings for companies with more than 5000 employees was estimated to be one vacancy for every two applicants in 2017. Among companies with fewer than 300 employees, however, the estimate was four jobs for every applicant. In recent years, through job fairs organised by the government and online portals, small and medium size firms have begun to target recruitment of foreign students. Because of their dire need for labour, our interviewees reported that, small firms are less rigid in recruitment processes, with many administering simplified written tests, and others only requiring interviews. Although such firms offer less pay and security, foreign students, under pressure to secure a work visa within a year after graduation, are often willing to enter this sector.

Foreign graduates we interviewed also reported other advantages in working for smaller firms. Some wanted to avoid the rigid internal labour markets in larger firms, and believed that in small firms they could learn more, their skills would be put to better use, or that they would enjoy more autonomy. An increasing number of smaller firms in the media, gaming and design industries are especially attractive for foreign students, whose decision to study in Japan is often motivated by someday entering these world-famous Japanese culture sectors.

Fitting in – experiences of foreign graduates in German and Japanese workplaces

German employers seek graduates with readily usable and specific occupational skills, while Japanese employers expect to train new recruits for broader occupational roles. A similarity, however, is the expectation that skills are developed through work practice over a long-term employment relation. In Germany, especially in the engineering and science fields, this involves operational experience in successive projects, using different technologies and development processes, and directed at different sets and types of clients or applications. Japanese personnel management practices tie on-the-job training to regular job rotations and personnel assessments, a significant part of which are personalised and subjective (Endō 1994). Gaining operational knowledge in Germany, and organisational experiences in Japan are the practices through which career relevant skills are constructed for post-graduates in employment. Moreover, careers in both systems are structured internally by enterprises, rather than by job hopping on the external labour market, thus taking the form of internal advancement over a long-term employment relation. How do foreign graduates fit into these practices of career advancement?

Specialisation through operational and project experiences in Germany masks a vulnerability faced by foreign graduates in small firms, as shown in Ali's case. Ali is a mechanical engineer from Egypt working after graduating with a BS degree from an English-taught engineering programme at a German university. His company, with just 50 employees, has positioned itself in the German engineering market through its specialisation in a particular engineering process. Ali completed a *Praktikum* with this same company, and also wrote his thesis in cooperation with them. Ali was not particularly interested in the firm's engineering specialisation, but this was the only *Praktikum* and job he could find. At the time of our interview, Ali voiced many complaints about his job and work environment. For one, he felt relatively isolated, due not only to his limited language capacity but also his

Muslim background and the practices connected with this. By not drinking alcohol or eating pork he felt at odds with the German culture at work. Moreover, he felt his co-workers were technologically outdated. As he recounted, they 'still used the manual they were using in the 1970s!' There was not much more he could learn from them. Ali also experienced a lack of recognition for his research ability and contributions to the projects, which, he felt, meant that he was not considered for new projects or other skill development opportunities. Nonetheless, it was hard for him to change jobs because all his experiences and skills were tied to this specific engineering process. Ali expressed his situation as feeling suffocated. As a result, he was considering abandoning engineering altogether and starting his own trading business.

Foreign graduates in Japanese firms were not expected to specialise in this way, but they were expected to move through all their firms' functions, and to be very flexible about rotations. With a more international outlook on their future career development, foreign graduates working in Japan perceived such a long-term employment track with slow but steady advancement through internal labour markets as a career disadvantage. This was as much the case for foreigners like Mark, a young Australian graduate with a degree from an elite Japanese university, as for graduates positioned in special 'foreigner tracks'. Speaking fluent Japanese, Mark was recruited after he delivered his CV at a job fair to a large Japanese corporation, with supply chains in his home country, Australia. Mark was the only 'white guy', and, as he reported to us, was not treated differently from his Japanese co-workers. Mark received continuous on-the-job training by his superiors, from the manner of exchanging business cards, to pouring drinks for his older co-workers, and learning how to mix each of their preferred cocktails. He chanted the company slogans every morning with his work group, in synchronised fashion with employees nationwide, often with a hangover from business dinners the night before. Mark stayed in the company for three years before leaving. In his own words,

> I just felt there was no growth. It was very stable, almost too stable. I couldn't see myself ever being promoted to manager level because I was non-Japanese, I felt. ... So I was like, "What am I doing here? I can't get promoted." No matter how hard I worked, my salary was the same. ... . I increased the sales by 300% and they just patted me on the back. Well done, Mark, well done. It's like, okay, I'm done. I want to be recognised for my hard work, which is why I looked for something else.

We heard many different versions of such stories of frustration among foreign employees in Japan. Similar to Mark, many are worried by the slow progression of in-house careers and the seemingly useless skills they are expected to require along the way (see also Tseng 2021). In the first years of employment, new recruits are often required to do tedious clerical tasks in order to become familiar with the company's business operations from the bottom up. However, this skill building process is unfitting for skilled migrants who often consider each job as a learning experience with hopes of acquiring some transferable human capital to further their career. Staying in one firm in one country too long can be the end of future career chances.

Foreign graduates in Japanese 'foreigner tracks' confront similarly slow skill formation processes, but sometimes end up in more precarious situations. Abandoning her engineering training and joining an apparel company through the 'foreigner track', Haruka's career did not progress well. Together with other new recruits, she started her training in retail stores – a practice she understood and accepted. After four months, she was brought back to the overseas marketing department at headquarters, as initially promised by the human resource department. However, she spent the next year and a half doing very routine work, entering sales data. She repeatedly requested a new role in overseas marketing, but her supervisor's reply was always, 'still early, too early'. In the meantime, due to mismanagement, the company's overseas sales declined, and one of the retail branches was closed. She and 27 other foreign employees who were hired around the same time as Haruka were sent back to the storefront, where they repeated their training, with the excuse that they would benefit from being 'trained a bit more'. Haruka inquired in the human resources department about a role in overseas business in the future, but received ambivalent responses. Although she was indeed hired as a regular employee and received the same pay as her Japanese peers, she could no longer expect to develop a career in overseas business in this firm. She left the company after less than two years of employment.

Even if Haruka was placed in an overseas business role immediately, prior research suggests that foreign employees in foreigner tracks have limited career advancement opportunities. With the majority of foreign employees in Japan coming from neighbouring Asian countries, their overseas roles are often to deal with business in their own countries (Liu-Farrer 2011). This sort of specialisation takes foreign employees off the normal track for career mobility, which is tied to the accumulation of broad work experiences, knowledge and skills through firm-wide rotations. In the case of foreign business, this would at least mean job roles in different world regions. Moreover, as Haruka's case shows, foreign businesses are faced with uncertainties of their own. Citing a 2008 JILPT enterprise and employee survey, Holbrow and Nagayoshi (2018) find that employment institutional arrangements such as foreigner tracks and diversity training – seemingly affirmative measures – negatively impact on individuals' earnings and usually do not lead to long term career progression within Japanese firms.

In Germany and Japan, those who enter smaller firms tend to face more vulnerable employment situations and have shorter and steeper career mobility ladders within the firm. As a result, foreign graduates employed in small firms often attempt to build careers by job hopping. Jiewei, a Taiwanese graduate working in Germany had changed jobs four times in the five years since graduating, including one job in China. Her employer at the time we interviewed her was a family-run firm in Cologne with ten employees. In Japan, the ex-engineering student, Haruka who quit after being reassigned to the shopfront, was 'a bit rushed' to find another job, and turned to online job forums, where she entered 'Chinese language skill' as a key phrase for her job search. A small company with eight employees specialising in translation services invited her to take a written test and interview, and hired her the same day because they urgently needed a replacement. While Haruko liked her job, she reported that the firm 'had been doing the same thing for ten years, and their business hadn't changed. The size of the company didn't change either'. After one year, she left for yet another small Japanese company with five regular and one part-time employee. This time the owner was a naturalised Chinese woman. Haruka liked her egalitarian management style, and was hopeful about assuming a decision-making role in the new workplace. If this did not work out, Haruka told us she would open her own company in a similar field of business.

Conclusion

With liberalised immigration controls for skilled labour and foreign students, large supplies of foreign graduates, and strong demand from enterprises experiencing labour shortages, Germany and Japan represent countries with favourable conditions for integrating foreign graduates into skilled employment. Yet, only a moderate percentage of foreign graduates are able to find jobs upon graduation, and remain in employment. This article has sought to explain this phenomenon by examining the experiences of foreign graduates who have entered these labour markets and attempted to develop careers within the institutional context of their firm-specific skill formation systems. Like native students in Germany, foreign students do *Praktika*, and like native Japanese students, foreign students in Japan participate in the long run-up of the recruitment process, job fairs, assessments and interviews. Yet in both cases, our analysis has shown that foreign graduates confront structural and cultural barriers to career development in these host country labour markets.

In Germany and Japan, recruitment and training practices reveal homophilous tendencies, expecting foreign graduates to possess the same skill sets or act exactly as native workers do. Despite the advantage of having studied in the host country and acquired at least some language and cultural skills, foreign graduates experience differentiated outcomes because of formidable cultural expectations and labour market structural changes. Due to culturally inflected selection, a process of labour market segmentation in the primary labour market takes place. We observe that it is more likely for foreign engineering graduates in Germany to enter temporary agency employment. In Japan generally, and in the case of economics or social science graduates in Germany, foreign applicants often end up in niche positions for which their native languages as well as English ability become the specific skills making them employable. In both cases, the lesser known, and often lower paying small and medium sized enterprises have become a major employment destination.

After being employed, foreign graduates working in Germany and Japan report frustrations with pressures for cultural conformity and the perceived long-term outcomes of adapting to the firm-specific logics of careers. The obvious alternative, job hopping, brings few returns in such skill formation systems, since firm-specific skills are often non-transferable. Firm-specific training regimes make sense in a primarily domestic labour market and in a growing national economy where employment is stable. They are less suited to generating diverse cultural skills, or for adapting to the more volatile international business context. Moreover, to varying degrees, workplaces in both countries remain ethno-centric and consequently socially and culturally unattractive for foreign employees.

Our study underlines how skills are constructed within specific employment contexts, which immigration policies, despite attempting to support skilled migration, fail to account for. It shows that even foreign graduates, for whom cultural and language factors have been relatively attenuated, are unable to transform their skills into forms of employment that support their development and advancement. The high proportion of foreign graduates who never enter the labour market, the experience of cultural isolation and differentiation of those who do, and who thus intend to soon exit their jobs and possibly the country, suggest that employers in firm-specific skill formation systems have yet to break their rigid delimitation of employees' skill and come up with strategies to effectively incorporate skilled foreign labour, regardless of where they obtain their higher education.

There have been efforts in both countries to ameliorate this situation. The German *Sachverständigenrat* (2015) proposes that universities begin much earlier, at the beginning of study, to prepare foreign students for local labour markets, and that more public funding is made available to expand career services tailored specifically to foreign students. In Japan, the Asian Human Resources Funding Plan (2007–2012) sponsored by the economics and education ministries (METI and MEXT) initiated a Career Support Network for International Students in Japan in 2011, with the aim of training foreign students in the 'Japanese way of job-hunting and how to prepare for it' and to provide 'information about job openings' through 'guidance, seminars, combined information sessions'.[6] These solutions, though constructive, indicate the persistent tendency noted by van Riemsdijk, Basford, and Burnham (2016) that incorporation is still seen predominantly as a one-way process, whereby migrants are expected to bear the responsibility for their socio-cultural incorporation into the host working environment. Our study clearly indicates that in order to retain foreign graduates, employers need to shift away from practices assuming migrants will 'fit in' to existing social cultural environment and career patterns, and initiate adaptations to their training and advancement practices, which enable the development of diverse skills and international career paths. Enterprises in both countries are no longer dealing with a domestic labour force in a national economy. Future business strength in a globalising economy lies in developing a diverse and mobile labour force, whose skills and competencies become competitive advantages as individuals and organisations cross cultural boundaries and incorporate the unfamiliar.

Notes

1. In Japan, foreign graduates are given the 180-day 'Designated Activity' visa, which can be extended to one year (http://www.moj.go.jp/nyuukokukanri/kouhou/nyukan_nyukan84.html) (accessed August 1, 2019). In Germany, Section 16 of the Residence Act (AufenthG) permits non-EU foreign students, upon completion, an extension for purposes of job search for 18 months. Employment is allowed during the 18-month extension after graduation (https://germanlawarchive.iuscomp.org/?p=1464 (accessed July 22, 2019).
2. In Germany these included statistics, prognoses and reports published by the German Statistical Bureau, the Ministry of Education and Research (BMBF), the Institute for Work and Employment (IAB), the German Academic Exchange Service (DAAD), the Stifterverband (Foundation) for the German Economy, The Sachverstaendigenrat (Expert Office) of the German Bureau for Integration and Migration, the Bertelsmann Foundation, and McKinsey and Company. In Japan, we draw on official statistics provided by Ministry of Culture, Education, Sports and Technology (MEXT), Ministry of Justice (MOJ), and surveys conducted by MyNavi Corporations, Japanese Institute of Labour Policy and Training (JILPT) and the Japan Student Services Organization (JASSO).
3. This is a lower grade in Germany, where 1,0 is very good, the highest grade, and 5,0 is a fail.
4. Only 13.2% of the international student currently enrolled in Japanese universities are in science and engineering. The majority of them, 64.3%, are in humanities, social sciences and fine arts (JASSO 2019).
5. Although companies surveyed by MyNavi (2017) or JILPT (2013) generally indicated that they hire foreign and Japanese recruits in the same way, meaning that they hire both as regular employees with similar initial positions, this does not prevent foreigners from

being tracked into occupational niches in the long run. Some firms, in fact, set aside numerical targets to hire international graduates with such roles in mind.

6. Career Support Network for International Students in Japan, https://ajinzai-sc.jp/s_howtouse_en.html, accessed August 4, 2019.

Disclosure statement

No potential conflict of interest was reported by the author(s).

Funding

This study is funded by Japan Society for the Promotion of Science (JSPS)'s Promotion of International Joint Research Grant (2017–2019) [grant number 16KK0088].

ORCID

Gracia Liu-Farrer http://orcid.org/0000-0003-3241-8703

References

Basford, Scott, and Micheline van Riemsdijk. 2015. "The Role of Institutions in the Student Migrant Exerience: Norway's Quota Scheme." *Population, Space and Place* 23: 1–13. doi:10.1002/psp.2005.

Bauder, Harald. 2003. ""Brain Abuse", or the Devaluation of Immigrant Labour in Canada." *Antipode* 35 (4): 699–717.

Becker, Gary. 1964. *Human Capital: A Theoretical and Empirical Analysis, with Special Reference to Education*. New York: Columbia University Press.

Blackmore, Jill, Cate Gribble, and Mark Rahimi. 2017. "International Education, the Formation of Capital and Graduate Employment: Chinese Accounting Graduates' Experiences of the Australian Labour Market." *Critical Studies in Education* 58 (1): 69–88.

Brinton, Mary. 2005. "Education and the Economy." In *The Handbook of Economic Sociology*, edited by Neil J. Smelser, and Richard Swedberg, 575–602. New York: Russell Sage Foundation.

Conrad, Harald, and Hendrik Meyer-Ohle. 2017. "Overcoming the Ethnocentric Firm? Foreign Fresh University Graduate Employment in Japan as a New International Human Resource Development Method." *The International Journal of Human Resource Management* 30 (17): 2525–2543. doi:10.1080/09585192.2017.1330275.

DAAD (Deutscher Akademischer Austauschdienst). 2013. *Strategie DAAD* 2020. Bonn: DAAD.

Doi, Yasuhiro, and Ikutaro Enatsu. 2010. "Nihon kigyō no shokuba no kokusaika to ryūgakusei no kyaria kyōiku (The Internationalization of Japanese Enterprises and the Career Education for International Students)." *Ryūgakusei Kyōiku* 15: 27–34.

Endō, Kōshi. 1994. "*Satei* (Personal Assessment) and Interworker Competition in Japanese Firms." *Industrial Relations* 33 (1): 70–82.

Erel, Umut. 2010. "Migrating Cultural Capital: Bourdieu in Migration Studies." *Sociology* 44 (4): 642–660.

Ernst, Angelika. 1998. *Aufstieg — Anreiz — Auslese: Karriermuster und Karriereverläufe von Akademikern in Japan*. Wiesbaden: Springer VS.

Estevez-Abe, Margarita. 2005. "Gender Bias in Skills and Social Policies: The Varieties of Capitalism Perspective on Sex Segregation." *Social Politics: International Studies in Gender, State & Society* 12 (2): 180–215. doi:10.1093/sp/jxi011.

Estévez-Abe, Margarita, Torben Iversen, and David Soskice. 2001. "Social Protection and the Formation of Skills: A Reinterpretation of the Welfare State." In *Varieties of Capitalism: The*

Institutional Foundations of Comparative Advantage, edited by Peter A. Hall, and David Soskice, 145–183. Oxford: Oxford University Press.

Expert Council of German Foundation on Integration and Migration (SVR). 2015. *Train and Retain: Career Support for International Students in Canada, Germany, the Netherlands and Sweden*. Berlin: SVR Research Unit.

Fligstein, Neil. 2001. *The Architecture of Markets: An Economic Sociology of Twenty-First Century Capitalist Societies*. Princeton: Princeton University Press.

Fukuoka, Masako. 2015. "*Ryūgakusei no shūshoku ni kansuru ishiki chōsa to bijinesu nihongo he no shisa* (Survey Regarding International Students' Career Aspirations and Lessons for Business Japanese Education)." *Mie University International Center Kiyō* 10: 1–18.

Giardini, Angelo, Rüdiger Kabst, and Michael Müller-Camen. 2005. "HRM in the German Business System: A Review." *Management Revue: The International Review of Management Studies* 16 (1): 63–80. doi:10.5771/0935-9915-2005-1-63.

Hawthorne, Lesleyanne. 2005. ""Picking Winners": The Recent Transformation of Australia's Skilled Migration Policy." *International Migration Review* 39 (3): 663–696.

Hawthorne, Lesleyanne. 2008. *The Growing Global Demand for Students as Skilled Migrants*. Washington, DC: Migration Policy Institute.

Hawthorne, Lesleyanne. 2010. "How Valuable is "Two-Step-Migration"? Labour Market Outcomes for International Student Migrants to Australia." *Asian and Pacific Migration Journal* 19 (1): 5–36.

Heinrich, Steffen. 2010. "Facing the 'Dark Side' of Deregulation? The Politics of Two-Tier Labour Markets in Germany and Japan After the Global Financial Crisis." *Social Policy Review* 22: 151–176.

Holbrow, Hilary J., and Kikuko Nagayoshi. 2018. "Economic Integration of Skilled Migrants in Japan: The Role of Employment Practices." *International Migration Review* 52 (2): 458–486.

Ishida, Hiroshi. 2001. "Educational Credentials and Labour-Market Entry Outcomes in Japan." In *From School to Work. A Comparative Study of Educational Qualifications and Occupational Destinations*, edited by Yossi Shavit, and Walter Muller, 287–310. Oxford: Oxford University Press.

JASSO (Japan Student Services Association). 2016. "*JASSO Heisei 28 Gaikokujin ryūgakusē shinro jōkyō/gakui jyuyo jōkyō chōsa kekka* (JASSO 2016 Survey on the Situations of Post-Graduate Mobilities and Degree Conferrals of International Students)." https://www.jasso.go.jp/about/statistics/intl_student_d/data17.html#no1.

JASSO (Japan Student Services Association). 2019. "Result of an Annual Survey of International Students in Japan 2018." https://www.jasso.go.jp/en/about/statistics/intl_student_e/2018/__icsFiles/afieldfile/2019/01/11/data18_e.pdf.

JILPT (Japan Institute for Labour Policy and Training). 2013. *JILPT Chōsa Shirīzu No. 110 (JILPT Survey Series No. 110*. https://www.jil.go.jp/institute/research/2013/documents/0110.pdf.

Kariya, Takehiko. 2001. "From High School and College to Work in Japan: Meritocracy Through Institutional and Semi-Institutional Linkages." In *From School to Work. A Comparative Study of Educational Qualifications and Occupational Destinations*, edited by Yossi Shavit, and Walter Muller, 311–336. Oxford: Oxford University Press.

Liu-Farrer, Gracia. 2011. "Making Careers in the Occupational Niche: Chinese Students in Corporate Japan's Transnational Business." *Journal of Ethnic and Migration Studies* 37 (5): 785–803.

Liu-Farrer, Gracia, Brenda S. Yeoh, and Michiel Baas. 2021. "Social Construction of Skill: An Analytic Approach Toward the Question of Skill in Cross-Border Labour Mobilities." *Journal of Ethnic and Migration Studies* 47 (10): 2237–2251. doi:10.1080/1369183X.2020.1731983.

Mayer, Michael C J., and Richard Whittington. 1999. "Strategy, Structure and 'Systemness': National Institutions and Corporate Change in France, Germany and the UK, 1950-1993." *Organization Studies* 20 (6): 933–959.

MEXT (Ministry of Education, Culture, Sports, Science and Technology). 2018. *Heisei 20nendo Daigaku nado sotsugyo yotēsha no shūshoku naitē jōkyō chōsa* (A Survey of 2018 Graduating

Cohort' Job Offer Situations) http://www.mext.go.jp/b_menu/houdou/31/01/__icsFiles/afieldfile/2019/01/18/1412605_1.pdf.

MEXT (Ministry of Education, Culture, Sports, Science & Technology). 2008. *Outline of the Student Exchange System: Study in Japan and Abroad*. Tokyo: MEXT.

MHLW (Ministry of Health, Labour and Welfare). 2019. *Heisei 21nen 3gatsu Daigaku nado Sotsugyōsha no Shūshoku Jōkyō wo Kōhyō shimasu* (Announcing the Employment Situations of the 2019 March University and other Graduates). https://www.mhlw.go.jp/stf/houdou/0000205940_00002.html.

Mosneaga, Ana, and Lars Winther. 2013. "Emerging Talents? International Students Before and After Their Career Start in Denmark." *Population, Space and Place* 19 (2): 181–195.

MyNavi Corporation. 2017. 2018 *Nensotsu kigyō gaikokujin ryūgakusei saiyō jōkyō chōsa* (Enterprise Survey about 2018 Foreign Graduates)" https://saponet.mynavi.jp/wp/wp-content/uploads/2017/03/[2017年卒]企業外国人留学生採用状況調査.pdf.

Nohl, Arnd-Michael, Karin Schittenhelm, Oliver Schmidtke, and Anja Weiss. 2014. *Work in Transition: Cultural Capital and Highly Skilled Migrants' Passages Into the Labour Market*. Toronto: University of Toronto Press.

Nowicka, Magdalena. 2014. "Migrating Skills, Skilled Nigrants and Nigration Skills: The Influence of Contexts on the Validation of Migrants' Skills." *Migration Letters* 11 (2): 171–186.

OECD. 2011. *International Migration Outlook: SOPEMI 2011*. OECD Publishing. http://dx.doi.org/10.1787/migr_outlook-2011-en.

Oishi, Nana. 2021. "Skilled or Unskilled? The Reconfiguration of Migration Policies in Japan." *Journal of Ethnic and Migration Studies* 47 (10): 2252–2269. doi:10.1080/1369183X.2020.1731984.

Plöger, Jörg, and Anna Becker. 2015. "Social Networks and Local Incorporation—Grounding High-skilled Migrants in Two German Cities." *Journal of Ethnic and Migration Studies* 41 (10): 1517–1535. doi:10.1080/1369183X.2015.1015407.

Recruit Works Institute (Rikurūto Wākusu Kenkyūjō). 2016. *"Dai 33-kai Rikurūto Wākusu Daisotsu kyūjin bairitsu chōsa. 2017-nensotsu (33th Comprehensive Recruit Works Survey on Ratio of College Graduate Job-seekers to Job Vacancies. 2017 Graduating Cohort)."* http://www.works-i.com/pdf/160421_kyuujin.pdf.

Reich, Michael, David M. Gordon, and Richard C. Edwards. 1973. "A Theory of Labor Market Segmentation." *The American Economic Review* 63 (2): 359–365.

Reitz, Jeffrey G. 2001. "Immigrant Skill Utilisation in the Canadian Labour Market: Implications of Human Capital Research." *Journal of International Migration and Integration* 2 (3): 347–378.

Robertson, Shanthi. 2013. *Transnational Student-migrants and the State: The Education-Migration Nexus*. Basingstoke: Palgrave Macmillan.

Samers, Michael. 1998. "'Structured Coherence': Immigration, Racism and Production in the Paris Car Industry." *European Planning Studies* 6 (1): 49–72.

Statistisches Bundesamt. 2018. "13% ausländische Studierende an deutschen Hochschulen." Pressemitteilung Nr. 46 vom 13. November 2018. https://www.destatis.de/DE/Presse/Pressemitteilungen/Zahl-der-Woche/2018/PD18_46_p002.html.

Stifterverband. 2016. *Hochschul-Bildungs-Report 2020: Hochschulbildung für die Arbeitswelt 4.0*. Essen: Stifterverband für die Deutsche Wissenschaft e.V.

Støren, Liv Anne, and Jannecke Wiers-Jenssen. 2010. "Foreign Diploma Versus Immigrant Background: Determinants of Labour Market Success or Failure?" *Journal of Studies in International Education* 14 (1): 29–49.

Streeck, Wolfgang. 2001. "Introduction: Explorations Into the Origins of Nonliberal Capitalism in Germany and Japan." In *The Origins of Nonliberal Capitalism: Germany and Japan in Comparison*, edited by Wolfgang Streeck, and Kōzō Yamamura, 1–38. Ithaca: Cornell University Press.

Studying-in-Germany.org. 2019. "Germany International Student Statistics 2019", https://www.studying-in-germany.org/germany-international-student-statistics/.

Thelen, Kathleen, and Ikuo Kume. 2003. "The Future of Nationally Embedded Capitalism." In *The End of Diversity? Prospects for German and Japanese Capitalism*, edited by Kozo Yamamura, and Wolfgang Streeck, 183–211. Ithaca, NY: Cornell University Press.

Tseng, Yen-Fen. 2021. "Becoming Global Talent? Taiwanese White-collar Migrants in Japan." *Journal of Ethnic and Migration Studies* 47 (10): 2288–2304. doi:10.1080/1369183X.2020.1731986.

van Riemsdijk, Micheline, Scott Basford, and Alana Burnham. 2016. "Socio-Cultural Incorporation of Skilled Migrants at Work: Employer and Migrant Perspectives." *International Migration* 54 (3): 20–34.

VDI (Verein Deutsche Ingenieure). 2019. Demografischer Wandel: Nachwuchsmangel bei Ingenieuren – was zu tun ist. https://www.vdi.de/news/detail/demografischer-wandel-nachwuchsmangel-bei-ingenieuren-was-zu-tun-ist.

Waldenberger, Franz. 2016. "In-House Careers: A Core Institution of the Japanese Firm in Need of Reform." *Journal of Strategic Management Studies* 8 (1): 23–32.

Intermediaries and transnational regimes of skill: nursing skills and competencies in the context of international migration

Margaret Walton-Roberts

ABSTRACT

Market-based migrant intermediaries play an important role in skilled migration. Skilled workers, especially in regulated professions such as nursing, face increasingly complex testing and credential assessment systems. 'Regimes of skill' control and filter membership to these professions by reproducing already existing power imbalances in the global regulation of skilled labour. This paper examines these processes in the case of Indian trained nurses who use educational brokers to enrol in Canadian post-graduate programmes with the intention of practising in the Canadian health care system. The study elaborates on the 'regime of skill' in nursing, revealing its maintenance through interactional and transnational connections between intermediaries, educators and regulators in terms of codifying and translating skills and competencies between jurisdictions with different cultural and professional histories and norms of nursing. Findings reveal that intermediaries operate transnationally in a symbiotic manner with more powerful actors in order to exploit regimes of skill and expand their market share.

Intermediaries and skill regimes in international migration

When skilled workers embark on international migration journeys they rarely do so alone. Private market based immigrant intermediaries (service providers who contribute to the international mobility and labour market integration of migrants) are increasingly active in all phases of skilled migration, from attraction and mobilisation, labour market entry, and integration (Groutsis, van den Broek, and Harvey 2015; c.f. Salt and Stein 1997). Scholarly interest in the role of intermediaries has increased significantly (Lindquist, Xiang, and Yeoh 2012; Cranston, Schapendonk, and Spaan 2018; Deshingkar 2019). This has produced greater analysis of the role of intermediaries that details their transnational operation and organisation, thereby escaping methodological and conceptual nationalism (Cranston, Schapendonk, and Spaan 2018). Furthermore, as the introduction to this special issue outlines (Liu-Farrer, Yeoh, and Baas 2021), migrant intermediaries arbitrate migrants' skill by working symbiotically with states, educators, employers and professional regulators to interpret, evaluate and convert skills from one context to another. Recent research has certainly demonstrated the full spectrum of intermediaries' potential influence on migrants, migration systems and the regulatory frameworks that direct, facilitate, and constrain human mobility. On the one hand, intermediaries support migrants' agency in embracing international migration opportunities, but on the other, they contribute to increased migrant precarity, and this realisation results in deeper appreciation of how the two seemingly contradictory processes actually work together in the practices and performativity of migrant brokerage (Deshingkar 2019). Migrant intermediaries also play a central role in producing the ideal subject for certain labour market niches by being transnationally networked into wider brokerage and labour market institutional structures (Polanco 2017; Deshingkar 2019). Overall it is evident that, 'research on the migration industries as not just as a research field in itself, but as a vehicle for understanding contemporary processes of migration' (Cranston, Schapendonk, and Spaan 2018, 551–552).

In order to comprehend these processes in more detail, a focus on the relationship between migrants and intermediaries in specific geographic and occupational sectoral contexts is warranted (Groutsis, van den Broek, and Harvey 2015). Research by sector permits deeper analysis of skill specific regulations that inform occupational norms and channels of access via migration. Shan and Fejes (2015, 227) conceptualise this channelling of migrant access as a 'regime of skills':

> a new mode of control and modulation that defines the desirability of individuals in the labour market ... rather than providing a fixed set of reference points, the regime of skill is rather a shifting ground that affords opportunities to some while closing doors to others.

The conceptualisation of a 'regime of skill' raises awareness of the multiple forces that contribute to constructing and regulating the parameters of skill. When intermediaries mobilise and facilitate international skilled migration into regulated occupations, we need to understand their role in the 'shifting ground' of the regime of skill more broadly. Skilled migrants must purchase relevant information and guidance from market based intermediaries in order to increase their chances of entry and integration in the destination labour market, and their ability to satisfy the regime of skill governing their occupational sector. This need for guidance is more profound in regulated occupations where multiple agents – state actors, professional associations, consumer groups, employers and unions – have an interest in controlling who gains access to the profession (Sweetman, McDonald, and Hawthorne 2015). The manner in which intermediaries fit into this regime provides a window into understanding, 'the evolving role of the state, the day-to-day operation of globalisation and how we can understand the economy' (Cranston, Schapendonk, and Spaan 2018, 552).

Groutsis, van den Broek, and Harvey (2015) argue that the tendency toward more active roles for market-based intermediaries is important because it can increase structural inequality; the purchasing power of the migrant determines the quality of guidance they can afford. Moreover, market based intermediaries are of variable quality in an often unregulated realm, forming part of a system of network governance where the state withdraws from delivering some public services, or works in combination with market intermediaries. To appreciate the significance of this process, Groutsis, van den Broek, and Harvey (2015, 1571) suggest; 'Future research could further investigate the changing transactional exchanges between the migrant and the intermediary by examining each of the intermediaries and their relationship with particular groups of migrants in different geographic and sectoral contexts'. Skills are socially and contextually constructed, and the shifting ground of the regime of skill will reflect this. Moreover, a closer analysis of intermediaries in specific occupations assists us in understanding, 'how migrant identities are produced in different ways through migration industries, from representations to practices' (Cranston, Schapendonk, and Spaan 2018, 548).

This paper addresses the call for more sector specific research on migrant intermediaries, and furthers Shan and Fejes (2015) skill regime conceptualisation by drawing on a case study of Indian migrants using the services of a nursing education-migration intermediary for a study-work migration pathway that will ideally allow them to practice nursing in Canada. Study-work migration pathways reflect the increasing significance of 'two-step' migration policy routes, where receiving states provide international students with an opportunity to transition into a work visa and in some cases provide pathways for permanent residence when their skills are in demand (Hawthorne 2010; Walton-Roberts and Hennebry 2019). The paper demonstrates how intermediaries react to, reshape and reinforce the regime of skill related to nursing in Canada, and the central role intermediaries play in all phases of migration, from mobilisation, labour market entry, and integration that accompany migration and the construction of the relevant regime of skill in immigrant receiving countries. The analysis details the complexity of international skilled migration, including the navigation of immigration policies, educational programmes and occupational and workplace hierarchies in the case of one regulated profession, nursing.

A focus on nursing incorporates analysis of how professional regulators shape the expression and codification of necessary skills and competencies, highlighting the socio-spatial construction of skills for specific gendered occupations (Iredale 2005; Raghuram 2000). Moreover, it reveals how the codified skills and competencies migrants' embody variably transfer across landscapes of labour marked by cultural and historical differences in professional identity and the variable level of power exercised by the many agents involved in the process. Pushing the concept of a 'regime of skill' further, the paper examines how intermediaries outside of the 'hegemonic West' actively contribute to the reproduction and reformulation of the regime of skill in their effort to increase their market share and promote their knowledge and expertise in specific occupational fields.

The next section of the paper briefly details why nursing is an important occupation to explore for the purposes of understanding the central role of intermediaries in skilled migration and how their actions intersect with relevant regimes of skill. The paper then expands on the particular focus of Indian trained nurses in Canada, and outlines the research methods used. The next three sections explore intermediaries and their role in building the regime of skills, from the attraction and mobilisation phase, to labour market entry, and workplace integration. Finally, the paper examines how intermediaries exploit and actively contribute to the regime of skill in place in order to assist clients in their navigation of complex occupational testing and verification processes. Intermediaries must be cognisant of relevant regimes of skill because migrants' have an intense need for relevant guidance in order to secure their inclusion in regulated occupations. In effect, there is a symbiotic relationship between the degree to which policy and occupational regulations act as barriers for migrants, and the need for intermediaries to assist migrants in navigating these barriers.

Nursing skills and international migration

Nursing is a 'mobile profession' (Kingma 2006, 1282), where the direction and scope of migratory flows are traditionally seen as determined by a set of 'push' and 'pull' motivators (Connell 2010), that are reinforced by and reflected in global uneven development. On the one hand, political, social, and economic insecurities, substandard working conditions, and an undesirable quality of living are commonly attributed factors that drive nurses to emigrate from locations in the Global South (Horne 2011). The convergence of these 'push' and 'pull' motivators, on both an individual and institutional level, gives shape to a 'global nursing care chain' (Yeates 2010, 426), a phenomenon wherein poorer countries situated at the lower end of the chain export valuable nursing human resources upwards along the chain to richer countries. This results in distinctive migratory patterns of nurses from the Philippines, India, China, and countries in sub-Saharan Africa to developed countries in the Global North (OECD 2017). A major complication to this migratory circuit is the global differences that exist in nurse training. The International Council for Nursing has promoted the idea of common standards for nursing education worldwide, but:

> achieving that goal remains unrealized and is complicated by the variations in nursing education throughout the world. Many countries specify university-level education as the minimum entry requirement for nursing – but the idea of university education for nursing remains challenging, with disparities being common in the programs currently offered in different parts of the world. Compounding the issue is the number of countries that still consider initial nursing education at the secondary school level to be adequate. (IOM 2011, 571)

Despite the challenge of nationally distinct training systems, OECD nations have adopted various strategies to attract internationally educated nurses (IENs) in order to address their labour market shortages. These include; active international nurse recruitment campaigns, bilateral state agreements (including mutual recognition agreements), favourable immigration regulations (including opportunities to apply for permanent residence, citizenship, and family reunification), and regional foreign credential recognition and licensing policies targeting the successful integration of IENs (Yeates 2010). In the OECD, overseas nurses represent 5.9% of the combined nursing workforce of member countries; this varies from over 25% in New Zealand to between 10% and 20% in Switzerland, Australia and the United Kingdom (OECD 2017). Global South countries, especially the Philippines, India, and China, have also engaged in a deliberate effort to overproduce nurses for overseas employment (Brush and Sochalski 2007). The private sector increasingly provides this export-directed education in key sending nations, often resulting in lower quality training and poor regulatory oversight (Reynolds et al. 2013). This has resulted in concern regarding the emerging spatial and temporal dynamics of nurse migration, with high-level dialogues on health worker migration noting concern about, 'the accelerating and dynamic nature of international health worker movement', increasingly temporary migration, and increased source country production that is often disconnected from labour markets (WHO 2017, 1).

The increased production of nurses for export correlates with a growing focus on defining and operationalising more rigorous occupational competency frameworks in key receiving nations (Hodges 2012). Recommended standards for nursing and midwifery include; prequalification and education requirements for registration, processes for achieving and maintaining registration, and practice standards that include language competency requirements (Brownie et al. 2015). Such standards improve the nursing workforce, improve healthcare practice and management and increase public confidence in healthcare safety. However, such frameworks can limit access, progression and mobility of health care workers within and between national labour markets (Bourgeault et al. 2010; Sweetman, McDonald, and Hawthorne 2015; Salami, Meherali, and Covell 2018). One outcome of such codified regimes of skill is the potential for international migrants to experience foreign credential devaluation. This deskilling contributes to the global flexibilisation of labour (Bauder 2006), which Valiani (2012) argues corporate health systems exploit, in that they hire IENs to increase labour flexibility within their organisations. Other scholars regard this global skills transfer as evidence of a new form of unequal exchange that 'delineates the contours of a new international division of labour that implies an asymmetric model based on the reintegration of peripheral nations into the global capitalist system' (Wise and Covarrubias 2012, 131). Liu-Farrer, Yeoh, and Baas (introduction to this special issue) also detail how seemingly neutral immigration policy designed to attract skilled immigrants results in practices that 'facilitate the de-facto import of various kinds of gendered and racialized labour' (XX). The increasing complexity of credential and regulatory frameworks in receiving nations does not dull the potential rewards of securing such employment. Rather the presence of labour market barriers combined with potential reward generates a strong incentive for the use of intermediaries to assist in integrating workers from the periphery into the core nations of the global capitalist system. The case of IENs illuminates this uneven transnational landscape of skilled labour mobility, and the work of market based intermediaries who intervene in the process (Gabriel 2013; Yeates 2009).

Indian trained nurses in Canada: forging a transnational regime of skill

The nursing occupation has historically provided female migrants from south India an opportunity for movement to the Global North and Middle East (George 2005; Walton-Roberts 2012). More recently northern India has also become active in the training and migration of nurses (Walton-Roberts, Bhutani, and Kaur 2017), and Canada, a settler society with an active and highly selective permanent immigration system (Banting 2010), has emerged as an important destination. One migration route increasingly used by Indian nurses to enter Canada is the two-step pathway of first entry as an international student, then subsequent conversion into a working visa and entry into the labour market as an IEN (Hawthorne 2010; Covell, Neiterman, and Bourgeault 2015; Covell et al. 2019; Walton-Roberts and Hennebry 2019).

The number of international students in Canada has almost tripled the last 10 years to over 500,000 (El-Assal 2018), and India is a prominent source region (Williams et al. 2015). The Government of Indian facilitates, even encourages, this two-step pathway through its support for private sector investment in nurse training (Walton-Roberts 2015). Research on this two-step pathway suggests it offers some advantages over other migration channels for IENs interested in gaining the right to work in Canada (Covell, Neiterman, and Bourgeault 2015). By entering the two-step migration pathway, IENs engage with the national training systems they wish to find employment within, and from this position, they can more effectively negotiate the regime of skill. In Canada, this regime includes spatial and sectoral variation by province and cadre of nursing rank, reflected in different credential evaluation, verification and related competency testing procedures.

In 2009, IENs made up 8.3% of the overall Canadian nursing workforce (Horne 2011, 40). This figure is relatively small compared with other groups of health professionals such as physicians and pharmacists. Nearly half of all IENs practising in Canada in 2010 were working in Ontario. Based on immigration and labour force data, Williams et al. (2015) estimated that about 17,500 IENs entered Canada in 2011. According to their final visas, the three largest classes by which IENs immigrated were temporary foreign worker (49%), economic immigrant (43%), and family class (3%), with at least 11% of these initially entering Canada as international students. IENs in Canada are mostly women, between ages 24 and 44, who reside and work in Ontario (43%). The top source countries for Canadian IENs include India and the Philippines. Research on international students in Canadian regulated health professional programmes (nursing, medicine, dentistry and pharmacy) showed that 71% remained in Canada after their studies, contrasting with 55% for international students in all health care programmes of study (Covell, Neiterman, and Bourgeault 2015). This suggests the use of two-step migration pathways for immigrants interested in working in regulated health care professions is a promising strategy.

The empirical material this paper draws on emerged from a multi-sited research project conducted over the last decade. Methods used included 48 key informant interviews and focus groups in India (Punjab) and Canada (Ontario) with nurses, nursing faculty, bureaucrats and intermediaries, and surveys with nursing students in India ($n = 1000$) (Walton-Roberts, Bhutani, and Kaur 2017). When permitted, interviews were audio recorded, transcribed, and analysed using Nvivo qualitative data analysis software. In India, surveys and focus groups were conducted with nursing students to examine their background and interest in migration; in Canada, qualified Indian nurses enrolled in a college educational programme answered questions about their experiences and their long-term migration intentions. Pseudonyms are used for individuals, but not for the intermediary interviewed, since public data about related programmes and services are referenced.

This data reveals how market-based intermediaries (construed as both the migrant-education placement agency and the public college providing the training programme in Canada) engage with and influence the regime of skill (Shan and Fejes 2015). Immigration policy and professional nursing regulators control the entry of skilled workers by assessing their credentials and competencies (including language), and intermediaries (in migration and education domains) intervene in this process by assisting candidates to meet these demands. The data and analysis presented goes further, however, to reveal a dynamic transnational landscape of skill reconstruction and development where migration and educational intermediaries across source and destination regions reinforce the contours of specific regimes of skill. The next section of the paper examines this argument in more detail, highlighting the stages of transnational formation of this regime of skill, beginning with the connection between the household and the educational cum migration intermediary in the phase of attraction and mobilisation.

Households and recruiters in India: attraction and mobilisation

Surveys with 1000 Indian nursing students in northern India 2010–2012 revealed over 52% identified advice from family or friends as the main reason behind their choice to enter nursing, and 32% already had a relative in the nursing field. Moreover, 66% of the Indian student sample stated that they intended to go overseas once they had completed their studies. For the majority of these students, nursing is an occupational choice framed by a combination of family advice and the potential for overseas migration. About one third (31%) of the sample indicated their intention to use networks of family or intermediaries to seek overseas migration opportunities once their studies were completed. For many of these students, it was possible to migrate directly to the Middle East for a nursing position just a few years after graduating, but this is more challenging to achieve in OECD nations. This has resulted in many nurses using employment in the Middle East as a stepping stone to help them move 'up' the chain into Europe, North America or Australia (Percot 2006). The risks associated with international migration and the use of intermediaries are well documented in the case of nursing, which can include misinformation and fraud concerning contract conditions and ethno-specific exploitation in terms of fees charged and occupational placement (van den Broek, Harvey, and Groutsis 2015). In India, the public are well aware of the risks associated with using the services of intermediaries (Irudaya Rajan, Varghese, and Jayakumar 2011). To circumvent the risks associated with migration, especially to the Middle East, one strategy adopted by recent nursing graduates is the two-step visa migration method. Rather than engaging in lengthy strategies of stepping from one location to another to secure better employment and residency rights, nurses use the services of educational intermediaries to place them into programmes where the immigration system permits two-steps in terms of moving from a study to work visa, allowing migrants to enhance their educational qualifications at the same time as they submit their credentials to the relevant regulatory agencies (Walton-Roberts and Hennebry 2019).

While there are numerous Indian intermediaries specialising in nurse migration opportunities, one group was explicit in its attention to education, rather than migration. Mentioned by numerous students and faculty interviewed for this research (in Canada and India), the intermediary advertised their programmes as allowing nurses to 'pursue a Foundation or Enhancement programme as per their career goal and to work in top healthcare facilities in countries like Canada/U.K./U.S.A./ AUS/ NZ'.[1]

While the risks associated with the use of international migration intermediaries are legion in India, interest in migration opportunities remains high. The intermediary examined here recognised this demand, and used the threat of insecurity posed by the wider intermediary sector as a way to promote their specific approach to mobility, a dedicated migration channel for education purposes that offers more security for migrants and their families:

> We basically prepare them to succeed … migration always has its own challenges with people going and staying and taking care of themselves, and the culture issue … in all of our programs, they always go in cohorts or groups, and we have tutors. So that makes all the difference. (Recruiting company director, July 6, 2011, Chandigarh India)

The intermediary promoted international educational opportunities for recently trained nurses by grouping them into cohorts and offering a full spectrum of support before, during and after the transition, something clearly important to migrant nurses and their parents when contemplating the decision to migrate. Presented as a protective corridor, the enhanced focus on personal security and protection certainly attracts migrants and their families:

> they see more or less a secured way for them to progress. And we have shown that in Punjab we get more than four thousand – five thousand nurses who have come out of Punjab over the last ten years who have been doing that. But they now see a secured way into nursing, and they can go through the proper pathways that they can settle down and become a nurse. But the decision is still the families' and exactly because the family is still funding all the activity … we have been able to establish the kind of goodwill that we would take good care of them … We are recruiting them and preparing them in India and supporting them here. As well we have the staff moving around supporting them and they know it. The other thing is that they know they all are moving in a cohort … and that's a very, very big comfort … [this includes] the preparatory course done in India prior to departing for international studies, for six weeks. They form new relationships and friendships … And that is a very big comfort for everyone … in our case we are sending a cohort; it's always a cohort, it is never one or two nurses going anywhere … there's much more security for the parents and also because they are mostly young girls. (INSCOL Director (Canadian campus) October 8, 2013)

When families agree to send their daughters and sons with INSCOL, they expect them to provide secure options for living arrangements such as home stays or campus living when they arrive in the destination, but in some cases, services combine with an already existing overseas Indian diaspora network. The intermediary acknowledged that extended kin networks were an important factor that encouraged families to send their daughters and sons to specific overseas locations:

> most of the time the people who send them, they have one or two relatives over there … And they send them under some supervision or if they are sure that their daughters will be safe from here, then they send them. (Recruiting company director, July 7, 2010, Chandigarh India)

Indian nurses enrolled in programmes in Canada discussed how the recruiter was 'vetted' by their parents, who made the decision to engage them (and paid the fees):

> I had met with that [recruiter] and my parents said okay then go with [them]. Daddy said it's a good thing to do … [the recruiter] was getting in the system to Canada … so I think that was a good experience … . (Indian student registered in Canadian College April 19, 2011 Interview)

The educational intermediary argued that their focus was not migration *per se*, but they understood international migration was the intention of the majority of their clients. They highlighted that fact that Indian trained nurses needed to develop more skills to be able to meet the regulatory requirements for entry into Canadian nursing:

> To apply for a PR [in Canada] they need to show at least 2 years work experience. If the candidate does not have the experience of two years … they prefer that they should go to Canada so that they can just take the education and then to get PR on their own. So this is one of the reasons that some students prefer to study with us … the Indian education system and Canada education system is different. So the nurses who are going on PR from India …

they don't want to waste their time by taking experience in India .... (INSCOL consultant, Chandigarh India July 2013)

Newly graduated Indian nurses understand that the regime of skill in Canada demands they have some relevant in-country experience. Rather than 'waste' their time working in India and imagining that this experience will benefit them, they are aware that a two-step migration process allows them to negotiate with the skill regime in situ, by meeting some requirements through the Canadian educational system. The regime of skill is complex, and while the majority of candidates are aware of this, they are less aware of how rapidly changes might occur in immigration and professional credential policy, and how this will make their journey even more complicated. Recognising the complexity of the assessment process helps to explain the value proposition intermediaries' offer to those IENs keen to work in Canada, and furthermore, it explains their singular role in comprehending, explaining, and meeting the demands of the prevailing regime of skill for the regulated nursing profession.

Entering the regime of skill: labour market entry for IENs in Canada

Canada's nursing professions are self-regulated. As such, to practice nursing in Canada, IENs are only eligible for licensure when they have successfully met the requirements of the relevant regulatory body, and have an appropriate immigration visa. Several aspects to the licensing process are a major impediment to IENs' successful completion of licensure in Canada. The assessment of an IEN's foreign credentials (the evaluation of the equivalency of their educational qualifications and professional skills), is often cited as one of the most common barriers that significantly delays or prevents IENs from completing their licensure process altogether (Kolawole 2009, 185). For example, between 1 January and 31 December 2012, the College of Nurses of Ontario received 5517 new applications from IENs (not including the U.S.). Of these, 1761 or 32% completed their registration within 1 year. In comparison, of the 10,458 Ontario trained nurses who applied, 7736 (or 74%) resulted in full licensure by the end of the year.

The amount of time it takes an international applicant to obtain the necessary documentation from their institution of study, and the time it takes a regulator to complete credential assessment both depend on the specific nursing programme and institution in the source country. Programme assessment is also dependent on when the applicant completed their training, so assessment is time as well as location specific. As such, the period for assessment varies significantly between applicants (NNAS 2017). The provincial regulator may require the applicant to undertake further study before they can even complete an entry to practice exam. This leaves IENs often unclear and unprepared to develop a realistic expectation regarding the financial costs and time required to complete the process if they are attempting this individually.

In 2015, there was a streamlining and integration of Canadian nursing national testing frameworks with a move toward a single registration exam rather than distinct provincial examinations. In June 2012, all Registered Nurse provincial regulators, with the exception of Quebec, entered into an agreement with the U.S.-based National Council of State Boards of Nursing (NCSBN) to replace the Canadian Registered nurse examination (CRNE) with the computerised adaptive test the NCLEX-RN (National Council Licensure

Examination) as the entry-to-practice examination for RN licensure effective January 2015 (CCRNR 2013, 8). The CRNE was previously only administered in Canada, and the new agreement allowed applicants to write the NCLEX-RN in any permanent test site located in Canada or sites in the U.S. (CCRNR 2013, 8). Moreover, NCLEX-RN examination sites exist in several countries outside the U.S., including Germany, India, Hong Kong, Mexico, Puerto Rico, the Philippines, Taiwan, and the U.K. This shift to a different testing system was encouraged by the Canadian federal government to 'ensure timely access of graduates to the profession in order to facilitate labour mobility' (Rowshan and Singh 2014, 47). In addition, during this time, there was a notable collaboration between regulatory bodies to harmonise licensure processes and credential equivalency assessments across Canada, to create bridging programmes, and provide comprehensive and transparent workforce and regulatory information for IENs at the pre-arrival stage. For example, an Offshore Examinations Study explored the feasibility of offering licensing examinations to IENs outside of Canada. Countries that send nurses to Canada have responded to these developments favourably (Santiago 2013, 207).

Becoming a nurse in Canada: skills and integration

The complexity of the regime of skill in the case of nursing makes the completion of one or two years of post-graduate education in Canada a worthy investment if it can assist the individual with the process of integrating into the workforce as a registered nurse. In addition, Canada's own immigration policy approach has prioritised international students. International students are viewed as 'ideal immigrants' or 'future citizens of Canada' who tend to have higher levels of English or French proficiency, academic credentials that are easily recognised by employers, and higher success rates of integration compared with their counterparts in the foreign worker category (Tamburri 2013). Strategic policy shifts capitalise on international students in Canada, allowing them to enter the workforce and contribute to the economy. The Canadian government uses their express entry immigration process as a means to absorb international students into the country as permanent residents, though challenges admittedly remain (Dam, Chan, and Wayland 2018). Express entry operates as a competitive pool, where those with the highest comprehensive ranking scores rise to the top of the pool and have a stronger chance of being invited to apply for permanent residence.

Public colleges have also embraced the international student option as a means to increase their revenues. They are well aware that the intention of the majority of international students is to seek an opportunity to work, and in most cases apply for permanent residence in Canada (Williams et al. 2015). Canadian colleges become the lynchpin between migrants, Indian intermediaries and the Canadian nursing labour market. Only university baccalaureate (degree) programmes qualify for Registered Nurse (RN) and Nurse Practitioner (NP) credentials. The number of university spaces available for training IENs tends to be less than those available at colleges. College programmes are eligible for Registered Practical Nurse (RPN) programmes, but they are also very active in the provision of professional bridging programmes for immigrants, including nurses, who already possess a foreign nursing credential. These programmes assist IENs to prepare for the College of Nurses Ontario (CNO) assessment of their credentials and offer additional training to help candidates meet potential competency gaps and any further examination that may be required in order to have their credentials recognised. Instructors recognise that student skills depend upon where and when they gained their nursing credentials; instructors assess the strengths and weaknesses of various cohorts in light of this and adjust their programming accordingly. They also inform the intermediary of any universal skill deficiencies they identify. The public college must also be responsive to the professional association's entry to practice regulations in order to maintain their programmes' verification; they must also be receptive to changes in the labour market in terms of changing geographical and sectoral demand. College instructors also develop a strong understanding of the formal, cultural and tacit skill set resulting from the Indian training context. Senior college instructors participate in overseas visits to the Indian intermediaries' offices, as well as visiting several Indian nursing colleges and hospitals, in order to understand the practice context of Indian trained nurses. In light of the knowledge developed from these trips, instructors strategically redesign their programmes. For example, Canadian instructors placed foundational knowledge assessment and language preparation at the start of their gerontology and critical care programmes for Indian trained nurses in order to identify any weaknesses at the outset of the programme. Part of the college training includes preceptor clinical training in local hospitals, so the instructors also made sure to brief their hospital partners about the skill sets of the Indian trained nurses they were working with. Clinical training is vital to the success of IEN students, both for meeting the requirements of the regulator, but also in terms of finding potential employers. The instructors regularly engaged with nursing officials from their local hospital partners, sharing with them their experiences of visiting India:

> Instructor 1: If they [nurse mentors in hospital] hear that these are postgraduate BScN [Bachelor of Science in Nursing] they're gonna come in thinking they are at this level right? And the reality is no – they've got a lot of anatomy/physiology/pathology and are very book smart, but how it works and is delivered here in Canada from a nursing role is very, very different …
>
> Instructor 2: You know, it's difficult with these students because maybe they have been doing IV push medications over in India in ICU, so they come here and think 'well, I'll just do it', right? Well, no you're here as students and you need to be supervised and watched, so it's very different … they give meds in India but here we have our eight checks … with every single patient and every single med … And we're adamant about that and they get tested on that …
>
> Instructor 1: Exactly. We are all really concerned about our control practices. They know, they understand the theory, but you and I have both been to India, we know that they understand the principles, but to be able to implement with resources best practices regarding infection control, so that's a huge issue for our community partners … We don't feel [we] can pull out our clinical components, because we think it's so integral, that they not only learn theory … you know, you need to be able to apply it. (Canadian College Instructor interview April 16, 2013)

The instructors' exposure to the Indian context provides them with a transnational professional habitus; they understand where the students come from, their skills, their strengths, but also the weaknesses that will make them vulnerable in a Canadian context. The Canadian college is also an intermediary, offering a service for purchase. In order to retain market interest, they must deliver, but they work with what the

Indian educational system produces, what Canadian employers expect of students in preceptor training, and what professional regulators demand. They provide feedback to the Indian intermediary about what they see as student deficiencies relative to the demands of the Canadian health systems and the professional regulator. The Indian intermediary uses this feedback, as well as the knowledge they gain from their international partner visits, to revise pre-departure training to address technical and cultural differences that emerge:

> the first cohort that we [sent out] in 2003 was there was no training ... and we were not setting them up to succeed. That is how we learned ... before you leave you have to do a certain skill ... So once we brought that in we saw the success rate dramatically go up in terms of education in Canada ... [For example] in math there's a calculation for dosage in which the nurse has to calculate how much dosage has to be given to a patient and it involves algebra, and if they make a mistake the dosage and the outcome, the medication can become fatal. Now, in India a nurse would not do that, the doctor would do that, so that was new for them, and the first cohort struggled with that ... They would have that in their primary education, but you have not practised it in so many years. For those students we did the module for algebra. (INSCOL Offices Canada, February 23, 2015)

Calculating a dosage is a technical skill, but the context of its use is also cultural, since in India the expectation is that the doctor will deal with it. In Canada, the nurse has the responsibility to do this. Part of the skills training process involves awareness of the regulatory differences in the scope of practice, and building awareness of the responsibilities a nurse practicing in Canada has compared to the norms associated with nursing in India. Seemingly minor differences in the training and education of nurses in India versus Canada illustrate the point about the immense complexity in assessing and transferring apparently standard skills (IV and dosage calculations) across contexts with different cultures and histories of professional nursing practice. We can see how important these intermediaries (the Indian agent and the Canadian college) are in framing the success of these migrants. Their role is at the intersection of multiple agents who are more powerful, the Canadian government who grants the visa, and the professional regulator who controls entry to practice. However, as Groutsis, van den Broek, and Harvey (2015) argue, the intermediary is not a neutral or passive actor in this process; instead, the regime of skill is about how 'skill and competency, as relational constructs, join hands with other social relations to produce differences while maintaining the power and practices of the hegemonic West' (Shan and Fejes 2015, 227). However, intermediaries not in the hegemonic West can also position themselves to join hands with the regime of skill.

Exploiting the regime of skill

The Indian intermediary reacts to information they gain from their international education partners by redesigning their preparatory pre-departure courses, but they also learn from the Canadian professional regulatory body about restrictions and requirements. In mid-2013, the CNO introduced the IENCAP (IEN Competency Assessment Program), which included an Objective Structured Clinical Examination (OSCE), a series of simulations designed to test competencies in live practice conditions. Similar to equivalency examinations in other jurisdictions, the IENCAP is a one-time high stakes test, and if unsuccessful, applicants are required to complete additional training to address identified competency gaps. IEN bridging programme practitioners have expressed concern regarding the OSCE's difficulty level, the low pass rate, and expressed concern regarding how IENs will access and afford the necessary training to address identified competency gaps, considering the small number of educational spaces available to address such gaps. The director of INSCOL saw his clients struggle with these changes in the assessment process, and understood that there was a demand for something to help manage the increasingly drawn out assessment and credential process the OSCE had introduced:

> Earlier most of them [IENs from India], there was no need for them to go to any remedial courses just be eligible to write the [entry to practice exam]. But now it's plus 6 months to one year ... we are seeing our students may not get [to the point] and they can write the exam. (INSCOL Director (Canada campus) October 8, 2013)

In reaction to this significant change in the regime of skill associated with nursing, INSCOL's Director decided to open an institution in Canada specifically geared toward training IENs for CNO's mandated IENCAP assessment tests. INSCOL exploited the opportunity presented by these assessment demands by making an investment in Canada. The director saw an opportunity to provide targeted training enhancement for all IENs who needed to complete the IENCAP, not just Indian IENs. He opened an institution in the Greater Toronto Area in Canada that uses simulation labs to train IENs for various CNO assessment tests. His plan includes working with Canadian college partners to offer preparatory programmes designed to help all IENs gain the knowledge and skills they will need to pass these high stakes examinations in order to become a RN in Canada. The long-term plan, according to the director, was to develop a career college that would become a designated institution by the Ontario government for the purposes of accepting international students from around the world. INSCOL Canada – 'A World of Opportunities to be a Global Nurse' was established in 2013 offering over 20 study programmes for nurses and nursing students. The stated mission is:

> Recognizing the need of skilled nursing professionals in medical facilities and hospitals across the globe, INSCOL laid the foundation of INSCOL Canada – A World of Opportunities to be a Global Nurse in 2013. The prime objective of setting this initiative was to transform IEN (Internationally Educated Nurses) into global nurses so that they can be part of best medical facilities on global front. Within a short span it became an international hub for the Global Nurse Program catering to Middle East, South East Asia, and Africa in addition to India and Canada.[2]

What has happened here is that a barrier, the IENCAP examination, has been converted into an opportunity for this Indian intermediary, who is now effectively not just an Indian-based intermediary. As stated at the start of the paper, there is a symbiotic relationship between the policy and occupational regulation agencies that control the barriers migrants must negotiate, and the intermediaries who emerge in order to assist migrants to navigate them. This admittedly single example suggests that intermediaries are not only active in creating the networks to entice migrants (and their families) to participate in the process of international skilled migration, they also become transnationally located in order to address the specific skill demands made by regulators in the receiving country, in this case, Canada. This intermediary expanded the range and influence of their expertise, in the process transforming this skills adaptation practice into a transnational one, with Indian educational brokers becoming transnational agents located in Canada providing training for IENs from around the world in order to pass Canadian entry to practice exams. This Indian intermediary reacted to the development of more stringent testing regimes – the intensification of the regime of skill – by investing in Canada and building a new institution to serve not only Indian trained nurses, but also other IENs in Canada who have to meet the demands of the IENCAP process.

Conclusion

Building upon the regime of skill concept (Shan and Fejes 2015), and Groutsis, van den Broek, and Harvey's (2015) call for greater geographical and sector analysis of intermediaries in skilled migration, this paper offers detailed analysis of occupationally specific skills, educational upgrading, bridging and testing that connects nurse training and labour markets across multiple jurisdictions. Drawing from empirical data on the international migration of nurses, the paper illustrates how hegemonic forces (CNO) construct the competency frameworks migrants must satisfy (IENCAP). This example demonstrates how intermediaries position themselves as transnational agents able to exploit the regime of skill in their effort to assist IENs to meet its demands.

Nursing is an important profession to assess through the lens of a regime of skill. Despite the desire for global standards of nursing education and regulation, nationally specific barriers to entry exist for IENs based on a range of factors, and this has important material consequences for migrants and states. Nursing, however, is an in-demand occupation globally, and several sending nations have invested in overproducing nurses so some may find opportunities overseas. In the case of India, families play an important role in directing young people toward this profession. Intermediaries understand the risk, the investment and the need to protect the young people who opt for these international migration pathways. They also understand and communicate the potential reward offered by being a 'global nurse'. They, together with the public, are well aware of the stringent regime of skill presented by a regulated profession such as nursing. The potential gains, however, mean a significant interest in international migration remains.

In the Canadian context, state policy in the form of international student migration with an option for conversion to permanent residence creates a nexus with this professional migration route. INSCOL responds to this context by creating a particular strategy for skilled migration, one that protects the individual who moves, and partners with colleges offering relevant programmes of study that can lead to credential recognition. When the regime of skill becomes more stringent, with the creation and adoption of new testing regimes such as IENCAP, the amount of time clients take to complete requirements increases. In response, the intermediary moves in to exploit the demands made by a hardened regime of skill. IENs embody skills that are created, transferred and reintegrated across a diffuse global health landscape that incorporates a range of actors with different roles and powers. Understanding the components of this landscape reveals a complex chain of actors that includes households, state and non-state educational cum migration intermediaries and professional regulators who play variable roles in the formation and enforcement of the regime of skill. The relationship between actors can be symbiotic. This suggests the hegemonic West is not the only actor involved in the formation and maintenance of the regime of skill, nor is it the only actor to benefit from its imposition.

Intermediaries are concerned with expanding their market share and providing services to an ever larger market, this motivation requires they operate transnationally and where possible, deeply integrate themselves into the process of skill construction, codification, testing and regulation. The development of such expertise embeds the intermediary more deeply into the regime of skills, while simultaneously promising to open it up for IENs who use their services. Interaction between these actors keeps the skills regime in play at any particular time, and while the distribution of power is unequal, intermediaries are not neutral or passive actors in the process. The state controls the policy pathways for migration purposes, the professional regulators control the regime of skill, including the credential evaluation and testing processes. Other actors in this network arguably react to the forces being imposed (educators and intermediaries be they in India or Canada), but in some cases they can co-construct and exploit the opportunities created by distinct regimes of skill.

Notes

1. http://www.inscol.com/canada/.
2. http://www.inscol.com/canada/about-us/overview Accessed July 30, 2019.

Disclosure statement

No potential conflict of interest was reported by the author(s).

ORCID

Margaret Walton-Roberts http://orcid.org/0000-0002-6789-5350

References

Banting, Keith G. 2010. "Is There a Progressive's Dilemma in Canada? Immigration, Multiculturalism and the Welfare State: Presidential Address to the Canadian Political Science Association, Montreal, June 2, 2010." *Canadian Journal of Political Science* 43 (4): 797–820. doi:10.1017/s0008423910000983.

Bauder, Harald. 2006. *Labor Movement: How Migration Regulates Labor Markets.* Oxford: Oxford University Press.

Bourgeault, I. L., E. Neiterman, J. LeBrun, K. Viers, and J. Winkup. 2010. *Brain Gain, Drain and Waste: The Experiences of Internationally Educated Health Professionals in Canada.* CIHR/Health Canada Research Chair in Health Human Resource. Ottawa: University of Ottawa.

Brownie, Sharon M., Lyndal H. Hunter, Salah Aqtash, and Gary E. Day. 2015. "Establishing Policy Foundations and Regulatory Systems to Enhance Nursing Practice in the United Arab Emirates." *Policy, Politics, & Nursing Practice* 16 (1–2): 38–50. doi:10.1177/1527154415583396.

Brush, Barbara L., and Julie Sochalski. 2007. "International Nurse Migration Lessons From the Philippines." *Policy, Politics, & Nursing Practice* 8 (1): 37–46. doi:10.1177/1527154407301393.

CCRNR (Canadian Council of Registered Nurse Regulators). 2013. "NCLEX Frequently Asked Questions for Canadian Educators and Students". NCSBN Examinations. CCRNR. http://www.nanb.nb.ca/media/resource/NCLEX-RNFAQsCanadians-2013-E.pdf.

Connell, John. 2010. *Migration and the Globalisation of Health Care: The Health Worker Exodus?* Cheltenham: Elgar.

Covell, Christine L., Elena Neiterman, Jelena Atanackovic, Yaw Owusu, and Ivy Lynn Bourgeault. 2019. "The Study-Migration Pathway". A Pathways to Prosperity Project. Pathways to

Prosperity. http://voiesversprosperite.ca/wp-content/blogs.dir/1/files/2015/12/Study-Migration-Pathway.pdf.

Covell, Christine L., Elena Neiterman, and Ivy Lynn Bourgeault. 2015. "Forms of Capital as Facilitators of Internationally Educated Nurses' Integration into the Registered Nursing Workforce in Canada." *Canadian Public Policy* 41 (1): S150–S161.

Cranston, Sophie, Joris Schapendonk, and Ernst Spaan. 2018. "New Directions in Exploring the Migration Industries: Introduction to Special Issue." *Journal of Ethnic and Migration Studies* 44 (4): 543–557.

Dam, Huyen, Joyce Chan, and Sarah Wayland. 2018. "Missed Opportunity: International Students in Canada Face Barriers to Permanent Residence." *Journal of International Migration and Integration* 19 (4): 891–903. doi:10.1007/s12134-018-0576-y.

Deshingkar, Priya. 2019. "The Making and Unmaking of Precarious, Ideal Subjects – Migration Brokerage in the Global South." *Journal of Ethnic and Migration Studies* 45 (14): 2638–2654. doi:10.1080/1369183X.2018.1528094.

El-Assal, Kareem. 2018. "Huge Surge in International Students Coming to Canada to Study". *Canadian Immigrant.* https://canadianimmigrant.ca/careers-and-education/international-students/studyincanada/huge-surge-in-international-students-coming-to-canada-to-study.

Gabriel, Christina. 2013. "NAFTA, Skilled Migration, and Continental Nursing Markets." *Population, Space and Place* 19 (4): 389–403. doi:10.1002/psp.1780.

George, Sheba Mariam. 2005. *When Women Come First: Gender and Class in Transnational Migration*. Berkeley: University of California Press.

Groutsis, Dimitria, Di van den Broek, and Will S. Harvey. 2015. "Transformations in Network Governance: The Case of Migration Intermediaries." *Journal of Ethnic and Migration Studies* 41 (10): 1558–1576. doi:10.1080/1369183x.2014.1003803.

Hawthorne, Lesleyanne. 2010. "How Valuable is "Two-Step Migration"? Labor Market Outcomes for International Student Migrants to Australia." *Asian and Pacific Migration Journal* 19 (1): 5–36. doi:10.1177/011719681001900102.

Hodges, Brian D. 2012. "The Shifting Discourses of Competence." In *The Question of Competence: Reconsidering Medical Education in the Twenty-First Century*, edited by Brian Hodges and Lorelei Lingard, 14–41. Ithaca, NY: Cornell University Press.

Horne, Glenn. 2011. "Canada's Policy Framework for the Utilization of Internationally Educated Nurses." *Queen's Policy Review* 2 (2): 37–53. https://www.queensu.ca/sps/qpr/sites/webpublish.queensu.ca.qprwww/files/files/15%20canadian%20foreign%20policy%20framework%20foreign%20nurses.pdf.

IOM (Institute of Medicine). 2011. *The Future of Nursing: Leading Change, Advancing Health.* Washington, DC: The National Academies Press. https://www.ncbi.nlm.nih.gov/pubmed/24983041.

Iredale, Robyn. 2005. "Gender, Immigration Policies and Accreditation: Valuing the Skills of Professional Women Migrants." *Geoforum; Journal of Physical, Human, and Regional Geosciences* 36 (2): 155–166. doi:10.1016/j.geoforum.2004.04.002.

Irudaya Rajan, S. V, J. Varghese, and M. S. Jayakumar. 2011. *Dreaming Mobility and Buying Vulnerability: Overseas Recruitment Practices in India*. Delhi: Routledge.

Kingma, Mireille. 2006. *Nurses on the Move: Migration and the Global Health Care Economy.* Ithaca, NY: Cornell University Press.

Kolawole, B. 2009. "Ontario's Internationally Educated Nurses and Waste in Human Capital." *International Nursing Review* 56 (2): 184–190. doi:10.1111/j.1466-7657.2008.00666.x.

Lindquist, Johan, Biao Xiang, and Brenda S.A. Yeoh. 2012. "Opening the Black Box of Migration: Brokers, the Organization of Transnational Mobility and the Changing Political Economy in Asia." *Pacific Affairs* 85 (1): 7–19. doi:10.5509/20128517.

Liu-Farrer, Gracia, Brenda S. Yeoh, and Michiel Baas. 2021. "Social Construction of Skill: An Analytical Approach Toward the Question of Skill in Cross-border Labour Mobilities." *Journal of Ethnic and Migration Studies* 47 (10): 2237–2251. doi:10.1080/1369183X.2020.1731983.

NNAS (National Nursing Assessment Service). 2017. *National Nursing Assessment Service (NNAS) Annual Report 2017.* NNAS. https://static1.squarespace.com/static/5303cd1de4b0c4df8d27e4ce/t/59b2b091a9db0927a1ee7ca6/1504882838063/NNAS-Booklet+for+Communication+%281%29.pdf.

OECD. 2017. "Foreign-trained Doctors and Nurses." In *Health at a Glance 2017: OECD Indicators*. Paris: OECD. doi:10.1787/health_glance-2017-59-en.

Percot, Marie. 2006. "Indian Nurses in the Gulf: Two Generations of Female Migration." *South Asia Research* 26 (1): 41–62. doi:10.1177/0262728006063198.

Polanco, Geraldine. 2017. "Culturally Tailored Workers for Specialized Destinations: Producing Filipino Migrant Subjects for Export." *Identities* 24: 62–81.

Raghuram, Parvati. 2000. "Gendering Skilled Migratory Streams: Implications for Conceptualisations of Migration." *Asian and Pacific Migration Journal* 9 (4): 429–457. doi:10.1177/011719680000900402.

Reynolds, Jaratdao, Thunthita Wisaijohn, Nareerut Pudpong, Nantiya Watthayu, Alex Dalliston, Rapeepong Suphanchaimat, Weerasak Putthasri, and Krisada Sawaengdee. 2013. "A Literature Review: The Role of the Private Sector in the Production of Nurses in India, Kenya, South Africa and Thailand." *Human Resources for Health* 11: 1. doi:10.1186/1478-4491-11-14.

Rowshan, A., and M. Singh. 2014. "A New Era on the Horizon-Challenges and Implications of the NCLEX-RN Exam in Canada." *International Journal of Nursing and Health Science* 1 (6): 46–54. http://www.openscienceonline.com/journal/ijnhs.

Salami, Bukola, S. Meherali, and C. L. Covell. 2018. "Downward Occupational Mobility of Baccalaureate-prepared, Internationally Educated Nurses to Licensed Practical Nurses." *International Nursing Review* 65 (2): 173–181.

Salt, John, and Jeremy Stein. 1997. "Migration as a Business: The Case of Trafficking." *International Migration* 35 (4): 467–494. doi:10.1111/1468-2435.00023.

Santiago, Mark Lawrence. 2013. "Spaces of Expertise and Geographies of Ethics : Health Worker Recruitment and Migration from the Philippines to Canada." PhD diss., University of British Columbia. https://open.library.ubc.ca/cIRcle/collections/ubctheses/24/items/1.0166828.

Shan, Hongxia, and Andreas Fejes. 2015. "Skill Regime in the Context of Globalization and Migration." *Studies in Continuing Education* 37 (3): 227–235. doi:10.1080/0158037x.2015.1074895.

Sweetman, Arthur, James Ted McDonald, and Lesleyanne Hawthorne. 2015. "Occupational Regulation and Foreign Qualification Recognition: An Overview." *Canadian Public Policy* 41 (Suppl. 1): S1–S13. doi:10.3138/cpp.41.s1.s1.

Tamburri, R. 2013. "Changes to Immigration Rules are a Boon to International Student Recruitment." *University Affairs*. http://www.universityaffairs.ca.

Valiani, Salimah. 2012. *Rethinking Unequal Exchange: The Global Integration of Nursing Labour Markets*. Toronto: University of Toronto Press.

van den Broek, Di, William Harvey, and Dimitria Groutsis. 2015. "Commercial Migration Intermediaries and the Segmentation of Skilled Migrant Employment." *Work, Employment and Society* 30 (3): 523–534. doi:10.1177/0950017015594969.

Walton-Roberts, Margaret. 2012. "Contextualizing the Global Nurse Care Chain: International Migration and the Status of Nursing in South India." *Global Networks* 12 (2): 175–194.

Walton-Roberts, Margaret. 2015. "The International Migration of Health Professionals and the Marketization and Privatization of Health Education in India: From Push-pull to Global Political Economy." *Social Science and Medicine* 124: 374–382.

Walton-Roberts, Margaret, Smita Bhutani, and Amandeep Kaur. 2017. "Care and Global Migration in the Nursing Profession: A North Indian Perspective." *Australian Geographer* 48 (1): 59–77.

Walton-Roberts, Margaret, and Jenna Hennebry. 2019. "Bumpy Roads: Tracing Pathways into Practice for International Students in Nursing." In *Outward and Upward Mobilities: International Students in Canada, Their Families, and Structuring Institutions*, edited by A. Kim and M. Kwak, 246–265. Toronto: University of Toronto Press.

Williams, Keegan, Gabriel Williams, Amy Arbuckle, Margaret Walton-Roberts, and Jenna Hennebry. 2015. *International Students in Ontario's Postsecondary Education System, 2000–2012: An Evaluation of Changing Policies, Populations and Labour Market Entry Processes*. Research Report for Higher Education Quality Council Ontario. http://www.heqco.ca/en-ca/Research/ResPub/Pages/International-Students-in-Ontario's-Postsecondary-Education-System-2000-2012.aspx.

Wise, Raul Delgado, and Humberto Marquez Covarrubias. 2012. "Strategic Dimensions of Neoliberal Globalization: The Exporting of Labor Force and Unequal Exchange." *Advances In Applied Sociology* 2 (2): 127–134. doi:10.4236/aasoci.2012.22017.

World Health Organization. 2017. *International Health Worker Migration: A High Level Dialogue.* PDF (Meeting Summary). World Health Organization. https://www.who.int/hrh/news/2017/high_level-dialogue-int-health-worker-migration-meeting-summary.pdf.

Yeates, Nicola. 2009. *Globalizing Care Economies and Migrant Workers.* Basingstoke: Palgrave Macmillan.

Yeates, Nicola. 2010. "The Globalization of Nurse Migration: Policy Issues and Responses." *International Labour Review* 149 (4): 423–440. doi:10.1111/j.1564-913x.2010.00096.x.

The work that brokers do: the skills, competences and know-how of intermediaries in the H-2 visa programme

Rubén Hernández-León

ABSTRACT

This article analyses the skills and competence acquisition of migration entrepreneurs in the H-2 visa programme, a U.S. temporary worker scheme. This programme, which nowadays largely recruits Mexicans, is managed by a migration industry of labour contracting agencies, recruiters, document processors, and transporters. This article focuses on recruiters, in charge of selecting workers, and document processors, responsible for completing visa application forms. Hailing mostly from the rural working class, recruiters derive expertise from membership in the social world of the migrant. The competences of document processors closely track their belonging in the urban middle class, reflecting experiences of formal education which prepare them to deal with the bureaucratic interface of the programme. These migration entrepreneurs also acquire skills by cooperating and competing with colleagues, migrants, contracting firms, employers, advocates, and government officials – interactions that expose them the risks and benefits of a more expansive role in the brokerage apparatus.

Introduction

Labour importation schemes, commonly known as temporary or migrant worker programmes, involve a panoply of intermediaries charged with the management of these systems. While state bureaucracies (i.e. labour and foreign affairs ministries, immigration bureaus) assume broad responsibility over regulation and administration, the day-to-day implementation and governance of these schemes are often devolved to private actors (Gordon 2017). Lawyers, contracting agencies, recruiters, document processors, transportation and lodging businesses and others, constitute a migration industry in charge of developing the material infrastructures and deploying the know-how that facilitates migration. As migration entrepreneurs, these private actors seek financial compensation in exchange for brokering cross-border mobility, a motivation that differs from that of state officials, who may be driven by political expediency and bureaucratic efficacy.

In this article, I analyse the skill acquisition process and development of social competences of migration entrepreneurs in the H-2 temporary worker programme, a scheme that every year brings hundreds of thousands of labourers to the United States. Despite the fact that citizens of more than 80 countries and jurisdictions can apply for an H-2 visa, nowadays the programme largely imports Mexican nationals in both of its two subcategories: the H-2A visa for agricultural labourers and the H-2B visa for non-agricultural workers. The precursor of the H-2 visa programme is the British West Indies (BWI) Temporary Alien Labor Program, created in the 1940s to import Caribbean workers for Florida's sugar cane harvest and other crops in the northeastern region of the United States. The H-2 visa category was formally introduced in the Immigration and Nationality Act of 1952 and its two subcategories were established in the Immigration Reform and Control Act of 1986 (Hahamovitch 2014; Martin 2017).

The H-2 visa programme has increased significantly in the aftermath of the Great Recession of 2007–2009, driven largely by demand of H-2A visas (agricultural workers). The decline of undocumented migration from Mexico, the ageing of the agricultural workforce, and the slow pace at which machines replace workers in the harvest, are some of the factors that account for a growing use of H-2A visas among U.S. farmers (Massey, Durand, and Pren 2015; Martin 2017). H-2B visas have also grown considerably over the past ten years. The H-2B visa has an annual quota of 66,000 workers, while the H-2A visa is uncapped. Over the years, the U.S. Congress has variably allowed for returning H-2B workers not be counted towards the annual cap. In 2017, Congress increased the H-2B limit to 81,000 but counted returning workers towards that annual cap (Fernández Campbell 2017). After granting additional increments, the number of H-2B workers was expected to reach 96,000 in 2019 (Long 2019). In Fiscal Year (FY) 2018, the U.S. Department of State issued 280,183 H-2 visas out of over 313,663 applications (U.S. Department of State 2019).[1]

Jamaicans were the preferred source of H-2 workers for about four decades until the late 1980s, when employers started to switch to Mexican labourers (Hahamovitch 2014). Over the past few years, Mexican citizens have received between 90 and 95 per cent of the H-2A visas and between 70 and 75 per cent of the H-2B visas. Despite the dominance of a single country-source, the H-2 visa programme is solely a unilateral programme of the United States that responds to its labour needs and it is not governed by a bilateral agreement with Mexico. The H-2 visa scheme stands in contrast with the Bracero Program (1942–1964), a temporary worker programme established between the United States and Mexico. As a partner of the agreement, the Mexican government sought to carry out domestic and foreign-policy goals, regulate the emigration of its citizen-workers and manage the implementation of the programme in the national territory, albeit it with limited success (Durand 1998). By comparison, the Mexican government is both formally and effectively absent from the H-2 programme. Instead, migration entrepreneurs operate unhindered throughout Mexico, substituting for the regulatory and organisational functions frequently assumed by the institutions of the sending state.

How do migration entrepreneurs who participate in the H-2 programme learn and develop the skills and competences needed to facilitate, sustain and profit from cross-border mobility? Specifically, how do cooperation and competition with each other and interaction with other social actors (i.e. migrants, consular officials, non-governmental organisations) allow migration entrepreneurs develop the know-how to operate the H-2 programme? I answer these questions by examining the careers, tasks and interactions between document processors and labour recruiters. While document processors are responsible for the seemingly trivial job of filling out forms required in the application of an H-2 visa, recruiters are in charge of identifying and selecting candidates for this temporary worker scheme. As I show below, document processors and recruiters occupy critical positions in the larger H-2 brokerage apparatus, which allow them to interact downstream with migrants, upstream with contracting companies, employers and consular officials, and laterally with colleagues (i.e. individuals who perform a similar task) and with ancillary service providers (i.e. transporters, hoteliers).

I begin by offering a theoretical framework that brings together the study of the migration industry and migration entrepreneurs, on the one hand, and research on the development of practical and hidden skills, on the other hand, in the specific context of the H-2 programme. I then move to discuss the methods of data collection for this study. In the analysis and discussion section, I present the findings of interviews with document processors, recruiters, migrant workers, U.S. consular and Mexican government officials, showing how migration entrepreneurs informally learn skills and develop the know-how to find and supply the H-2 labour force.

The skills and competences of migration entrepreneurs

Temporary labour migration schemes are devised and regulated by state institutions and bureaucracies broadly responsible for the legal frameworks and rules governing the importation of foreign workers. But on the ground, labour importation schemes are often managed by a migration industry composed of entrepreneurs who variably incentivise, facilitate and sustain cross-border mobility, extracting economic benefits (Hernández-León 2013). States legitimate the participation of migration entrepreneurs in the export and import of foreign workers through licensing and monitoring systems and devolve the day-to-day management functions to these actors, leading to varying forms of co-governance (Surak 2018; Kim 2018).[2] Migration entrepreneurs also work at the behest of employers and migrants. To employers, brokers offer the recruitment of workers, selecting, mobilising and socialising them into the expectations of the job, modulating their aspirations and monitoring their behaviour on the job. To migrants, intermediaries facilitate cross-border mobility and access to jobs (Shrestha 2018; Kim 2018).

By outsourcing these tasks to brokers, the state and employers save on recruitment costs. For example, by authorising the involvement of labour agents in the recruitment and processing of migrants, governments avoid maintaining costly state bureaucracies. Similarly, employers economise resources by relying on specialists and by hiring them only when services are needed.[3] By delegating these functions to migration entrepreneurs, both state and employers deflect legal and political responsibility on various forms of abuse and exploitation taking place during the migratory journey and at the workplace (Hernández-León 2008). In the United States, temporary staffing firms and agricultural grower associations often appear as the employer on record, assuming legal responsibility for insurance and worker's compensation in case of workplace accidents (Chauvin 2010). Ultimately, the value of contractors and other migration entrepreneurs in temporary worker schemes rests on their ability to produce a flexible labour force that can be mobilised when required and laid off when deemed unnecessary (Griffith 2015).

Commonalities aside, temporary worker programmes also vary significantly along multiple lines. These schemes differ on the level of involvement of sending states in the regulation of emigration, monitoring and reintegration of returnees, interventions frequently arranged through bilateral agreements with the governments of destination countries (Xiang and Lindquist 2014). These programmes also diverge in terms of the mix of public and private actors running them and the formal rules and gender ideologies that produce flows alternatively dominated by either men or women (Goss and Lindquist 2000; Silvey and Parreñas 2019; Durand 1998; Hellio 2013). Contract worker programmes also vary on the prevalence of deception and participation of predatory and criminal actors, who participate in the control and extraction of additional rent from workers, often with the acquiescence of governments and employers (Goss and Lindquist 2000; Muñoz, Sandoval, and Hernández-León 2018; Perrotta and Sacchetto 2012).

This article contributes to the growing body of studies analysing the work migration entrepreneurs do for the day-to-day management of temporary worker programmes and the skills, know-how and competences they develop to proficiently create and mobilise a migrant labour force across borders (Lindquist 2012; Chee, Yeoh, and Vu 2012; Shrestha 2018). I use a total human capital perspective to understand how migration entrepreneurs 'acquire, transfer and apply ... skills, competences and knowledge,' including 'working knowledge and technical skills learned through observation and interaction' (Hagan, Hernández-León, and Demonsant 2015, 9), which allow them to engage not only in the profit-driven facilitation of cross-border mobility but also in the long term regeneration of the temporary worker scheme as a migration infrastructure (Shrestha 2019). Inspired in the study of hidden and devalued work, the total human capital approach focuses on making visible skills and competences developed in non-formal settings, through on- and off-the job learning, by means of cooperation and other forms of interactive labour (Star and Strauss 1999; Hagan, Hernández-León, and Demonsant 2015). I apply this perspective to understand and make visible the 'labour involved in managing, facilitating and controlling migration' (Cranston, Schapendonk, and Spaan 2018, 544).

I identify skill sets as those that enable brokers to (1) engage the state and the bureaucratic regulations of migration, and (2) connect with migrants, shape their aspirations and instrumentalise their ties to other migrants; and as competences derived from (3) competition and collaboration with fellow intermediaries and other actors in the brokerage structure. The first two sets of skills closely track the social class background of migration entrepreneurs and often remain latent until they are activated in the context of brokerage; the third set references how intermediaries develop know-how by competing and cooperating with others and by turning knowledge about the process of migration into profit-seeking facilitation. This third skill set is also derived both from tasks that are intrinsic to the role of broker (i.e. connecting two or more parties) and from competences acquired elsewhere in the structure of intermediation and mobilised in the context of role transitions (i.e. shifting from advocacy and protection work to for-profit facilitation) (Stovel and Shaw 2012).

In his studies of the *padrone* (labour broker) in the context of Italian migration to the Americas, historian Robert Harney identified the middle classes, at home and destination, as the brokers of transatlantic migration. These members of the middle classes 'specialised in performing as brokers between labour and capital, as transmitters of remittances and pre-paid tickets, and as steamship agents, while engaging, because the migrants' dependence of them, in many other businesses' (Harney 1979, 73). Holding middle-class occupations, these brokers possessed a vital and, at the time, relatively scarce skill: literacy and, in some instances, biliteracy (the ability to read and write in two languages). According to Harney, 'literacy was a form of capital and the basis of the brokerage system itself.' Specifically, 'it was their ability to correspond and communicate with the American employer which made padroni powerful' (1979, 73–74). Today, distinct forms of literacy become valorised in the migration industry apparatus that mediates temporary worker programmes, particularly the broker's expertise in the 'economy and micro-politics of documentation' (Lindquist 2012, 88), which include the procurement of documents, completion of forms, handling changing procedures, and dealing with government officials. While these competences are often learned on the job, they also stem from the educational experiences of the middle class.

Scholars have also identified the experience of migration as a source of broker competences. Embedded in strong and weak networks connecting them to fellow sojourners and to employers, migrants valorise trust and social capital to become migration entrepreneurs. The skills, know-how and cultural competences migrants use to assume the role of brokers arise from the embodied experience of cross-border sojourning and, above all, from a deep understanding of the migrants' social world (Lindquist 2012; Chee, Yeoh, and Vu 2012; Hernández-León 2008). Migrants often start careers as migration entrepreneurs when their employers assign them the task of recruiting new workers (Waldinger and Lichter 2003; Krissman 2005). This is the case of many farm labour contractors (FLCs) in the United States, who replenish the ranks of the agricultural labour force by recruiting co-ethnics, earning the pejorative name of 'graduated farm workers.' Their most prised skill is their ability to deal with fellow migrants (Krissman 2000).

Migration entrepreneurs of different social origins do not operate in isolation. They come together in the brokerage structure's own division of labour and the broader field of actors facilitating international migration (Krissman 2005; Hernández-León 2013). Brokers learn and develop additional skills by interacting with other service providers, representatives of the state, employers, migrant and migrant advocates in relations of competition and cooperation. It is through these interactions that, for example, migration entrepreneurs become exposed to new opportunities to expand their operations and learn about changing regulations (Chee, Yeoh, and Vu 2012).

In the context of guest-worker schemes, it is not uncommon for government regulators, consular officials and NGO staffers, to 'shift roles and mobilise previously acquired knowledge to become migration entrepreneurs' (Hernández-León 2013, 34; Krissman 2005; Kim 2018; Lindquist 2012). Advocates and government officials also learn and develop migration-facilitating skills and know-how '[which] can then be translated into actionable knowledge to establish different kinds of migration-related businesses' (Hernández-León 2013, 35). These actors cultivate these competences through formal and informal learning processes but come to know about money-making opportunities by interacting with sojourners, employers and migration entrepreneurs in the field of migration facilitation.

In sum, brokerage requires that migration entrepreneurs deploy skills and know-how to efficiently and effectively do their jobs. Some of these competences are acquired formally and informally in contexts pegged to the class origin of the broker but others result from on-the-job learning, and through competition and collaboration with other brokers and stakeholders of the process of international labour recruitment.

Methods

The site of this study is the city of Monterrey in northeastern Mexico, where thousands of workers arrive every week to apply for an H-2 visa at the local U.S. consulate. In FY 2019, this consulate handled almost 68 per cent of the 260,546 H-2 visas issued in Mexico (U.S. Department of State 2019). This consular office processes as many as 2,000 H-2 visas applications in a day, explaining why Monterrey is a major hub of the temporary worker migration industry, boasting a concentration of contracting agencies, recruiters, document processors, transportation companies and other migration entrepreneurs. While Monterrey is the most important hub of the H-2 migration industry in Mexico, document processors and recruiters search and enlist workers throughout the country and apply for the actual visa at a U.S. consular representation convenient to them. For example, the border city of Nuevo Laredo, some 136 miles north of Monterrey, hosts another U.S. consulate where large numbers of H-2 visa applications are processed. At times, the H-2 team at the Monterrey consulate diverts visa applications to the consular site in Nuevo Laredo when too many requests overwhelm its capacity.

The process of recruiting H-2 visa workers actually starts when U.S. employers interested in hiring foreign labourers submit a job order to the state workforce agency (SWA) to demonstrate their effort to first employ domestic workers and then file a labour certification with the Department of Labor (DOL). After receiving certification from the DOL, an application is made to the Department of Homeland Security to import foreign workers (Rousmaniere 2013). Although some firms might complete these steps on their own and recruit new hires tapping into the networks of current employees, many resort to lawyers and labour contracting agencies specialised in the H-2 visa process. Labour contracting agencies work simultaneously with document processors and recruiters based in Mexico.

The final phase of the visa application process lasts three-to-four days and begins when, shortly after arriving in Monterrey, applicants line up outside the offices of document processors scattered in the city centre to complete forms. Then, a photo and biometric information (i.e. fingerprints) are taken at a large processing centre (Applicant Service Centre or CAS for its initials in Spanish) subcontracted by the U.S. government. Meanwhile, recruiters and visa processors, acting as representatives of the applicants, take passports and forms to the U.S. consulate. There, a team of about 12 consular officials and staffers, exclusively dedicated to processing H-2 visas, checks documents and conducts interviews with prospective temporary workers. Once approved, successful applicants receive their passports stamped with the H-2 visa, and within a few hours, board buses and vans destined for myriad workplaces north of the border.

This article draws from qualitative and ethnographic data primarily collected in this city, between 2013 and 2019, where a team of researchers and I conducted interviews with document processors, recruiters, representatives of contracting agencies, transportation companies, hotels and shelters, street vendors, migrants and migrant advocates, and U.S. consular and Mexican government officials. The large number of businesses created around the recruitment of H-2 visa workers has produced an urban economic enclave in Monterrey with several city blocks concentrating on these services. The research team also observed aspects of the recruitment process that unfold during the time migrants spend in this city, specifically the work and interactions that take place at document processing agencies. We followed the activities of 10 of the approximately 20 document processors that operate in the city; several of these processors and three recruiters they work with were interviewed multiple times following an unstructured protocol. A member of the research team conducted a brief stint of participant observation at a document processor's office, helping fill out forms, and also conducted fieldwork in a community of origin in north-central Mexico and in two companies in hire H-2 workers in Louisiana, for the sugar cane harvest, and Indiana, for melon and vegetable-picking (Muñoz 2016). In addition to primary qualitative data, I use quantitative data from the U.S. government, official documents that describe the H-2 programme, reports of advocacy organisations analysing various forms of abuse and newspaper articles informing of changes in the programme.

Breaking into the world of recruiters and document processors in Monterrey is no easy feat. These migration entrepreneurs operate in a grey area, constantly crossing the blurry lines of formality and informality, legality and illegality and, not surprisingly, are suspicious of outsiders. While labour brokerage is seen as a legitimate practice by many of the actors involved in the H-2 visa programme, this activity often involves obfuscated exchanges, deception, and resistance to government regulation. When first approached, document processors and recruiters negate that they perform brokerage functions or simply deny access to researchers. These brokers also compete intensely with each other and fear that their clients – contracting firms and migrants – will be taken from them should they divulge information about contacts and business strategies.

Gaining the trust of intermediaries took a long time and demanded an extended presence at the site, requiring a kind of low-intensity fieldwork, instead of a concentrated period of data collection. This extended engagement allowed the observation of new modalities of worker recruitment, such as the use of Facebook and other social media, tools that potentially circumvent established recruitment practices (see below). Given these circumstances, I have decided to omit gender and approximate age, among of other characteristics, when quoting most informants, sacrificing some ethnographic texture and specificity. Various gaps in knowledge remain, such as exactly how much profit different intermediaries extract from enrolling labourers in the programme. This has to do with the fact that some brokers pass onto the worker recruitment costs that are supposed to be covered (or at least reimbursed) by employers, such as the cost of the visa.

Consistent with studies that seek to uncover hidden forms of labour (Star and Strauss 1999), I identify and analyse inductively the skills, competences and practices of brokers, exposing how their know-how is developed partly on the basis of their social background, cultivated on the job, and derived from interactions with other actors of the brokerage structure.

Analysis and discussion

The work that document processors and recruiters do

This article focuses on document processors and recruiters, two actors of the system of recruitment of H-2 visa workers. Although in principle these brokers perform different tasks in the recruitment apparatus, as I show below, the roles blur and blend as each actor potentially takes on a more expansive set of tasks in the structure. Recruiters are the frontline migration entrepreneurs in charge of identifying, selecting and mobilising H-2 visa workers, often working-class men who hail from rural areas in Mexico and have experience migrating to the United States; their expertise is intertwined with their sociability and networks.[4] For example, a recruiter interviewed for this study is a former undocumented migrant from Central Mexico who used to work for a relative and farm labour contractor in the United States before being detained and deported by immigration authorities. This recruiter works exclusively on the Mexican-side of the operation and enlists H-2s for different U.S. labour contractors and a large visa-processing firm, depending on the season. Another recruiter interviewed is a third-generation farm labour contractor. Although this person pursued university education in Monterrey, he sports a cowboy look and remains connected to the region where his family is from and where he finds new workers.

Recruiters use their familiarity with migrants and their social world to create and shape the labour force employers seek. In order to do so, recruiters function as information brokers, disseminating the availability of H-2 jobs but also acting as gatekeepers to the programme. They also have to informally assess the personality, labour skills, and social background of the candidate, becoming what the authors of the introduction to this special issue call, 'arbitrators of skill' (Liu-Farrer, Yeoh, and Baas 2021). As they do in temporary worker programmes elsewhere (Lindquist 2012; Shrestha 2019), recruiters mould the aspirations of migrants, explaining that an H-2 visa is, as a third-generation farm labour contractor put it, 'an opportunity for the workers and their families to improve their lives.' Recruiters purposefully travel to regions of Mexico with low levels of outmigration with the objective of getting workers with minimal social capital in the United States, who are therefore disinclined to abscond from the programme. However, recruiters also enlist labourers from regions with a long history of both legal and undocumented migration and veritable diasporas in the United States. The aspirational work recruiters perform with these migrants with extensive social capital abroad involves convincing them, as a visa processor who also recruits workers stated, that 'it is better to return [to Mexico] and then be able to go back to the United States, instead of staying there [without authorisation].'

In principle, document processors occupy a circumscribed position in the H-2 visa recruitment apparatus. Their main task is to fill out a DS-160 non-immigrant visa application, for each person. The form prompts the applicant to provide detailed biographical and family data, travel plans and companion information,[5] record of prior visas and previous stays in the United States, and education and employment history in the home country. The form also includes questions about health, social and political affiliations and criminal background of the applicant and immediate family members. Processors also collate the documents required in the visa application and, at times, represent the employers vis-à-vis consular authorities.

The main task of document processors is to comply with the formal bureaucratic requirements of the H-2 visa application and stay abreast of its changing regulations. While document processors are not a homogeneous category, many are women with middle-class origins and high school or college diplomas. The careers of these migration entrepreneurs often begin elsewhere in the brokerage apparatus, as government officials and advocates. In these jobs, they acquire skills and competences that they later convert into actionable knowledge to launch careers as migration entrepreneurs (Hernández-

León 2013). For example, a former staffer at the H-2 visa section at the U.S. consulate in Monterrey established a document processing service after quitting their post but not before spending some time at a state government agency overseeing migrant rights. Working at these posts – especially with the consular team in charge of H-2 visas – offered exposure to discrete skills but also broad knowledge about how the programme works and how the U.S. government oversees it. In a different case, a former representative of an NGO advocating for the rights of guest workers, a job in which they helped with H-2 visa applications (free of charge), established a small firm to process different types of visas. Tellingly, the advertisement of their 'personalised advisory' services included a legend that appeared to count the years spent at the non-profit organisation: 'Ten years of experience are behind us.'

Document processors vary drastically according to the size of the operation. Some processors function as a one-person entity, handling a few hundred applications annually, while others, providing services to large U.S.-based contracting and temporary labour agencies, are staffed with a dozen employees and process as many as 10,000 cases per year. Furthermore, large contracting agencies with presence in multiple cities in Mexico do not outsource document processing, conducting this step of the process internally. These companies still rely on recruiters who bring workers to processing offices throughout the country.[6]

Recruiters and document processors are recognised by U.S. consular authorities as representatives of the employers and can legally charge them fees for finding workers. But many recruiters also extract money from applicants as a condition to include them on their lists. According to U.S. regulations of the H-2 programme, these fees are illegal and, if consular officials find out, they can revoke the petition for visas. However, recruiters often coach applicants so that they say as little as possible during the interviews with consular staff.[7] Workers have very little to gain and much to lose by denouncing these illegal charges, including mistreatment by U.S. employers, because a revocation (even if it is first initiated to investigate a complaint) freezes the visa application process and cancels the opportunity of obtaining a job abroad. Both recruiters and document processors work with H-2 applicants to decide whether to reveal a prior undocumented stay in the United States. At times, brokers urge workers not to reveal information about prior unauthorised sojourns during the interview with consular officials. But they also 'play the honesty card,' as a document processor put it, volunteering evidence of earlier undocumented presence, especially when the applicant has had a recorded encounter with law enforcement officials, and hoping that the consular officer will file an administrative pardon on behalf of the worker.

In Mexico, contracting agencies, recruiters and document processors are nominally regulated by the federal labour code but, due to the weak infrastructural power of the state, the corresponding government institutions (i.e. the secretaries of labour, treasury and interior) do not exercise any effective oversight of their activities. This regulatory vacuum adds to the fragmented and opaque nature of the recruitment system, opening numerous opportunities for fraud and creating an economy of deception. Every few months, news outlets inform of massive fraud schemes committed by pseudo recruiters who promise visas and jobs, collect fees, summon workers to Monterrey (to process their documents) where they ask for more money, only to disappear and leave their victims stranded and owing money to loan sharks (Muñoz, Sandoval, and Hernández-León 2018).

Learning skills through interaction, cooperation and competition

Document processors and recruiters also acquire skills and competences through the interactions and relations of cooperation and competition they sustain with each other and with other migration entrepreneurs (i.e. transporters), with migrants, migrant advocates and government functionaries, particularly U.S. consular officials. These brokers use these interactions to obtain vital information not only to successfully run their businesses but also to shield their operations from risks that come from intermediation and to learn about opportunities to increase profit.

Learning from migrants and from fellow brokers

Although U.S. companies and contracting agencies are the clients paying for the services of document processors and recruiters, these migration entrepreneurs deliver these services interacting with migrants and with fellow brokers. Recruiters and document processors sustain a distinctly intense interaction as both need to coordinate the workers' arrival in Monterrey, the visa application process and subsequent departure close to the date workers are needed in the United States. A document processor's office actually functions as the de facto headquarters of the recruiter while in Monterrey, and therefore as the locale where these two actors solve any problems arising during the visa application process.

It is through these interactions that document processors learn about the pitfalls and advantages of expanding and offering recruitment services downstream. Some document processors interviewed in Monterrey characterised recruitment as a 'thorny affair' and 'a trap' because any mistake could get them in trouble with U.S. consular officials who, in turn, could veto them from bringing workers to the consulate and in, extreme circumstances, cancel their U.S. visa. These document processors also saw recruitment as an inherently precarious endeavour because of workers who jump their contracts, abandon their jobs and leave employers angry at untrustworthy recruiters.[8] These document processors viewed the entire recruitment scheme as a 'corrupt system' and 'necessary evil' that guarantees legal access to a temporary job in the United States but that includes malfeasance on the part of various actors, such as migrants who charge friends and relatives for referring them to a recruiter and employers who, in turn, try to recoup visa-processing expenses from their workers. This ambivalence pointedly reflects what scholars have called the broker's dilemma: while brokerage offers financial and status gains to those who perform this role, it also entails risks that might translate into the loss of trust of one or more parties (Stovel and Shaw 2012). Sensing the perils of a more expansive role in the brokerage structure, these 'risk averse' document processors stay within the confines of their position and turn down opportunities to expand their services to become recruiters.

Other document processors, however, choose to expand and include recruitment as part of their menu of services.[9] By becoming recruiters, document processors can charge contracting agencies fees for finding workers *and* for assisting with their visa applications.[10] This opportunity not only requires tolerance to risk but also necessitates a different set of skills and social competences. Document processors need to venture from the world of the office and respective clerical skills to the world of migrants, their communities of origin and local labour markets, blurring the boundaries between these two types of brokerage. Because the H-2 programme requires a minimum of experience in the job for which the temporary worker is hired, document processors-turned recruiters need to canvas local economies in Mexico that provide labourers with such characteristics. In their new capacity, these brokers need to develop knowledge about Mexico's economic geography, labour markets and the skills associated with particular occupations.

Document processors who double as recruiters also hone social competences to assess an individual's skills, experience and general trustworthiness. A document processor whose sole task is to complete forms has a limited interaction with the applicant but a recruiter sustains a prolonged and potentially multidimensional relationship with the worker, especially if the individual is requested by the employer year after year.[11] Recruiters operate in a segment of the labour market in which resumes and diplomas are not the means to determine ability. Instead, they rely on referrals using the networks of current employees, various forms of mass regional advertisement and interviews they conduct in communities of origin.[12] As one recruiter put it, 'even a handshake can tell you about a person.'

These means of finding and selecting H-2 applicants (i.e. networks and word of mouth) not only serve recruiters but also empower workers.[13] Document processors and recruiters learn that the way they treat workers during the recruitment process is shared with contacts downstream, with friends and family members, and upstream, with employers in the United States. Workers who feel either cheated (e.g. charged high or illegal fees) or mistreated (e.g. housed in dilapidated hotels, transported in substandard buses) during the recruitment process can complain to employers, who in turn might break the relationship with their service providers and find new ones. Some document processors described long term relationships with workers who stayed with them even when lawyers, contracting agencies or recruiters had been replaced by the employer. It is likely that this dynamic affects particularly small and medium-sized document processors and recruiters who process a relatively low number of visas and who depend on referrals by both workers and employers. Because of their size and dependence on 'good reviews,' small operations try to place H-2 applicants in good hotels, transport them in clean and reliable vehicles and minimise their exposure to predatory intermediaries (e.g. taxi services charging exorbitant fares for a ride to the consulate).[14]

While the referral system is an efficient way to identify H-2 candidates, it turns some workers into for-profit intermediaries, creating problems for established brokers. Several document processors and recruiters relayed multiple cases of workers who charge friends and family members for referring or including them on a list they would later hand in to a broker. Intermediaries are not always aware that the workers they recruit are charging other workers and if news of these proscribed fees reach consular authorities, brokers and employers can be penalised and asked to remedy the harm by reimbursing the workers. In response, document processors and recruiters reengineer their workforce by shedding veterans and enlisting new workers – incidentally, the least informed about wages and conditions. As mentioned above, document processors who used to recruit directly, are now using Facebook to find and screen new labourers, eliminating the use of referrals. These practices also reflect the tensions and contradictions of the recruitment of temporary workers. The ideal labourer is a novice who is dependent on brokers and employers and willing to passively accept the terms of the contract. Instead, many of the actual workers are veterans who have accumulated information about wages, labour conditions and even the possibility of extracting rent from other workers.[15]

Through their interactions with workers, document processors and recruiters also learn about additional opportunities to profit from the labourers' travels in and out of Monterrey and the lodging services they need in this city. Although some of these services are arranged by contracting agencies, document processors and recruiters can also partner with hotels and transportation companies to take workers to the United States after their visas are approved, offering commissions and additional revenue streams (Hernández-León and Sandoval Hernández 2017).

Document processors and recruiters also learn from each other. Document processors interviewed in Monterrey, in particular, reported receiving support from colleagues, sharing office space and other resources, particularly during critical times: when the online system stopped working and when the demand for visas outstripped anyone's capacity to process them. Of course, subordinates working at document processing firms learn the ropes from owners and supervisors, completing forms, talking to workers, driving them to the consulate and coordinating various moments of the visa application process. However, this cooperation is overshadowed by a prevailing narrative of competition, rivalry and mistrust. Document processors gossip about each other's activities and reputations but also fear that sharing too much information will lead to losing clients to another firm. For example, sharing with others how much they charge per visa processed might give a competitor an opportunity to offer a contracting agency, law firm or employer a lower bid. This sense of intense competition is exacerbated by the fact that while some document processors work for a single large contracting agency, most have to process visas for multiple clients.

Intense competition and mistrust extend to subordinates. As explained above, owners fear that these subordinates might leave them and establish their own operations or extract money from workers without the knowledge of the document processor. For instance, a processor I interviewed in Monterrey had just fired a driver who was taking workers to the consulate without the approval of his boss. Not long after letting him go, the owner found that he had already started working for another visa processing agency located in one of the migrant hotels. In another case, a document processor who used to own a contracting agency in Texas, parted ways with a long-time assistant when he found out that the aid was charging recruitment fees to workers.

Learning from employers, contracting agencies and consular officials

Upstream, document processors and recruiters interact primarily with consular officials, contracting agencies and less frequently with employers.[16] As mentioned above, document processors and recruiters act as the employer's representative in the visa application process at the U.S. consulate. Exposure of abuse or irregularities during the interview that consular officials conduct with individual workers can have dire consequences for these migration entrepreneurs, from revocation of the employment petition, to the vetoing of the broker, to the cancellation of the agent's U.S. visa. Any of these actions can severely hamper the ability of these agents to offer services to contracting agencies, law firms and employers, and eventually put them out of business.[17] To minimise exposure, recruiters coach workers on volunteering as little information as possible during the interview with consular staffers, often invoking gender norms of manliness and toughness. For example, before travelling to Monterrey, a recruiter operating in central Mexico summoned workers and admonished them to 'behave like men' during the interview.[18] Consular authorities in Monterrey have recently created a registry of agents, have begun to conduct visits to the offices of brokers, and have organised information sessions with firms that process H-2 workers. These are monitoring mechanisms that extend the regulatory capacity of state authorities over these intermediaries but that also provide opportunities for migration entrepreneurs to interact with consular officials, with each other, and to learn about best practices and potential pitfalls.

It is important to restate here that these migration entrepreneurs, from the contracting agency to the document processor to the recruiter, help realise the employers' demand for temporary workers. However, this mandate is not just about finding a certain number of labourers; it is also about selecting workers with distinct characteristics. As previously discussed, document processors and recruiters select workers for skill. Recruiters also use gender as part of this selection process. For example, women are recruited to work as crab pickers (removing the meat from the crab's shell), to cook for agricultural labourers,[19] and to clean rooms in hotels. In contrast, men are recruited for all sorts of agricultural work, from apple and orange picking to cutting and drying tobacco leaves, and tree-planting, construction and landscaping jobs (with the H-2B visa).

Document processors and recruiters learn from employers (via the contracting agencies in some instances) that ranchers prefer workers from parts of Mexico without a long history of migration to the United States. In the words of a document processor-turned recruiter, 'the bosses don't want people from Jalisco [in Mexico's historic region of migration] because [these workers] make trouble, are lazy and leave their jobs.' Workers from high areas of emigration have a long history of labouring in the United States and have extensive social networks. If they experience abusive conditions and significant downtime, which is not paid, these workers can abandon their jobs and turn on their networks to find alternatives (Griffith 2005).[20] The strategies of brokers include searching for labourers in new areas of emigration, such as the heavily indigenous state of Chiapas in southern Mexico and Tlaxcala in the southcentral part of the country. As a recruiter I interviewed twice stated, workers from Chiapas 'are needier [than people from other states], have fewer resources and prefer to go back and forth [instead of staying in the United States].'

At the behest of employers, recruiters also seek to weaken solidarity and collective resistance among workers by mixing H-2 applicants from different places of origin, 'so that they don't know each other,' as an interviewee put it. The recruiter in question went on to explain that, 'if the group functions well, we call the [same] workers again the following year.' As previous studies have shown, these migration entrepreneurs commonly carry out the mandate of employers of culling groups of workers by not calling some of labourers again and even blacklisting individuals deemed to be 'trouble makers' (Griffith 2005). These practices extend to workers who have suffered accidents, have become ill on the job and who, as stated by one of my interviewees, are perceived as 'not working as hard as the others.'[21] These strategies speak to the fundamental tasks of selecting, filtering and controlling workers, which brokers execute for the broader system of recruitment.

Conclusion

The work document processors and recruiters do as part of the H-2 brokerage apparatus requires different skill sets and social competences. In this article, I take a total human capital perspective to examine how these two types of migration entrepreneurs acquire skills and develop the know-how to perform vital tasks in the H-2 visa programme – find guest workers and deal with the bureaucratic requirements of the visa application. Consistent with the studies that track the origins and careers of brokers, the document processors and recruiters analysed in this article derive skills and know-how from their social class experiences (Lindquist 2012; Shrestha 2019; Krissman 2000). Hailing from the urban middle classes and exposed to formal education, document processors are well prepared to deal with the bureaucratic interface of a temporary worker programme: completing forms, keeping up with new regulations and interacting with consular officials. In contrast, recruiters derive skills and know-how from close exposure and participation in the social world of the migrant. While these migration entrepreneurs hone skills informally, on the job, it is not uncommon for some of them to first learn about the intricacies of the H-2 programme performing advocacy and regulatory functions, to then valorise this knowledge in the context of profit-seeking ventures.

Document processors and recruiters also learn and develop crucial social competences through their relations with other actors of the brokerage apparatus, including other migration entrepreneurs (e.g. contracting agencies, lawyers), employers, migrants, migrant advocates and consular officials. These interactions entail varying forms of cooperation, competition and even exploitation that can be mined for profit, each bringing opportunity but also peril. From their interactions with migrants, downstream, document processors, in particular, learn about opportunities to go beyond the processing of visas and become recruiters themselves. As document processors-turned recruiters, these migration entrepreneurs assume a more expansive role in the brokerage structure, finding, selecting and filtering workers while shepherding them through the visa application process, and delivering them to contracting agencies and employers in the United States. While a more expansive role offers the chance to increase profits, it potentially entangles document processors in exploitative relations with migrant workers and, if complaints are filed, exposes them to inquiries and sanctions on the part of consular authorities. Becoming a recruiter entails risks that not all document processors are willing to assume.

From their nexus upstream, document processors and recruiters learn about the demands of employers and contracting agencies to forge a pliable workforce of labourers with skills and prior experience, who perform according to the expectations, do not abandon their jobs, return to Mexico at the end of their contracts and who are willing to return to the United States the following season. In order to form this workforce, recruiters canvas the country's regions and, as a result, learn about its economic geography and labour markets. But to comply with the desires of employers, these migration entrepreneurs might also select candidates from localities and states without a deep history of cross-border migration, with limited social networks and minimal capacity to counter abuse.

Finally, document processors and recruiters acquire skills by interacting with other migration entrepreneurs in dense relations of cooperation and competition. Some visa processors begin their careers as aids or employees, learning the intricacies of this occupation from established colleagues. But the possibility that subordinates set up their own visa processing firm, taking away valuable deals with employers and contracting agencies casts an aura of tension and mistrust over relations with others in the field. Similarly, the possibility of document processors underbidding each other ends up emphasising a narrative of competition over one of collaboration. Clearly, brokering cross-border mobility offers opportunities for profit. However, such opportunities are only realised through a complex and fractious learning process in which visa processors and recruiters, two distinct kinds of migration entrepreneurs, interact, cooperate and compete with multiples actors of the social process of international migration.

Notes

1. These numbers represent an approval rate of 89.3 per cent. A U.S. fiscal year goes from 1 October of the previous calendar year (2017) to 30 September of the year of reference (2018).
2. Some states temporarily absorb this migration industry, turning it a branch of the government, only to reprivatize it later on (see Siracusa and Acacio 2004).
3. Employers often pass on to workers the cost of recruitment, recouping from them the fees paid to brokers and to government agencies (see Silvey and Parreñas 2019).
4. Recruiters do not constitute a homogeneous category; some are, in fact, women of varied social class backgrounds (see Griffith 2015).
5. Even though H-2 workers are allowed to bring families using an H-4 visa, recruiters rarely inform migrants of this opportunity. Occasionally, employers consent to workers laboring in year-round supervisory positions to bring in families with the H-4 visa.
6. These variations reflect the diverse paths of H-2 worker recruitment (Muñoz 2016).
7. Some recruiters and document processors ask workers to sign a paper stating that they have not been charged any fees in Mexico.
8. Some employers have workers pay the cost of recruitment (e.g. visa processing, transportation) upfront as a way to make them stay for the duration of the contract and then reimburse them at the end.
9. These brokers have larger operations, allowing for an internal division of labour with part of the staff undertaking recruitment and part remaining as document processors.
10. Some recruiters try to expand upstream by becoming document processors and capturing the fees associated with completing forms. This creates tensions between these two types brokers, given that this course of action displaces document processors with whom recruiters collaborate.
11. Conducting fieldwork in Monterrey, I encountered workers who had laboured in the United States with an H-2 visa for more than 20 years.
12. These recruitment strategies have led some communities of origin to specialise in sending H-2 temporary workers abroad.
13. Workers are also consumers of brokerage and mobility services (Harney 1979). Seizing on this notion, advocacy organisations have launched websites where workers can evaluate brokers. See Contratados.org, by the Centro de los Derechos del Migrante.
14. To be sure, improved recruitment conditions do not necessarily translate into good workplace conditions in the United States.
15. On the imaginaries recruiters and employers construct of the ideal worker, see Shubin, Findlay, and McCollum (2014) and Hellio (2013).
16. Some document processors explained that they do not have any contact with employers.
17. During the interview, consular officials check various data sets to verify that the applicant has not crossed into the United States or worked in the country without authorisation. This information can be used by U.S. authorities to deny the visa.
18. This interaction was observed by a member of the research team (see Muñoz 2016).

19. As per my interviews with recruiters and migrant women in Monterrey, this appears to be done informally. Women are processed as H-2A visas workers to labour in agriculture but, in reality, they are brought with groups of men to cook and clean at dormitories and camps.
20. Some H-2 candidates from traditional sending states in Mexico have conducted prior undocumented sojourns to the United States but hide these experiences from intermediaries. If these unauthorised stays are flagged by consular authorities and the visa is denied, the broker loses time and money, while scrambling to replace the workers whose applications were turned down.
21. Migrant advocates fight these practices and have established agreements with large contracting agencies so that these workers are not excluded from future calls (Hernández-León and Sandoval Hernández 2017).

Disclosure statement

No potential conflict of interest was reported by the author(s).

References

Chauvin, Sébastien. 2010. *Les Agencies de la Précarité. Journaliers à Chicago*. Paris: Le Seuil.

Chee, Heng Leng, Brenda S.A. Yeoh, and Thi Kieu Dung Vu. 2012. "From Client to Matchmaker: Social Capital in the Making of Commercial Matchmaking in Malaysia." *Pacific Affairs* 85 (1): 91–115.

Cranston, Sophie, Joris Schapendonk, and Ernst Spaan. 2018. "New Directions in Exploring the Migration Industries: Introduction to Special Issue." *Journal of Ethnic and Migration Studies* 44 (4): 543–557.

Durand, Jorge. 1998. *Política, Modelos y Patrón Migratorios. El Trabajo y los Trabajadores Mexicanos en Estados Unidos*. San Luis Potosí: El Colegio de San Luis.

Fernández Campbell, Alexia. 2017. "Trump Lifted the Cap on H-2B Worker Visas. Then His Businesses Asked for 76 of Them." *Vox*. https://www.vox.com/policy-and-politics/2017/7/20/16003254/trump-h2b-visa-program.

Gordon, Jennifer. 2017. "Regulating the Human Supply Chain." *Iowa Law Review* 102 (2): 445–504.

Goss, Jon, and Bruce Lindquist. 2000. "Placing Movers: An Overview of the Asian-Pacific Migration System." *The Contemporary Pacific* 12 (2): 385–414.

Griffith, David C. 2005. "Rural Industry and Mexican Immigration and Settlement in North Carolina." In *New Destinations: Mexican Immigration in the United States*, edited by V. Zúñiga and R. Hernández-León, 50–75. New York: Russell Sage Foundation.

Griffith, David C. 2015. "Labor Contractors, Coyotes and Travelers: The Migration Industry in Latin America and the U.S. South." *Eutopía* 9: 115–125.

Hagan, Jacqueline M., Rubén Hernández-León, and Jean-Luc Demonsant. 2015. *Skills of the 'Unskilled': Work and Mobility among Mexican Immigrants*. Berkeley: University of California Press.

Hahamovitch, Cindy. 2014. "'Risk the Truck': Guestworker-Sending States and the Myth of Managed Migration." In *Mismanaging Migration: Guestworkers' Experiences with North American Labor Markets*, edited by D. C. Griffith, 3–32. Santa Fe, NM: School for Advanced Research Press.

Harney, Robert F. 1979. "Montreal's King of Italian Labour: A Case Study of Padronism." *Labour/Le Travail.* 4: 57–84.

Hellio, Emmanuelle. 2013. "We Don't Have Women in Boxes: Channelling Seasonal Mobility of Female Farmworkers Between Morocco and Andalusia." In *Seasonal Workers in Mediterranean Agriculture. The Social Cost of Eating Fresh*, edited by J. Gertel and S. R. Sippel, 141–157. London: Routledge.

Hernández-León, Rubén. 2008. *Metropolitan Migrants: The Migration of Urban Mexicans to the United States*. Berkeley: University of California Press.
Hernández-León, Rubén. 2013. "Conceptualizing the Migration Industry." In *The Migration Industry and the Commercialization of International Migration*, edited by T. Gammeltoft-Hansen and N. Nyberg Sorensen, 25–45. London: Routledge.
Hernández-León, Rubén, and Efrén Sandoval Hernández. 2017. "El Reclutamiento de Trabajadores Temporales Mexicanos Para Estados Unidos: Infraestructura Burocrática, Industria de la Migración y Economía del Engaño en el Programa de Visas H-2." In *Migración Internacional, Interna y en Tránsito. Nuevos Actores, Procesos y Retos. Vol. I: Nuevos Procesos en la Migración Internacional y Mercados de Trabajo*, edited by M. Barros Nock and A. Latapí, 184–208. Mexico City: CIESAS.
Kim, Jaeeun. 2018. "Migration-Facilitating Capital: A Bourdeusian Theory of International Migration." *Sociological Theory* 36 (3): 262–288.
Krissman, Fred. 2000. "Immigrant Labor Recruitment: U.S. Agribusiness and Undocumented Migration From Mexico." In *Immigration Research for a New Century*, edited by N. Foner, R. Rumbaut, and S. Gold, 277–300. New York: Russell Sage Foundation.
Krissman, Fred. 2005. "Sin Coyote Ni Patrón: Why the "Migrant Network" Fails to Explain International Migration." *International Migration Review* 39 (1): 4–44.
Lindquist, Johan. 2012. "The Elementary School Teacher, the Thug and his Grandmother: Informal Brokers and Transnational Migration from Indonesia." *Pacific Affairs* 85 (1): 69–89.
Liu-Farrer, Gracia, Brenda S. Yeoh, and Michiel Baas. 2021. "Social Construction of Skill: An Analytical Approach Toward the Question of Skill in Cross-Border Labour Mobilities." *Journal of Ethnic and Migration Studies* 47 (10): 2237–2251. doi:10.1080/1369183X.2020.1731983.
Long, Heather. 2019. "Trump Administration Nearly Doubles H-2B Guest Visa Program, Which Brings Many Mexican Workers." *Washington Post*. https://www.washingtonpost.com/business/2019/04/06/trump-administration-nearly-doubles-h-b-guest-visa-program-which-brings-many-mexican-workers/?utm_term=.ab53068d9f42.
Martin, Philip. 2017. *Immigration and Farm Labor: From Unauthorized to H-2A for Some?* Washington, DC: Migration Policy Institute.
Massey, Douglas S., Jorge Durand, and Karen A. Pren. 2015. "Border Enforcement and Return Migration by Documented and Undocumented Immigrants." *Journal of Ethnic and Migration Studies* 41 (7): 1015–1040.
Muñoz, Lidia. 2016. *Permanentemente Temporales. Un Análisis Sobre las Prácticas de Contratación del Sistema de Visas de Trabajo Temporal H2 en México. Tésis de Maestría en Antropología Social.* Monterrey: CIESAS.
Muñoz, Lidia, Efrén Sandoval, and Rubén Hernández-León. 2018. "A rio Revuelto, Ganancia de Reclutadores: El Fraude en el Reclutamiento del Programa de Visas H2." In *Cruces y Retornos en la Región del Noreste Mexicano en el Alba del Siglo XXI*, edited by S. Arzaluz and E. Sandoval, 173–208. Tijuana: COLEF.
Perrotta, Domenico, and Devi Sacchetto. 2012. "Il Ghetto e lo Sciopero: Braccianti Stranieri Nell'Italia Meridionale." *Sociologia del Lavoro* 128: 152–166.
Rousmaniere, Peter. 2013. *Introduction to H-2A Temporary Agricultural Labor Program*. http://www.workingimmigrants.com/2013/01/introduction_to_h2a_temporary.html.
Shrestha, Tina. 2018. "Aspirational Infrastructure: Everyday Brokerage and the Foreign-Employment Recruitment Agencies in Nepal." *Pacific Affairs* 91 (4): 673–693.
Shubin, Sergei, Alan Findlay, and David McCollum. 2014. "Imaginaries of the Ideal Migrant Worker: A Lacanian Interpretation." *Environment and Planning D: Space and Society* 32 (3): 466–483.
Silvey, Rachel, and Rhacel Parreñas. 2019. "Precarity Chains: Cycles of Domestic Worker Migration From Southeast Asian to the Middle East." *Journal of Ethnic and Migration Studies*. doi:10.1080/1369183X.2019.1592398.
Siracusa, Christina, and Kristel Acacio. 2004. "State Migrant-Exporting Schemes and Their Implications for the Rise of Illicit Migration: A Comparison of Spain and the Philippines." *Journal of International Migration and Integration* 5 (3): 321–342.

Star, Susan L., and Anselm Strauss. 1999. "Layers of Silence, Arenas of Voice: The Ecology of Visible and Invisible Work." *Computer-Supported Cooperative Work: Journal of Collaborative Computing* 8: 9–30.

Stovel, Katherine, and Lynette Shaw. 2012. "Brokerage." *Annual Review of Sociology* 38: 139–158.

Surak, Kristin. 2018. "Migration Industries and the State: Guestwork Programs in East Asia." *International Migration Review* 52 (2): 487–523..

U.S. Department of State. 2019. "Non-Immigrant Visa Statistics." https://travel.state.gov/content/travel/en/legal/visa-law0/visa-statistics/nonimmigrant-visa-statistics.html.

Waldinger, Roger, and Michael Lichter. 2003. *How the Other Half Works: Immigration and the Social Organisation of Labor*. Berkeley: University of California Press.

Xiang, Biao, and Johan Lindquist. 2014. "Migration Infrastructure." *International Migration Review* 48 (S1): S122–S148.

From cooks to chefs: skilled migrants in a globalising culinary field

James Farrer

ABSTRACT

Migrants do not simply move across physical spaces but within institutionalised social fields, including occupational fields. This ethnographic study takes a globalised culinary field – the social and economic space of fine restaurant dining – as an example of an emergent transnational social field. Focusing on culinary migrants to Shanghai, it shows how the institutionalisation, professionalisation and globalisation of the culinary field create new opportunities for the mobility of workers. Transnational mobility can be advantageous to the career mobility of culinary workers at all levels, from line cooks, to head chefs, and further to celebrity chefs building global brands. More generally, the mobility of skilled labour is shown to depend on the transnationalisation of the fields in which skills are socially defined, and migrants themselves are key players in instantiating and expanding a field.

Culinary workers as skilled migrants

This paper explores the transnational mobility of highly skilled migrant culinary workers in an ascending global city, interrogating the relationship of geographic mobility to career mobility within a global city network. It uses the concept of a 'transnational culinary field' to explore this mobility, arguing that the mobility of culinary workers should not be conceptualised only as geographic mobility, but also as mobility within the culinary field. An integral point is that the mobility of skilled labour involves not only the mobility of individuals within a field, but the mobility of the field itself, or the expansion of specialised institutional networks within which specialised skills are defined, developed and recognised. In general, migrants do not simply migrate between physical spaces but across and within social fields, which include fields of employment, sexual fields, and educational fields (see Farrer 2019b). Migrants must consider the geographic portability of the forms of 'capital' – including human capital, social capital, cultural capital, even sexual capital – that are needed for success in a field. Some types of human capital are more portable than others, such as technical skills and degrees from prestigious universities, typically held by 'skilled migrants' (Kim 2015; Nohl, Schittenhelm, and Schmidtke 2014). However, many migrants are unable to hold on to various forms of human and cultural capital when crossing borders (Erel 2010; Oliver and O'Reilly 2010).

'Skill' is socially constructed, and geographic mobility may result in both the symbolic erasure and the practical acquisition of skills (see Liu-Farrer, Yeoh, and Baas 2021). Migration may lead to deskilling, with people regarded as 'skilled workers' in their old home, becoming 'unskilled labour' in their new one. 'Ethnic' restaurant work, is often regarded as one of these 'unskilled' migrant jobs, despite actually requiring many skills (see Ray 2016). However, ethnographic research on even low-skill migrant hospitality work shows that it can also be a pathway to acquiring skills. Migrants can use skills gained through mobility to enhance their position in the field – to get better jobs – or to provide conditions for further geographic mobility – for example, returning home to open a business that uses these new skills (Alberti 2014). In fine dining, geographic mobility to renowned 'creative hotspots' (Aubke 2014), famous restaurants (Stierand 2014), classic culinary regions (Sawaguchi 2015), or upcoming culinary destinations (Ferguson and Zukin 1998) may be regarded as key to building skills, a pattern also seen in artisanal sectors such as pizza-making (Ceccarini 2011). As one culinary school chairperson in the USA explained to me, moving among restaurants is the normative way that chefs acquire new knowledge. And while international mobility is not yet typical among US based chefs, it is increasingly common and desirable (April 2019 interview). Unlike traditional culinary centres like Paris, emerging nodes within the globalising culinary field – such as Asia's rising global cities – may provide both swifter job advancement as well as chances to acquire cross-cultural and culinary knowledge needed for cutting-edge culinary work.

Even in more highly credentialed professions such as academia, geographic mobility may be linked to field mobility. For example, Leung argues that geographical mobility itself is a form of Bourdieusian capital, as it reinforces career development, competency and competitiveness (Leung 2013). The loose professionalisation of the culinary profession may make such cross-border mobility even more important to career mobility than in more formally credentialed occupations, since experience in kitchens in various countries may signal an expansive culinary repertoire more effectively than a certificate. As discussed below, cross-cultural exposure could be regarded as a form of mobility capital for chefs, one closely linked to field-specific skills, both technical and managerial. I consider all of these as elements of *culinary capital*, since their relevance for culinary workers lies in their specific utility in the *culinary field*.

In short, this study is about the possibilities of upward social and economic mobility within the culinary field, and the relationship of career mobility to transnational geographic mobility. The study responds to a key question: Why would an aspiring chef of Western or Japanese cuisine, go to work in Shanghai, a city only recently known as an international culinary centre, and what does this tell us about culinary migration in general as a form of 'skilled migration'? Part of the answer, I argue, may lie in the mobility of the field itself, in other words, the extension of the culinary field across a transnational space that maps roughly onto a network of global cities. Cuisine is one of the 'creative industries' cultivated by city governments, and also a critical part of the urban infrastructure that attracts 'creative talents' to these cities (see Clark 2003; Farrer 2010; Lin and Baum 2016). However, the growth of a global culinary field is not simply the product of top-down government and industry initiatives but also the 'bottom-up' activities of migrants themselves (Farrer 2019a). For example, in the post-Soviet period, many Estonian cooks who moved to Finland to work as chefs brought the concept of the professional 'chef' back with them to Estonia, and subsequently founded the Estonian Chefs

Association in 2000 (Roosipold and Loogma 2014). Such migrants are not only seeking better positions in the culinary field but also extending the field to a new context, a field that in turn upholds their status as skilled workers.

The transnational culinary field as a space of mobility

The concept of 'fields' has been deployed in sociology as a way of describing the social organisation of strategic action among actors engaged in a common endeavour (Fligstein and McAdam 2015). Writing on the 'scientific field', Sidhu, Yeoh, and Chang (2015) draws on Robbins (2017, 268–269) who defines 'field' as a 'structured space of positions'. Those wishing to participate in the field are required to accept the rules, norms and regulations which characterise the field. There are three critical properties of a field: authority to impose its logic on those entering the field, a space of struggles, and the capacity to exercise a degree of autonomy. In gastronomy, we can think of the culinary field as a space of interactions among the actors who produce, sustain and also contest the 'rules of the game' of modern restaurant cuisine – investors, owners, chefs, critics, regulators, consumers, guidebooks, food media, etc. (Farrer 2015a; Ferguson 1998; Leschziner 2015). Business organisations are influential actors who control the 'hard' economic resources, but consumers, workers, governmental agencies, cultural authorities also foster culinary cultures. Within this expanding cultural field, we can see several trends that link the geographic mobility of culinary workers to the transformation and expansion of the culinary field itself: (1) broader recognition of the chef as a high-status occupation with creativity as a central value and increasing professional autonomy (Horng and Hu 2008; Leschziner 2015; Myhrvold 2011; Peterson and Birg 1988; Stierand, Dörfler, and MacBryde 2014); (2) the growth and diversification of the fine dining sector globally and the importance of a cosmopolitan fine dining scene to achieving 'global food city' status (Farrer 2010, 2015a); (3) the increasing (though still incomplete and contested) credentialization of the cooking profession, including recognition of culinary credentials across borders (Ceccarini 2014; Roosipold and Loogma 2014; UKNCPEQF 2016); (4) the growing importance of transnational authorities such as Michelin and 'World's 50 Best' in establishing culinary standards globally (Bouty, Gomez, and Drucker-Godard 2013; Chossat and Gergaud 2003; Farrer 2019c). All of these processes have created the potential for the transnational mobility of culinary professionals, who are also participants in expanding the culinary field. Migrant culinary professionals – including chefs, food writers, sommeliers, mixologists, etc – thus become not only beneficiaries but stakeholders in the expansion of this culinary field (Farrer 2019c; Wang 2019).

The first factor in the rise of a transnational culinary field is the recognition of cuisine as a creative industry, with the chef as a new type of creative professional. The elevation of the culinary profession is a long fitful process that arguably began in France in the nineteenth century with the advent of gastronomy as an autonomous field. Food critics, a new types of cultural authority, elevated the chef to an artist in his own right, a pattern much accelerated by food media in the twenty-first century (Ferguson 1998; Leschziner 2015; Trubek 2000). This emphasis on artistic creativity in restaurant cooking has been described as a 'modernist revolution' that redefined the relation between the chef and client, with the former gaining a prestige and authority never before enjoyed (Myhrvold 2011). The rise of fine dining restaurants outside of France since the 1970s, especially in the global financial centres of New York and London, reshaped and decentred this culinary field in the West, fostering greater freedom and variations in the careers of chefs and decreasing the grip of France on culinary authority (Ferguson and Zukin 1998). The high-end culinary field is now global, with many diverse interlinked subfields, including globalised Japanese and Chinese cuisines and other non-Western and fusion cuisines, though all influenced by the French-inflected ethos of modern fine dining, with its cultural icon – the creative celebrity chef (Farrer 2019c; Ho 2017; Khoo 2019).

The second factor is the rise of 'global food cities' (Farrer 2010). Since the 1970s, a network of fast-growing global cities has developed in which specialised and highly-skilled services are concentrated (Sassen 2013). These cities compete by offering amenities – including a cosmopolitan fine dining scene – to attract a mobile 'creative class' (Clark 2003). Mobile culinary professionals provide important amenities for this putative creative class, and are now regarded as 'creatives' themselves (Lin and Baum 2016). Culinary globalisation thus has redefined the profession of the chef in these emerging global cities. In Istanbul, for example, we see

> a fundamental change in the role of the chef: from a nameless and faceless kitchen worker to – frequently and in various combinations – cook, restaurateur, businessperson, author and researcher, media personality, celebrity and brand name, innovator or traditionalist, activist and campaigner.

Many of the new star chefs have more middle-class upbringings than traditional cooks (Yenal and Kubiena 2016, 64). Also in Moscow and St. Petersburg, we see that professional associations among chefs, culinary journalism, and culinary fairs have raised the profile of chefs (Shectman 2009). In East Asia's rising global cities, we see a new fine dining sector emphasising personal creativity, innovation and a greater focus on aesthetics (Farrer 2019c; Ho 2017; Khoo 2019). This expanding network of global food cities represent career opportunities for skilled culinary migrants. Whereas cross-border labour mobility may be limited within the fine dining scene in some established markets such as Germany (Lane 2011), in new global cities such as Shanghai, mobile talents may find new opportunities in sectors in which local chefs have less experience (Farrer 2015b, 2017, 2019a, 2019b; Thery, Le Bail, and Buchanan 2017). Beyond advantages in skill and experience, migrant chefs may possess ethnic, cultural or even racial attributes that local customers associate with authentic foreign cuisine, giving them a niche advantage in new markets (Farrer 2015b; Tzeng 2019). However, depending on their access to desirable forms of transnational cultural capital, such as English language ability and a middle class habitus, some migrants could find themselves stuck in an 'ethnic food' niche and unable to move to more prestigious culinary sectors (Ray 2016).

Third, the social recognition of skilled culinary professions has created new avenues for social and geographic mobility, making the field more attractive to entrants with middle-class backgrounds and academic credentials. This is less a story of the upward mobility of traditional culinary workers than one of middle-class and educated people redefining skilled jobs such as cooking and bartending as taste-making occupations (Ocejo 2017). Waiters, for example, have long been drawn from the middle classes. Preexisting cultural capital – beyond technical skills – thus plays an important role in establishing many culinary careers. Beyond such informal capital conversion, there is also a trend towards formal credentialization of culinary skills, which is especially important for migrant culinary workers who may need to show credentials for visa purposes or to gain employment in a new market. For example, Ceccarini shows that the standardisation of pizza making by the European Council Regulations has facilitated the migration of trained Italian *pizzaoli* to Japan, and also of Japanese *pizzaoli* to Italy, as a pathway towards professional recognition (Ceccarini 2014). Another pattern is the international sectoral qualification (ISQ), or the transnational recognition of occupational qualifications (UKNCPEQF 2016). As an example of ISQ, the organisation Worldchefs, a network of over 100 chef associations around the world, has set out to create globally recognised certifications for cooks, chefs and culinary educators, aiming to make their qualifications more transparent for employers across borders (https://www.worldchefs.org/Certification). Finally, many culinary schools now have a global footprint. Claiming to the world's largest culinary education institution, Le Cordon Bleu operates a global network of 35 institutes in 20 countries with 20,000 current students (https://www.cordonbleu.edu/home/en). The transnationalisation of culinary credentials enhances the mobility of skilled culinary labour, though employers and governments do not universally recognise these standards (UKNCPEQF 2016).

Fourth, the mobility of skilled culinary labour relies upon globalising culinary authorities. As a field in which experiential learning counts more than formal certificates, work in famous restaurants is the most important credential for mobile chefs (Aubke 2014). In turn, the reputations of these restaurants are increasingly dependent on ratings by food critics and other culinary authorities, the most prominent of which are the Michelin Red Guides, though Michelin now has many competitors, including 'Worlds 50 Best', Zagat, TripAdvisor, and food media (e.g. Netflix's 'Chef's Table'). Globalised culinary authorities are a key factor in the transnationalisation of the culinary field in Asia, with Michelin recently expanding to many Asian cities. Though particular ratings are often disputed, authorities such as the Michelin Guide and the World's 50 Best Restaurants provide certifications of quality and authenticity to both industry insiders and consumers (Bouty, Gomez, and Drucker-Godard 2013; Chossat and Gergaud 2003; Farrer 2019c). They also provide globally recognised credentials for chefs who pass through highly rated kitchens. In an applied creative field in which skills are difficult to measure, mobility through starred establishments becomes a key way of proving ability while also creating the basis for further mobility by chefs who learn to blend concepts, flavours and techniques in various kitchens around the world (Steirand 2014; Stierand, Dörfler and MacBryde 2014).

My study focuses on international culinary migrants to Shanghai working in Western cuisine and Japanese cuisines (i.e. not in the Chinese food sector in which inbound migrants are relatively rare). Based on this research, my basic question is how the expansion of a global culinary field fosters the mobility of skilled migrants in and out of Shanghai, and how this transnational mobility facilitates upskilling for migrants within the culinary field. More unique to this study is the question is how migrants actually participate in the expansion of this field, and how the mobility of the field itself creates career pathways for further culinary migrants, including Chinese chefs migrating abroad.

Data and context: ethnographic case study of the expanding culinary field

This paper is based on an ethnographic qualitative study, conducted from 2005 to 2018, of migrant culinary work and the field of culinary work in Western and Japanese restaurants in Shanghai. The data includes over 100 interviews with chefs, restaurant owners, food writers and others active in the restaurant and hospitality business in Shanghai. This data is supplemented by participant observation in industry events, kitchen observations in several restaurants and interviews with many chefs and restaurant owners in other cities, which though not the focus here, provide additional knowledge of the field. This is a purely qualitative study. The analysis of the data is based on the principles of grounded theory in which qualitative data is used to generate theoretical descriptions. The case studies are used to describe pathways of mobility. The method does not exclude the possibility of other patterns, nor can it generate statistical descriptions of the distribution of patterns in the population.

Methodologically, Shanghai is an advantageous context to study the expansion of a transnational culinary field. As recently as the late 1970s, Shanghai was relatively isolated from global flows under the Mao regime, but today, it is one of the largest centres of international trade and investment in the world. According to the Globalization and World Cities Research Network (GaWC), while New York and London are the only Alpha++ cities, Shanghai is among the next tier of seven Alpha+ cities that are 'highly integrated and fulfil advanced service needs' (GaWC 2019). Shanghai's precipitous rise into the ranks of global cities includes rapid developments in many 'hard' as well as 'soft' service industries. The latter includes gastronomy. Shanghai now has a diverse restaurant scene ranging from fast food chains to internationally acclaimed fine dining venues (Farrer 2010, 2019b). It is not clear how many migrant chefs are involved in this new globalised restaurant scene. One very rough indication of the size of this market in Shanghai is that the leading Chinese restaurant website Dianping.com in September 2018 listed over 220 Western restaurants and over 240 Japanese restaurants costing 300 yuan (US$ 45) or more per diner, and 12 Western and 35 Japanese restaurants costing over 1000 yuan (US$ 150) per diner. In such high-end establishments, foreign chefs are commonplace and even expected.

Establishing a transnational culinary field in Shanghai

The earliest and most significant pathway for the movement of skilled culinary labour was created by corporate investors aiming to serve corporate expatriates, business travellers, and tourists in the rising global city. International hotel chains were the earliest major actors in the creation of a cosmopolitan restaurant scene. Western and Japanese expatriate chefs were first hired at the Sheraton, Hilton and Okura hotels which all opened in 1988. Hotel restaurant executive chefs were the prime movers in establishing a transnational culinary scene in Shanghai, fostering the mobility of other foreign chefs as well as training a new generation of local Chinese chefs in Western and Japanese cooking techniques in the 1990s. They established new culinary standards that reshaped restaurant work in the city.

The next phase in the development of a transnational culinary scene was the opening of independent restaurants outside of hotels, some by migrant chefs who had started in hotels. A pioneer was Australian chef and restaurateur, Michelle Garnaut who had moved from Melbourne to cook in Hong Kong in 1984. In 1989, she opened her own Hong Kong restaurant called M on the Fringe. Inspired by an experimental stint producing modern Western cuisine at the Peace Hotel in 1996, she decided to open a fine dining Western restaurant independent of a hotel, a first for Shanghai. In 1999, Garnaut opened her restaurant M on the Bund on the top floor of the Number 5 Building, with spectacular views of the rising nightscapes of modern Pudong. Other early pioneers in the independent restaurant scene often stumbled, however, with common problems being a failure to secure adequate capital, insufficient experience in the restaurant business, and unscrupulous local partners (a kind of negative social capital). Successful cases typically had both strong transnational and local (PRC or Hong Kong-based) ties (Farrer 2019a).

M on the Bund became a legendary local success story, but by insider accounts, it also represented a transitional phase in the fine dining scene, which was increasingly characterised by simultaneous trends towards corporatisation and transnationalisation. By corporatisation, I refer to the scale of the investors and investments. By transnationalisation, I refer to the entry into Shanghai of restaurateurs with pre-existing global reputations bringing their culinary standards, tastes, staff and management styles to Shanghai. From now on, Shanghai would be closely integrated into the culinary trends in the global food city network, with New York often at the centre. This corporatisation and transnationalisation of Shanghai's foodscape was represented in the Three on the Bund that opened directly next door to M on the Bund in 2004. Three on the Bund was funded and controlled by the Singaporean based Giti Group, a privately owned conglomerate. Haute couture and haute cuisine were its main attractions, with the Western fine dining restaurants headed by expatriate executive chefs. Within the next decade, developers refurbished office buildings from the pre-war era all along the Bund, with many becoming home to high-end restaurants and retail outlets.

Many luxury fine dining restaurants in Shanghai were managed by global restaurant groups headed by culinary stars, such as Jean-Georges Vongerichten, Jason Atherton, or Joel Robuchon, whose global culinary careers were effectively the 'branding' for these restaurant chains. Although represented as the restaurants (or even 'ateliers') of Michelin-starred chefs, these are now global corporations managing restaurants worldwide from their bases in New York, London, and Paris, where most of the aspiring young chefs gain their experience before being sent abroad to work in these far-flung operations. The restaurants in Shanghai and other rising global cities are often owned by local real estate developers, and managed by global restaurant companies. This worldwide collaboration between developers and luxury restaurant brands is creating a transnational labour market for mobile chefs in ascending global cities such as Shanghai and Dubai. They bring new standards for cooking and service, while incorporating these restaurant scenes into a growing transnational culinary field centred in New York, London, Tokyo, and Paris.

Jean-Georges, as one of the earliest and largest restaurant groups to open on the Bund, illustrates the mobility opportunities created by these large players in the fine dining sector. Jean-Georges Management, which in 2018 runs 37 restaurants in over ten countries. The first chef at Jean-Georges Shanghai was American Eric Johnson, who arrived in 2004. A native of Long Island New York, he went to university in Colorado, returning to his home city to enter the restaurant business. He worked for Daniel Boulud (another New York-based star chef), then moved to Jean-Georges. Mobility was one reason why this culinary career appealed to him, he said:

> I was getting ready to leave, not because I was unhappy, but I spent four years there, and so I wanted to always travel around with work. So I went to him and said to him, 'Can you set me up with a job somewhere?' We went through various things. We had plans in Bangkok, and France, and so forth. And he ended up opening up a restaurant in Paris and so he said, 'Let's

open a restaurant in Paris' and ended up asking me if I would go there and be the chef. I went there and did that and stayed in Paris for two years. (2005 interview)

Paris was difficult in terms of relations with the staff, Eric said, but it was an important learning experience. It also put him in a position to open a new restaurant in the emerging market of Shanghai. He successfully headed Jean-Georges in Shanghai for six years. This was a steep managerial challenge, since none of the young chefs had cooked this type of high Western cuisine. Eric also learned some techniques from Chinese chefs, he said, including processes for crisping skins on roast meats, making tofu, and producing Chinese soup stocks (though his applications differed greatly from the traditional Chinese ones) (2005 interview). After another stay in Hong Kong, he returned to the USA to finally open his own critically acclaimed restaurant in Seattle, featuring a fusion French-Vietnamese menu, a cuisine he had long been interested in. That restaurant also features some of the dishes he picked up in Shanghai, including a classic braised pork dish (Holleran 2015).

By 2016, Vongerichten's company managed three acclaimed restaurants on the Bund, from Italian to Korean, receiving one Michelin star in 2018 for his flagship Jean-Georges in 2018. In turn, the company brought more and more migrant chefs into the city, creating many young rising stars. One of these mobile culinary talents was Bina Yu. Originally from South Korea, she moved to New York when she was eighteen to pursue a career in gastronomy. After studying English, she finished a course at the Culinary Institute of America. She was then able to land a job at Jean-Georges's restaurant Nougatine in New York City. After two years there, she went to work at Danji, a Michelin starred Korean restaurant with French influences. She then returned to Jean-Georges, where she was made a sous chef. At the seasonal sous chef dinners where young chefs show off their own cooking for the team, she impressed Vongerichten with her Korean fusion items and some Japanese styles she picked up from Danji chef Hooni Kim. Vongerichten then chose her to head his new Korean concept restaurant in Shanghai, which was entirely conceived in New York City. This was a very challenging project, Yu said. She found that Shanghai was not ready for her innovative fusion Korean cuisine, and after two years, the restaurant closed. Bina left the Jean-Georges group, and in 2018, she opened a new Asian-French fusion restaurant called Together, whose menu she designed with another expatriate chef, South African Kim Melvin, who had come to Shanghai to work for a Jason Atherton managed restaurant. Bina Yu went from entry-level cook in Vongerichten's empire to a well-known rising star in the Shanghai food scene. Like many other young migrant chefs, however, she sought further transnational mobility, and in 2019, she moved on to Paris for both personal and career reasons (2016, 2018, 2019 interviews).

This discussion illustrates the importance of corporate investment and corporate visa sponsorship in the initial establishment of a transnational culinary field in Shanghai. This began with hotels, but as luxury developments such as Three on the Bund started, global restaurant consultancies such as those led Jean-Georges Vongerichten and Jason Atherton have also become key players. Celebrity chefs are themselves transnational migrants – the gastronomic equivalents of Leslie Sklair's transnational capitalist elite (Sklair 2012) – who move from city to city weaving together the structures of career mobility for the next tier of highly skilled culinary migrants, like Erik Johnson, Bina Yu or Kim Melvin. For such skilled culinary migrants, transnational mobility becomes intrinsic to their mobility in the culinary field, often facilitating big jumps in field position; For

Bina Yu, for example, moving to Shanghai was her first shot at being a head chef in a Vongerichten restaurant. For Kim Melvin moving to Shanghai offered first a chance to lead the pastry section, then to open and head two other restaurants in the Atherton empire (2018 interview). Lucas, an Italian chef in his mid-twenties, described how he was promoted to head chef of a fine dining Italian restaurant when a Michelin-starred head chef suddenly departed, a swift career advance he could not have dreamed of in his last place of work in Australia (2019 interview).

For two decades, China has provided a relatively open doorway for such skilled culinary migrants, though it may be narrowing. During the early period of this research, foreign chefs could receive an employment visa if they could show two years of formal culinary training and four years of experience in the relevant culinary field. A sponsoring employer was the other necessary condition for an employment visa (and in actual practice, a sufficient one, since credentials were easily fudged). After the implementation of a new point-based work visa system in the PRC in 2016, however, requirements have tightened, including the need to certify formal qualifications with notarised documents (see Farrer 2019b, 104–105). This produces two effects. One is that chefs without formal culinary school qualifications report troubles obtaining or renewing their visas. Some resort to unscrupulous visa agents who forge or exaggerate qualifications, putting both the agent and the worker at risk of prosecution (One agent I interviewed was arrested for this). However, as one chef with a formal culinary school degree from South Africa explained, these changes also create incentives for qualified professionals like her. This is especially true for those with a bachelor degree, since a BA degree (or equivalent) brings the most points under the new system. Overall, chefs with transnational ties, Michelin-level resumes, corporate sponsorship, and certifiable culinary degrees have the strongest chances of mobility and success in this culinary field. Those who lack these elements – which represent transnational economic, cultural and social capital – have trouble both coming to Shanghai and successfully moving on to other markets in which these elements of 'skill' are also valued. In short, the state remains a key gatekeeper, and migrants from countries or regions where formal culinary certification is uncommon are disadvantaged. On the other hand, some countries provide documentation of degree-equivalency for vocational culinary training, facilitating mobility. Certification, is however, primarily a visa requirement; employers tend to value experience over credentials. In a market driven field, chefs working in prestigious and popular cuisines find more opportunities. For example, there are fewer South Asian chefs in Shanghai because South Asian cuisines are unpopular. There are, however, many highly skilled migrant chefs from Japan, France, Spain, and Italy, which are associated with popular, high status cuisines.

Creating a migrant entrepreneurial niche: from cooks to chefs to owners

With no previous connections to the city, expatriate chefs and restaurateurs often arrived in Shanghai as employees of hotels, large restaurant groups, or more rarely, in corporate jobs with little connection to food service. However, given the dynamic growth of restaurants in Shanghai, some of them found themselves not only experiencing upward mobility in a transnational culinary career, but also opportunities for entrepreneurship and ownership in the emerging culinary sector in Shanghai. In turn, their entrepreneurship has deepened the transnational occupational niche for skilled culinary migrants in Shanghai.

Several Shanghai restaurant entrepreneurs came into the business, not as cooks, but as designers, not an unusual starting point in image-focused gastronomy. One of these is Naoya Hirano, who grew up in Tokyo, where he studied design at Musashino Art University (Farrer 2017). Only a few years out of university, he was sent to China to manage the restaurant investment of a large Japanese company. The first concept was a high-end Japanese family style restaurant in a historic villa on Donghu Road. 'It completely failed. This was a bad time for me', Hirano said. He saved the business by converting the location into a trendy Spanish tapas bistro. The experience taught Hirano about the type of innovative, design-focused, bold style of marketing necessary to succeed in Shanghai. 'You have to be willing to do something outrageous to succeed in China', Hirano said. 'This is what the Chinese expect. It has to be an interesting experience. The food must be good, but it doesn't need to be spectacular'. Having acquired the company for himself, Hirano now heads his own Fulu Restaurant Group that operates kaiseki, sushi, kappo cuisine, and a Peruvian restaurant in the city. However, even a successful entrepreneur such as Hirano, sees himself moving onward, perhaps to Europe, perhaps to Japan, where he is exploring the idea of culinary-related ecotourism ventures. Hirano brought a limited set of skills to Shanghai but developed many others, including menu and interior design, videography, service styles, Chinese language, financial management, and investor and public relations.

One of Hirano's earliest protégés was 'Willy' Trullas Moreno, a chef from Barcelona, with a long transnational resume. He had worked in restaurants in Paris, New York and Barcelona, before taking an offer to go to China with a team from the Torres winery to promote Spanish wine and food. For a year, he travelled the country, cooking and learning the ways of Chinese kitchen staff, management and customers in multiple hotel kitchens (Farrer 2015b). Like Hirano, Willy brought with him a specific set of skills – linguistic and culinary – but developed many others in interaction with business partners and the Chinese kitchen staff. His big break came in 2007, when Hirano sought his help in creating the new restaurant concept. Offering him a minority stake in the business, Hirano suggested that Willy use his English nickname to create the eponymous restaurant. The figure of the celebrity chef was relatively new to Shanghai, but the expatriate population in Shanghai appreciated Willy's offbeat character. Chinese chefs usually stayed put in the kitchen, labouring anonymously while the owner of the restaurant earned the reputation. Riding on the global interest in Spanish food, a Chinese appreciation for dishes that are easily shared, and Shanghai expatriates' affection for his public persona, the original el Willy was an immediate success, garnering numerous awards from the local English press. By 2014, Willy was developing his Tomatito casual dining tapas restaurant into an Asian brand, opening restaurants in Manila and Ho Chi Minh City. Willy himself moved his residence to Bangkok (2017 fieldnotes). In just a few years, Willy had gone from being a migrant cook, living off a meagre salary, to becoming a transnational migrant entrepreneur. He largely attributes his success to the transnational culinary networks he formed in Shanghai. Hirano and Willy have also created mobility ladders for other migrant chefs.

One of the people who started with Willy and Hirano was an ambitious young Peruvian chef Carlos Satomayor. Starting out working a sous chef in Willy's flagship restaurant, Carlos became head chef of his more casual Mediterranean restaurant Elefante, and in 2018 opened a new Peruvian restaurant in that same location with Hirano as a partner.

Carlos' career shows the utility of transnational mobility in building up a chef's resume, a complex culinary repertoire, and the cosmopolitan habitus necessary to succeed in this competitive business. Like many great chefs, he started young, first leaving Peru at age fifteen to work in an uncle's Tex-Mex restaurant in New York City. Peru has a booming culinary school sector, with students banking on the popularity of Peruvian cuisine abroad. While in culinary college, Carlos cooked at various restaurants in Lima, occasionally returning to the US to work for his uncle and perfect his English, a key ingredient of a global chef's career. He worked at a fine dining restaurants in Lake Tahoe in the US, and interned at restaurants in Germany and France. One of the greatest influences, he said, was his teacher in France, who taught him many of the finer points of technique:

> It is when I realize that if you go around the world, outside of your comfort zone, then you have a different vision and a different way to explain things. So, this chef in Bordeaux in particular, he used to work for Alain Chapel, and he is the one who opened 'Chapel' in Kobe. (2018 interview)

Inspired by his famous teacher, Carlos also leapt at the chance to come to Asia, sponsored by Willy's company. His stint as a head chef in Elefante was challenging, especially managing a team of Chinese cooks:

> At the beginning, it was very difficult. I couldn't speak a word of Chinese. I had like a team with 16 to 18 cooks. So how do you manage to teach someone right? I had to force myself to learn Chinese to know how to say tomato, how to say onion, what's good, what's bad. Little by little. So today I would focus on my recipe, how I wanna make my chicken stock. I would come earlier than them, set up all the ingredients on the table, very beautifully organized and they are looking at me like, 'what's this?' So, I would say, 'this is how we make chicken stock with me'. (2018 interview)

Intercultural management skills are key to developing careers of the new global migrant chefs and part of the skill package developed through transnational mobility. Carlos is one many younger expatriate chefs I have met who speak quite good 'kitchen Chinese', unlike the first generation who relied entirely on an English-speaking Chinese sous chef to convey ideas to the line cooks. Another part of culinary skill is self-marketing, an amorphous and difficult-to-acquire package of capacities. Carlos sees Shanghai as a place to build his own brand. In 2017, he was nominated Chef of the Year by *Time Out Magazine*, and became a name in his own right in the Shanghai international food scene. As he put it, it is not enough to cook good food, people have to eat the food and know he made it. 'The question is', he said, 'how do you get Carlos in the food'. (2018 interview) For him, the new Peruvian restaurant Ekeko, named for a pre-Columbian Peruvian dynasty was a chance to create those personal flavours using the fusion cuisine of his home country. However, it closed after only a few months in 2018, leaving him looking for next steps. For Carlos, the first was consulting for numerous restaurants in the city and organising pop-up events that built his personal brand. In the process, he has become a well-known figure locally while building ties within a broader culinary field. Most recently he was contemplating a move to Europe, aiming to increase his managerial experience (2019, 2020 interviews).

For all these established and rising chef-entrepreneurs, key factors in initial success were pre-existing skills – culinary, linguistic and artistic – and transnational corporate support that could provide visa sponsorship and a first job. Mid-term factors were the establishment of bonding social capital within the burgeoning expatriate community (e.g. intra-ethnic ties) and bridging social capital with Chinese staff. Especially among male chefs, marriage to Chinese spouses offered a particularly useful form of bridging social capital, bringing ties to local Chinese networks to which these men otherwise had little access. Finally, access to international capital markets allowed a small group of these migrant men and women to develop major businesses (see Farrer 2019b). Upward mobility within this expanding culinary field – and the acquisition of relevant cultural, social and economic capital – not only entailed but facilitated the acquisition of specialised and flexible skills, including technical, managerial, promotional and creative competencies specific to transnational culinary work. This acquisition of culinary capital was facilitated by growing opportunities in Shanghai's expanding international culinary sector.

Global legitimating authorities: Michelin and mobility

The first Michelin city guide to a Mainland Chinese city was published in Shanghai in September 2016. The imprimatur of the most important global culinary authority had now put Shanghai on the map of global food cities. Shanghai restaurants were also featured in the even more selective list of 'Asia's 50 Best Restaurants' (an adjunct to the larger 'World's 50 Best Restaurants' list), in which the top restaurant in Mainland China was Ultraviolet (also a Michelin three-star) restaurant run by Paul Pairet, another migrant chef-entrepreneur. Overall, this image of Shanghai as a rising global food city is important for understanding the geographic and career mobility of chefs into this sector. Indeed, the aura of Michelin stars in Shanghai preceded the arrival of the guidebook in the city. Wealthy Chinese tourists already engaged in Michelin 'star collecting' in culinary destinations in Europe and Japan, and upon returning to China, many globe-trotting gourmets sought out chefs with an overseas Michelin pedigree (Farrer 2019c). It may even have been easier to make a career in Shanghai with Michelin stars before the guidebook actually arrived locally in 2016, than later. That is, if one already had worked at a starred restaurant in Europe, it was possible to market these stars in Shanghai, since no local guide existed to validate (or invalidate) them. One example is the French chef Nicolas Le Bec. In the summer of 2012, Nicolas, the former owner of an eponymous two-star Michelin restaurant in Lyon, shuttered his Lyon restaurant and moved to Shanghai with his Shanghainese wife. In April 2014, Nicolas opened in a sumptuous villa on Xinhua Road. Unlike other 'flying Michelin chefs', like Vongerichten or Robuchon, who simply put their name on the door while spending most of their time organising culinary ventures elsewhere, Nicolas had his feet planted firmly on Chinese soil. As the Lyonnaise manager Guillaume explained, 'We are changing the game of French cuisine in Shanghai. We have a two-star Michelin chef in the kitchen cooking lunch and dinner'. (2015 fieldnotes). Without any advertising, the pricey bistro attracted a stream of customers, 80% of whom were Chinese. So far, Nicolas has been frustrated in his attempts to win Michelin stars in Shanghai, but his early success clearly owes to the reflected glory of his French Michelin resume.

The arrival of Michelin has prompted even more culinary migrants. One of these is Joel Robuchon, the chef who, before his death in 2018, had more Michelin stars than any chef in the world. His restaurant in Shanghai earned a Michelin star only shortly after opening, attesting perhaps to the star power he already enjoyed globally. At the same time, these transnational culinary authorities may also make it more difficult for young migrant chefs to acquire culinary capital in the city in the ways they achieved in the 1990s and 2000s, which was largely through accolades in the local English-language press. Culinary authority in Shanghai is now increasingly transnational (e.g. Michelin) or national (e.g. the Chinese website Dianping) with local English-language media becoming less significant (see Farrer 2019b). Chinese food media – especially food bloggers – play a greater role in validating migrant chefs in Shanghai. In the long-run, the rise of more authoritative Chinese culinary media, even in areas of foreign cuisines, could change the standards within the transnational culinary field in (and even beyond) Shanghai. By 2019, we could see the increasing importance of 'internet celebrities' (*wanghong*) in setting restaurant trends, a new type of influencer who may be disrupting traditional notions of culinary authority.

The global culinary field as a mobility lattice

As the preceding ethnography shows, the transnational mobility of culinary workers relies on preexisting technical skills, credentials, and personal attributes (language, education, and ethnicity), but mobility itself can be a strategy for building broader skills. Moreover, these culinary migrants have not only benefited from the opportunities in the field, but also helped reproduce, enlarge and extend the field as a space of interlinked career and geographic mobilities – or a 'mobility lattice' – that can be used by many migrants (Farrer 2019b). This lattice consists of positions in space (expanding restaurant scenes around the world) linked to positions in the field (expanding transnational career opportunities) linked by social ties (networks of chefs) and formal organisations (restaurant corporations). These lattices are spaces in which migrants simultaneously move geographically and within the culinary field.

Skilled culinary migrants often start with significant resources. Their geographic mobility is enabled by existing *culinary capital* – the skills, knowledge, and symbolic resources that bring status in the field. Culinary capital might include credentials recognised in the industry and habitus particular to the field (Leschziner 2015; Naccarato and Lebesco 2013), but also more generic attributes such as nationality, language ability, and even embodied capital, such as gender, race or ethnicity, implicitly associated with authority in a cuisine (Farrer 2015b; Tzeng 2019). An Italian chef has much better chances gaining employment in Italian cuisine than in Japanese; though a Peruvian chef may ethnically 'pass' in a Spanish restaurant. Chinese chefs (despite advantages in cost and language) face disadvantages in Western cuisine in Shanghai in terms of ethnic profiling, but their biggest disadvantages are a general lack of cultural capital relevant to the culinary field. Most Chinese chefs in Shanghai are rural-to-urban migrants with little prior exposure to Western cuisine, advanced culinary training or fine dining in general (Farrer 2015b). Gender profiling also shapes mobile careers. Women are overwhelming found in pastry kitchens or in front house occupations (bartending or service). But women migrants I talked to did not see the culinary field in China as less friendly than in their own countries, and some saw greater opportunities in Shanghai, since culinary work in the West is also male-dominated, while in China their skills are still rare and more appreciated.

For migrant chefs, geographic mobility is also a strategy for field mobility, less for acquiring or enhancing narrow kitchen skills, and more for using existing skills to acquire broader cultural, social and economic capital, all part of the 'skill package' (or aggregate culinary capital) of an aspiring star chef. Social capital includes ties with other expatriate chefs as well as Chinese partners. Cultural capital includes intercultural skills (e.g. language ability) but also accolades from legitimating authorities in the field (reviewers, bloggers, employers, etc). Success can bring economic capital, a springboard to further ventures in Asia or elsewhere. Finally, mobility for many chefs has become a lifestyle, with highly skilled restaurant work in global cities being a 'transnational occupational niche', (Liu-Farrer 2011) one in which mobility itself is an additional form of capital, including the capacity to adjust quickly to new environments (Leung 2013). These field-specific forms of cultural, social, and mobility capital all are components of culinary capital accrued during migration.

One of the important lessons of this study is that the mobility of skilled migrants also entails the mobility of the fields in which these skills are recognised and developed. Beyond the culinary migrants themselves, other types of mobilities are essential to expanding the culinary field. My findings emphasise the mobility of capital, authority, and supporting personnel. Capital was essential to the rapid transformation of Shanghai into a global food city, including investments by hotel and restaurant chains. The second factor was the arrival of global legitimating authorities, such as the Michelin guide, which give 'starred' chefs from abroad a chance to succeed in an unfamiliar city such as Shanghai, which was already culturally 'prepped' for their arrival. Third, a variety of migrant professionals – including investors, architects, designers, marketers, food critics, journalists, and suppliers – were agents in extending the transnational culinary field (Farrer 2019b). The migrant chefs themselves also were key actors, not only employing other migrants from abroad, but training young Chinese chefs and organising internships (or *stage*) in restaurants abroad and other professional mobility opportunities for them (such as participation in global cooking and mixology competitions). Although young Chinese chefs face many barriers to entry into non-Chinese cuisines (see Farrer 2015b), some are using the mobility lattices created by foreign chefs to pursue transnational careers in non-Chinese cuisines (Thery, Le Bail, and Buchanan 2017). In short, this study shows that migrants not only employ transnational occupational fields for their own career and geographic mobility but participate in constructing fields that become mobility lattices, or opportunity structures, for others.

Disclosure statement

No potential conflict of interest was reported by the author(s).

ORCID

James Farrer http://orcid.org/0000-0002-9847-0347

References

Alberti, Gabriella. 2014. "Mobility Strategies, 'Mobility Differentials' and 'Transnational Exit': The Experiences of Precarious Migrants in London's Hospitality Jobs." *Work, Employment and Society* 28 (6): 865–881. doi:10.1177/0950017014528403.

Aubke, Florian. 2014. "Creative Hot Spots: A Network Analysis of German Michelin-Starred Chefs." *Creativity and Innovation Management* 23 (1): 3–14. doi:10.1111/caim.12044.
Bouty, Isabelle, Marie-Leandre Gomez, and Carole Drucker-Godard. 2013. "Maintaining an Institution: The Institutional Work of Michelin in Haute Cuisine Around the World". *SSRN Electronic Journal* ESSEC Working Paper, No. 1302. doi:10.2139/ssrn.2328259.
Ceccarini, Rossella. 2011. *Pizza and Pizza Chefs in Japan*. Leiden: Brill.
Ceccarini, Rossella. 2014. "Food Bureaucracy and the Making of Authentic Pizza." In *The Paradox of Authenticity in a Globalized World*, edited by Russell Cobb, 23–34. New York: Palgrave Macmillan.
Chossat, Véronique, and Olivier Gergaud. 2003. "Expert Opinion and Gastronomy: The Recipe for Success." *Journal of Cultural Economics* 27 (2): 127–141. doi:10.1023/a:1023432502059.
Clark, Terry Nichols. 2003. "Introduction: Taking Entertainment Seriously." In *The City as Entertainment Machine*, edited by Terry Nichols Clark. Bingley: Emerald Publishing.
Erel, Umut. 2010. "Migrating Cultural Capital: Bourdieu in Migration Studies." *Sociology* 44 (4): 642–660. doi:10.1177/0038038510369363.
Farrer, James. 2010. "Eating the West and Beating the Rest: Culinary Occidentalism and Urban Soft Power in Asia's Global Food Cities." In *Globalization, Food and Social Identities in the Asia Pacific Region*, edited by James Farrer. Tokyo: Sophia University Institute of Comparative Culture. http://icc.fla.sophia.ac.jp/global%20food%20papers/html/farrer.html.
Farrer, James. 2015a. "Introduction: Travelling Cuisines in and out of Asia: Towards a Framework for Studying Culinary Globalization." In *Globalization and Asian Cuisines: Transnational Networks and Contact Zones*, edited by James Farrer, 1–20. New York: Palgrave Macmillan.
Farrer, James. 2015b. "Shanghai's Western Restaurants as Culinary Contact Zones in a Transnational Culinary Field." In *Globalization and Asian Cuisines: Transnational Networks and Contact Zones*, edited by James Farrer, 103–124. New York: Palgrave Macmillan.
Farrer, James. 2017. "Domesticating the Japanese Culinary Field in Shanghai." In *Feeding Japan: Cultures and Politics of Food Identities*, edited by Andreas Niehaus and Tine Walravens, 287–312. New York: Palgrave MacMillan.
Farrer, James. 2019a. "Culinary Globalization from Above and Below: Migrant Entrepreneurs in Urban Place Making in Shanghai." In *Destination PRC: Immigration to China in the Post-Reform Era. New York*, edited by Angela Lehmann and Pauline Leonard, 175–199. New York: Palgrave Macmillan.
Farrer, James. 2019b. *International Migrants in China's Global City: The New Shanghailanders*. Abingdon: Routledge.
Farrer, James. 2019c. "Red (Michelin) Stars Over China: Seeking Recognition in a Transnational Culinary Field." In *Culinary Nationalism in Asia*, edited by Michelle King, 193–213. London: Bloomsbury.
Ferguson, Priscilla Parkhurst. 1998. "A Cultural Field in the Making: Gastronomy in 19th-Century France." *American Journal of Sociology* 104 (3): 597–641. doi:10.1086/210082.
Ferguson, Priscilla Parkurst, and Sharon Zukin. 1998. "The Careers of Chefs." In *Eating Culture*, edited by Ron Scapp and Brian Seitz, 92–111. Albany: State University of New York Press.
Fligstein, Neil, and Doug McAdam. 2012. *A Theory of Fields*. Oxford: Oxford University Press.
GaWC. 2019. "Gawc – The World According to Gawc". *Lboro.ac.uk*. http://www.lboro.ac.uk/gawc/gawcworlds.html.
Ho, Sana. 2017. "The Michelinization of Korean Food in Seoul." International Workshop: Scales of the Alimentation Between Europe and Asia: Connections, Syncretiisms, Fusions, Paris, Feb. 23.
Holleran, Leslie. 2015. "A Conversation with Seattle's New Top Chef, Eric Johnson". *Crosscut*. https://crosscut.com/2015/11/a-conversation-with-seattles-new-top-chef-eric-johnson.
Horng, Jeou-Shyan, and Meng-Lei (Monica) Hu. 2008. "The Mystery in the Kitchen: Culinary Creativity." *Creativity Research Journal* 20 (2): 221–230. doi:10.1080/10400410802060166.
Khoo, Gaik Cheng. 2019. "Defining "Modern" Malaysian Cuisine: Fusion or Ingredients?" In *Culinary Nationalism in Asia*, edited by Michelle King, 111–129. London: Bloomsbury Academic.

Kim, Jongyoung. 2015. "Global Cultural Capital and Global Positional Competition: International Graduate Students' Transnational Occupational Trajectories." *British Journal of Sociology of Education* 37 (1): 30–50. doi:10.1080/01425692.2015.1096189.

Lane, Christel. 2011. "Culinary Culture and Globalization. An Analysis of British and German Michelin-Starred Restaurants." *The British Journal of Sociology* 62 (4): 696–717. doi:10.1111/j.1468-4446.2011.01387.x.

Leschziner, Vanina. 2015. *At the Chef's Table: Culinary Creativity in Elite Restaurants*. Stanford: Stanford University Press.

Leung, Maggi W. H. 2013. "'Read Ten Thousand Books, Walk Ten Thousand Miles': Geographical Mobility and Capital Accumulation among Chinese Scholars." *Transactions of the Institute of British Geographers* 38 (2): 311–324. doi:10.1111/j.1475-5661.2012.00526.x.

Lin, Pearl M. C., and Tom Baum. 2016. "The Meaning of Applied Creativity in the Culinary Industry." *International Journal of Hospitality and Tourism Administration* 17 (4): 429–448. doi:10.1080/15256480.2016.1226153.

Liu-Farrer, Gracia. 2011. "Making Careers in the Occupational Niche: Chinese Students in Corporate Japan's Transnational Business." *Journal of Ethnic and Migration Studies* 37 (5): 785–803. doi:10.1080/1369183x.2011.559718.

Liu-Farrer, Gracia, Brenda S. Yeoh, and Michiel Baas. 2021. "Social Construction of Skill: An Analytic Approach Toward the Question of Skill in Cross-Border Labour Mobilities." *Journal of Ethnic and Migration Studies* 47 (10): 2237–2251. doi:10.1080/1369183X.2020.1731983.

Myhrvold, Bathan. 2011. "The Art in Gastronomy: A Modernist Perspective." *Gastronomica: The Journal of Food and Culture* 11 (1): 13–23. doi:10.1525/gfc.2011.11.1.13.

Naccarato, Peter, and Kathleen Lebesco. 2013. *Culinary Capital*. London: Bloomsbury Publishing.

Nohl, Arnd-Michael, Karin Schittenhelm, and Oliver Schmidtke. 2014. *Cultural Capital and Highly Skilled Migrants' Passages Into the Labour Market*. Toronto: Univerity of Toronto Press.

Ocejo, Richard E. 2017. *Masters of Craft: Old Jobs in the New Urban Economy*. Princeton, NJ: Princeton University Press.

Oliver, Caroline, and Karen O'Reilly. 2010. "A Bourdieusian Analysis of Class and Migration: Habitus and the Individualizing Process." *Sociology* 44 (1): 49–66. doi:10.1177/003803850 9351627.

Peterson, Y., and L. Birg. 1988. "Top Hat: The Chef as Creative Occupation." *Free Inquiry in Creative Sociology* 16 (1): 67–72.

Ray, Krishnendu. 2016. *The Ethnic Restaurateur*. London: Bloomsbury Publishing.

Robbins, Derek. 2017. "Pierre Bourdieu." In *Key Sociological Thinkers*. 3rd ed., edited by Rob Stones, 229–243. London: Palgrave.

Roosipold, Anne, and Krista Loogma. 2014. "Changes in Professionalism: The Case of Estonian Chefs." *Professions and Professionalism* 4 (3), doi:10.7577/pp.780.

Sassen, Saskia. 2013. *The Global City: New York, London, Tokyo*. Princeton, NJ: Princeton University Press.

Sawaguchi, Keiichi. 2015. "Japanese Cooks In Italy: The Path-Dependent Development of a Culinary Field." In *the Globalization of Asian Cuisines*, edited by James Farrer, 125–141. New York: Palgrave Macmillan.

Shectman, S. 2009. "A Celebration of Masterstvo: Professional Cooking, Culinary Art, and Cultural Production in Russia." In *Food and Everyday Life in the Post-Socialist World*, edited by Melissa Caldwell, 154–187. Bloomington: Indiana University Press.

Sidhu, Ravinder, Brenda Yeoh, and Sushila Chang. 2015. "A Situated Analysis of Global Knowledge Networks: Capital Accumulation Strategies of Transnationally Mobile Scientists in Singapore." *Higher Education* 69 (1): 79–101. doi:10.1007/s10734-014-9762-9.

Sklair, Leslie. 2012. *Transnational Capitalist Class*. Malden: Blackwell Publishing.

Stierand, Marc. 2014. "Developing Creativity in Practice: Explorations with World-Renowned Chefs." *Management Learning* 46 (5): 598–617. doi:10.1177/1350507614560302.

Stierand, Marc, Viktor Dörfler, and Jillian MacBryde. 2014. "Creativity and Innovation in Haute Cuisine: Towards a Systemic Model." *Creativity and Innovation Management* 23 (1): 15–28. doi:10.1111/caim.12050.

Thery, A., Helen Le Bail, and D. Buchanan. 2017. "The Migration of Experts and Savoir-Faire: The Case of French Cuisine Professionals in Shanghai." *China Perspectives* 4: 49.

Trubek, Amy B. 2000. *Haute Cuisine: How the French Invented the Culinary Profession*. Philadelphia: University of Pennsylvania Press.

Tzeng, Rueyling. 2019. "Beyond Palatable: White Privilege and Western Immigrant Restaurateurs in Postcolonial Taiwan." *International Area Studies Review* 22 (2): 168–185. doi:10.1177/2233865918815569.

UKNCPEQF (UK National Contact Points for the European Qualifications Framework). 2016. "International Sectoral Qualifications (Isqs) and Their Use in the UK". Qualifications Frameworks in the UK. European Commission. http://ccea.org.uk/sites/default/files/docs/accreditation/european/eqf/isq_report_nov2016.pdf.

Wang, Chuanfei. 2019. "Old Sake in New Glasses: Reframing Japan's National Drink Through Global Wine Culture." *Gastronomica: The Journal of Critical Food Studies* 19 (1): 79–90. doi:10.1525/gfc.2019.19.1.79.

Yenal, Z., and M. Kubiena. 2016. "Culinary Work at the Crossroads in Istanbul." *Gastronomica: The Journal of Critical Food Studies* 16 (1): 63–78. doi:10.1525/gfc.2016.16.1.63.

Index